Scott Burns has been a national sports reporter for more than 25 years. He has been with the *Scottish Daily Express* and *Scottish Daily Star* throughout that time and in recent years has come under the Reach plc umbrella, also working for the *Daily Record* and *Sunday Mail*.

Scott has travelled the globe covering all levels of football, from international games to cup finals and last day title deciders – but is in no doubt his sporting highlight was being able to report on Scotland's exploits at Euro 2020.

Scott has also been a long-suffering member of the Scotland Supporters Club for more than 30 years. He has been lucky enough to swap the stands for the press box but his wife, Amanda, boys, Ross and Aaron, along with his father-in-law, Bill, all continue to be Hampden regulars and active members of the Tartan Army.

WE CAN BOOGIE

Steve Clarke's Scotland Football Revival

SCOTT BURNS

First published in 2024 by
Arena Sport, an imprint of
Birlinn Limited
West Newington House
10 Newington Road
Edinburgh
EH9 1QS

www.arenasportbooks.co.uk

ISBN 978 1 91375 918 6

British Library Cataloguing-in-Publication Data
A catalogue record for this book is available from the British Library

Typeset by Initial Typesetting Services, Edinburgh

Papers used by Birlinn are from well-managed forests and other responsible sources

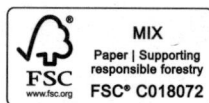

MIX
Paper | Supporting
responsible forestry
FSC
www.fsc.org
FSC® C018072

Printed and bound by Clays Ltd, Elcograf S.p.A.

In loving memory of Sam and Janet Hopkins
(Uncle Sam and Auntie Janet),
much-loved and well-travelled members of the
Tartan Army, who took me to my first Scotland game
and many more after that

CONTENTS

ACKNOWLEDGEMENTS

I would like to start by acknowledging all the people who have helped make this book possible. I would have to start with Steve Clarke and his various Scotland players and teams over the past five years who together have transformed the men's national team. Without them this book would not be possible.

I have to thank all the current and ex-Scottish internationals who willingly gave up their time to give a real insight into their manager and the job he has done with the Scotland team. There were also a number of opposition players, former players and teammates of Clarke who were also more than happy to assist.

There were a lot of players or staff who wanted to keep under the radar. They were more than happy to add some colour and off-the-record guidance but didn't want to go public. You know who you are and thank you.

I would also like to thank my wife, Amanda, and boys, Ross and Aaron, for their support throughout, via my early mornings and late evenings. Thanks to Amanda for all the proofreading.

Kenny Ramsay also deserves a massive thank you. He is one of the top sports photographers in the country and his photographs in the plate section brilliantly capture the big moments.

There are loads of other people who have helped me and I can only say thank you – your help is really appreciated.

Finally, I appreciate Reach plc giving me permission to work on this book and Birlinn for taking it on. Special thanks must go to Paul Smith for making this project a reality and to everyone involved at Birlinn for producing such a top-class book. I hope it does Steve Clarke and his Scotland team justice.

INTRODUCTION

METHODICAL, studious, determined, compassionate, knowledgeable and skilled. Steve Clarke has proved himself to be all of those things and more in a tenure as Scotland manager that has brought a remarkable revival in Scotland's football fortunes.

Since his appointment in 2019, the quiet man of coaching has restored the Hampden Roar. After a painful absence from football's top table that spanned more than two decades, Scotland can once again feast on tournament competition and sit side by side with the best in the game.

Euro 2020 was the appetiser. Euro 2024 is the tantalising main course. Who knows what's yet to be served up?

Successive European Championship qualifications have brought back belief and hope. The players feel it. The Tartan Army are revelling in it. The manager has created it, instilling the same steely confidence in his team that has been a hallmark of his distinguished career as a player and coach.

We Can Boogie is a celebration of a Scottish football renaissance, shining a light on the man at the helm and the players and staff who have been central to the success story. The chapters that follow chart the twists and turns of a long and eventful journey, through the eyes of those who have been there for the ride.

Interviews with Lyndon Dykes, Ryan Christie, Lawrence Shankland, Lewis Ferguson, David Marshall, Declan Gallagher, Stephen O'Donnell, Zander Clark, Andrew Considine, Ross Stewart, Max Johnston, Alex Dyer, Stevie Naismith, Alan McRae, Duncan Ferguson, Pat Nevin, Alex Gogic, Tony Fitzpatrick, Billy Dodds, Kirk Broadfoot, Charlie Nicholas and Charlie Adam have painted a colourful picture of life in and around Clarke's inner circle.

As a supporter and football writer I have been on that adventure with the manager and his squad, with extracts of interviews I have been part of in press conferences and mixed zones on home soil and across Europe woven through the pages that follow.

Steve Clarke's own words from those Scotland camps and post-match gatherings are featured alongside those of Andy Robertson, Kieran Tierney, Callum McGregor, John McGinn, Jack Hendry, Nathan Patterson, Billy Gilmour, Stuart Armstrong, Liam Cooper, Angus Gunn, Ryan Porteous, Ryan Fraser, Scott McKenna, Grant Hanley, Charlie Mulgrew, Kevin Nisbet, Jacob Brown, Mikey Devlin, Oli McBurnie, Anthony Ralston and Kris Ajer.

It's a tale of revival, of joy and of a nation reborn. Finally, we can say with confidence: we'll be coming!

Chapter 1

CALEDONIA IS CALLING FOR CLARKE

THE Scottish Football Association (SFA) confirmed on 18 April 2019 that Alex McLeish was to step down from his second spell in charge of the national team. Big Eck had delivered success in the Nations League and that had guaranteed a play-off place for the 2020 European Championships, but a poor start through the automatic qualifying campaign had cost him his job.

It was a tournament that Scotland was to co-host, with 11 cities across Europe to roll out the welcome mats and Glasgow selected as one of them. The SFA was determined that the Scotland national team were finally going to break the 22-year duck and qualify for a showpiece tournament again.

Former SFA president Alan McRae OBE said: 'It was massive due to the fact that it was the 60th anniversary of the European Championships and it was being held across so many different countries. It was fantastic that Hampden Park had been picked as one of the venues and of course we were all desperate to see Scotland qualify. We hadn't qualified for a major finals since the 1998 World Cup in France. We had come close a few times and made a few play-offs but we had never managed to get over the line. We knew the importance of being a host nation and trying to make sure we qualified for the finals. The last thing we wanted was to be hosting at Hampden Park and for Scotland not to be there.'

That was easier said than done. The Scots were drawn in Group I of the European Championship qualifiers, alongside a Belgian team who had finished third at the previous World Cup. You could also factor in a formidable Russia side and, for good measure, there were the potential banana skins of Kazakhstan, Cyprus and San Marino.

For Scotland to qualify, they had to finish in the top two and that was going to take a momentous effort. There was going to be very little room for error. The problem for McLeish was that his campaign got off to the worst possible start when Scotland crashed 3-0 away to Kazakhstan. It made an unlikely scenario look almost impossible after just one game. The Scotland team did manage to regroup and save some grace by beating the bottom seeds 2-0 away in San Marino. It was McLeish's final stand but it wasn't enough to save his job. There was too big a prize at stake and the incumbent manager, unfortunately, paid the price.

Suddenly, it was now about who was going to succeed him. Aberdeen manager Derek McInnes was heavily linked, as was Scotland under-21 boss Scot Gemmill and Steve Clarke, who had worked minor miracles in his transformation of Kilmarnock into a major force in Scotland again.

Clarke had raised eyebrows by returning to Scotland with Killie. He had taken them from a relegation fight to fifth place in a matter of months. He went on to add to his growing reputation by taking Killie to third place and back into Europe the following season. Clarke had also been named as the Professional Football Association (Scotland) and the Scottish Football Writers' Association manager of the year in that spell. He was very much Scotland's hot ticket in terms of the options and also had a wealth of coaching and managerial experience south of the border.

Clarke had been assistant to José Mourinho at Chelsea and held similar posts at Newcastle United, Liverpool and West Ham United. He also had his own spells in charge of West Bromwich Albion and Reading. The Kilmarnock success and that experience at the very top end of the English game was enough to convince the SFA that Clarke was the man to salvage Scotland's fading European Championship dream.

Alex Dyer was his assistant manager at Kilmarnock. He knew it was hard for his friend and colleague to walk away from what he had built at Rugby Park, but the lure of becoming the Scottish national coach was one his proud and patriotic boss just couldn't resist.

Dyer recalled: 'It was a difficult decision [in one sense] but it also wasn't that hard because it was the call from his country. It was the next step up. Steve had been down in the English Premier League and was working in the Scottish Premiership so the next step was to represent his country. Steve had a few caps as a player. He had done well at Kilmarnock. He had taken over a team that was struggling and ended up leading them back into Europe. That was why the SFA thought he was the best man for the job. He had done what he could do with Kilmarnock and Scotland was allowing him to go to that next level. When you are asked to manage your country you have to take it. Steve took the opportunity and there is no doubt, everyone will agree, he has grabbed it with both hands.'

Clarke was officially confirmed as Scotland's national head coach on Monday, 20 May 2019. Just a month after McLeish had departed. There were to be no prolonged managerial goose chases. The SFA had learned from their previous experiences and its hierarchy, much to their credit, had gone out and nailed down their top target.

Clarke, in the SFA's press release announcing his arrival in the job, stated: 'It is an honour to be appointed Scotland National

Head Coach and I will undertake those responsibilities with pride and commitment. I firmly believe we have a talented group of players who can achieve success on the international stage. I look forward to working with them and helping them to fulfil those ambitions. I appreciate the Scotland supporters have waited a long time for the national team to qualify for a major tournament. Now we have a Women's World Cup to look forward to in France this summer and it's my motivation to emulate the success of Shelley Kerr and her squad by leading us to Euro 2020. I believe we can qualify and look forward to that journey with the players and the fans, starting against Cyprus and Belgium next month.'

SFA chief Ian Maxwell was in no doubt that Scotland had got the right man this time around. Maxwell, in the same SFA media release, said: 'Steve's pedigree as a coach and manager of the highest regard set him apart in a high-calibre group of candidates. This season's achievements simply reaffirm the credentials we believe will be of huge benefit to the Scotland National Team. I am delighted that we now have the country's deserved Manager of the Year to lead the Scotland National Team and his experience over the past two decades will be integral to rejuvenating our UEFA Euro 2020 qualifying campaign, which resumes next month. It was important that we undertook the recruitment process diligently and respectfully, especially given the importance of the final games of the domestic season for Kilmarnock, Steve and his players. I would like to thank the Kilmarnock owner, Billy Bowie, and the club in general for their professionalism throughout the recruitment process.'

There was very little opposition to the appointment. It was universally welcomed and seen as a good fit.

Player turned pundit Pat Nevin knew Clarke well from their time together as teammates with Chelsea and Scotland. Nevin said: 'When he got the Scotland job he took over from Alex McLeish. Steve maybe wasn't as big a name as big Alex. People were coming to me and asking: "What do you think?" I told them all Scotland had won the biggest watch in their history, appointing Steve. I felt he was exactly what we needed. We don't need big names but a very good coach who knows how to build teams up over a period of time.'

Clarke went on to put his own backroom team together that included Dyer. That was no surprise. Dyer had worked with him at West Ham United and had been his trusted lieutenant at Rugby Park. The new Scotland boss also moved to bring in former Republic of Ireland midfielder Steven Reid as his other assistant coach. Reid had previously worked with Clarke at Reading. He was a well-respected, up-and-coming coach and Clarke felt, as the youngest member of the coaching group, Reid would have a better connection with the Scotland players.

There was some dubiety over the position of goalkeeping coach. Stevie Woods had been confirmed as having exited along with former boss McLeish and his backroom team. The Celtic goalkeeping coach, however, was convinced to stick around under the new regime and to be one of Clarke's key lieutenants. The new manager also brought in his Kilmarnock coach Billy Thomson to help, although he didn't hold the required goalkeeping licence. The pair, however, worked in tandem in those early camps.

Dyer didn't need to be asked twice to continue his coaching career under Clarke. He said: 'When Steve first got the job, he said: "Come with me," and I said: "Of course I will." It was never going to be a long-term situation, however. He knew I wanted to go into management in my own right. He asked me to give him a year or so and if something was to come up, like eventually it did at Kilmarnock, he wouldn't stand in my way. I wanted to go with Steve and to go to that next international level myself. I had spent two years with him and he took my coaching to another level. It was the next step for me. It was a joy to work with him.'

Clarke had less than a month to look at players and assemble a squad for his Scotland bow in the European Championship qualifiers at home to Cyprus and away to Belgium. It was time to lay the foundations and build for the future.

Chapter 2

THE LONG ROAD TO HAMPDEN: FROM BUDDIE TO STAMFORD BRIDGE BLUE

A YOUNG Steve Clarke was always destined to play football at some level. It was inevitable and unavoidable. Football was the main pastime for most Scottish boys growing up in the late sixties and early seventies. It was a time when televisions, if you were lucky enough to have one, were more than likely to be black and white and with just three channels to choose from. Outdoor life was what Clarke and his generation thrived on, jumpers for goalposts and playing under the dim glow of street lights.

He was also born into some decent footballing stock on 29 August 1963 in Saltcoats, Ayrshire. His dad, Eddie, was a very good amateur player, although injury curtailed him from playing at a much higher level. His Uncle Jimmy had come through the ranks at Celtic and went on to play professionally for Morton and Cambridge United.

Clarke's brother, Paul, was seven years older and was also a promising player, who went on to have a long and successful career with Kilmarnock from 1974 to 1986.

So the future Scotland boss was coming from a family with a real footballing pedigree, although it hardly helped him when he was a youngster and it came to family kickabouts at the local park. Clarke was never the biggest physically. He was a late developer and in his younger years was always playing catch-up in terms of physicality. When he played for his school his dad even asked if his son could play down a year to give the youngster a better chance. It was refreshing and in sharp contrast to the parents who push to see their boys fast-tracked up the age groups, through their academies and boys' clubs.

Clarke started playing for Saltcoats Star and Springside Colts before he caught the eye of St Mirren. He signed schoolboy forms, played for their under-16s and was then offered a provisional form, the step below signing a professional contract.

Clarke signed on at Love Street but his dad asked if he could be loaned to Beith Juniors to give him more first-team experience. His Uncle Jimmy was also at Beith and could keep a watchful eye on his development. Clarke freely acknowledged that spell in the juniors hardened him up and opened his eyes to the men's game.

The promising full back would eventually go on to sign for St Mirren, but his dad, from his own painful experience, knew how precarious football can be and insisted that Clarke junior signed part-time. That would allow him to serve his time as an apprentice instrument artificer at Beechams Pharmaceuticals in Irvine. It would give him a back-up if his football career didn't go to plan. Clarke worked at Beechams for four years but becoming a professional footballer remained his burning ambition. He continued to impress at St Mirren and went on to make a name for himself in Paisley under the then manager Rikki McFarlane.

Former St Mirren midfielder Tony Fitzpatrick recalled: 'He was a young boy from Saltcoats. Steve came right into the first team and you could see right away that he was a player who was going to have a good career. You just know when you see certain people and Steve fell into that category. He came in and played right back. He was a very good athlete and had a real determination. Steve looked like he could be a top player and he also got a few goals from right back. I know they talk about the modern wing backs now but Steve could have fitted into that role no problem. He could come out from the back, dribble past opponents and put crosses in. He was also a very solid defender, disciplined and he had good positional sense.'

Clarke came in and hit the ground running. He got a footballing education on and off the park. There were some big characters in that St Mirren dressing room, like Frank McDougall, Frank McAvennie, Chic Charnley and Doug Somner. They played hard on the pitch and at times even harder off it. Clarke, however, was determined to play at the highest level he could and that was his sole focus. The promising right back focused on his football and was always looking at ways to improve himself and his game.

Fitzpatrick recalled: 'Steve kept himself to himself in the dressing room. We had quite a mad group at St Mirren but Steve would just come in, do his work and get on with things. He was just a total professional. He was very career-driven. Steve was very much like he is today, very astute, thoughtful and wanting to be the best version of himself. He always wanted to improve as a player and he will be the same as a manager. He would do extra training, his work and then go home to his family.'

Clarke's progress in Paisley didn't go unnoticed. He was selected for Scotland's under-19s and progressed to the under-21s as he made a name for himself, starring for St Mirren in the Premier Division.

Former Celtic striker Charlie Nicholas said: 'I remember him coming through because he was just a wee bit older than Paul McStay. He was well thought of at St Mirren and he was attracting a lot of attention from clubs in Scotland and south of the border.'

Alex Miller came in as manager from Morton to take over from McFarlane and rewarded Clarke with a new contract. Miller also moved him in one to play as a central defender at times because he felt he could read the game and had the speed required.

Clarke was also part of a team that had two cracks at the UEFA Cup. Miller left for Hibs and Alex Smith replaced him as St Mirren boss. Clarke remained a key player for the Buddies and continued to see the bigger picture in terms of tactics, opposition and analysis of the game. He always looked outside the box to gain that wee edge or marginal gain – that could make all the difference and would later see him go on and become management material.

'You could see back then that Steve was a big thinker when it came to the game,' St Mirren legend Fitzpatrick said. 'I know it was early on in his playing career at St Mirren, but the signs were there that he would go on and become a manager one day.'

Clarke was going places and Celtic were keen to take him to the east end of Glasgow – but Chelsea came in and trumped them. The London club agreed to pay St Mirren around £400,000 for their star defender's services in 1987. It was a big fee but it was to prove to be something of a bargain, given the service he would go on and give the Stamford Bridge club as a player, coach and assistant manager.

Fitzpatrick acknowledged: 'Steve did very well at St Mirren. There were quite a lot of teams interested in him and I know Celtic were really keen, but he went to Chelsea. It was a lot of money but it was a bargain looking back now. What a playing career he had down in England. He deserved all the success he had and it is great to see him doing so well in management and now with the Scotland national team.'

The one downside for Clarke was that five months after he left Love Street, St Mirren went on to lift the 1987 Scottish Cup.

Clarke, by that time, was adapting to life south of the border. He would have felt at home with Chelsea having a big Scottish contingent. The blues had the likes of Joe McLaughlin, Doug Rougvie, John McNaught, Pat Nevin, David Speedie, Gordon Durie, Kevin McAllister and Les Fridge. There was also a fellow Ayrshire man coming through the Stamford Bridge ranks in Billy Dodds.

Dodds recalled: 'I was in the reserves when Steve came. Two boys from Ayrshire, it was great. St Mirren to Chelsea was a big step up. Chelsea was still a big club although not as big as it is today. They paid good money for him and there was a bit of expectation on Steve.'

Clarke certainly didn't look out of place in John Hollins's side. He made an immediate mark on his teammates. Fellow Scot Pat Nevin said: 'Steve came in and played right back and I was right wing. We had a really good understanding. He could also play centre back, left back or even centre midfield. Steve was one of those players; it didn't matter where you played him because you knew he would do a job and you could rely on him. He was a really good player.'

Dodds echoed those sentiments, adding: 'Steve was the complete full back; he could defend and get forward because of his pace, power and determination. He could also be a nasty so-and-so. He had that will to win. If I was a winger I wouldn't have fancied going up against him. He was aggressive, strong and quick. He was an unsung hero. There were bigger names than him at the club, like Kerry Dixon and David Speedie, but you knew if Steve was in your team then he would be Mr Dependable.'

His abilities didn't go unnoticed in the opposition ranks. Scotland and Arsenal striker Charlie Nicholas added: 'I played against Steve a couple of times when I was at Arsenal and he was a good, fast and solid defender. You never got much change out of him.'

Clarke was handed his Scotland debut in a 2-0 friendly win over Hungary in 1987. It was the first of his six caps, a pretty miserly tally considering the level he played at. He won the majority of his caps in his first couple of seasons at Chelsea, playing in wins over Belgium and Bulgaria and in draws with Saudi Arabia and Malta. Clarke then had to wait more than six years to make what was to be his final Scotland appearance in a 3-1 defeat to the Netherlands in 1994. It was a night where a certain Ruud Gullit, whom he would go on to work with, would bring a cruel end to his international career.

Nevin recalled: 'I remember his last game against the Netherlands. I was on the bench and Steve Clarke was directly up against Ruud Gullit who was wide on the left. Gullit was one of the best players on the planet at that time and it was fair to say Steve wasn't getting any help. I was thinking if I was on I would be trying to help and cover him, but he kept being left isolated. Steve got a bit of stick after the game and I remember thinking that was grossly unfair because Gullit, on form, could do that to anyone. I thought it was really harsh. It proved to be the last time he played for Scotland. Steve never really spoke up about it but I kind of gauged he felt a little bit let down by it all. I would have to agree with him on that. In fairness to Steve, he never went in a huff about it. He just got his head down, went back and continued to do well for Chelsea.'

I remember questioning the former Scotland boss Craig Brown about Clarke's lack of caps and he said that he had every right to be aggrieved!

It wasn't all a bed of roses for Clarke at Chelsea either because at the end of his first full season they were relegated to the Second Division. They came straight back up although Bobby Campbell had become Chelsea manager, and it is fair to say it wasn't exactly a match made in heaven for Clarke. He held his ground, typically stoic, and went on to play under Campbell's successors Ian Porterfield and David Webb. The First Division became the game-changing English Premier League in the 1992–93 season. Clarke didn't look out of place as he was named Chelsea's player of the year the following season. It was a time when English football was to hit the financial jackpot thanks to Sky Sports and Chelsea were manoeuvring into one of the more fashionable big guns, under Glenn Hoddle and then Ruud Gullit.

Clarke, during that period, was rewarded for a decade of Blues' service with a testimonial against PSV Eindhoven in 1996. It was a time when Chelsea really started to come alive. Clarke helped the Blues lift the 1997 FA Cup and the following season the Coca-Cola Cup and European Cup Winners' Cup arrived. That 1998 European final win over Stuttgart was to be Clarke's final competitive appearance for Chelsea.

Nevin acknowledged: 'Steve had a top career at Chelsea. Look at the changes at Chelsea, in terms of the quality of players they brought in, and Steve remained in the team. That's not luck; you have to be a very good player and Steve was. He stayed a long, long time at Chelsea. Steve, the way he was as a player and a manager, was just understated and just did his job. He wasn't looking for any big headlines or flashy moments. He was a bit like an old-school César Azpilicueta. He always did his job and was a top pro. His teammates really appreciated him and that is one of the biggest accolades you can get.'

Clarke made 421 appearances for Chelsea, scoring seven goals into the bargain. He currently sits ninth in Chelsea's all-time appearance list.

Chapter 3

GULLIT, THE SPECIAL ONE
AND KING KENNY

STEVE Clarke was given his first step on the coaching ladder by his former Chelsea manager and international tormentor Ruud Gullit. The legendary Dutchman had left the Chelsea manager's job and was handed his Premier League return by Newcastle United. Gullit had been impressed with Clarke as a senior player at Stamford Bridge, so much so that he took him to St James' Park as his assistant at the start of the 1998–99 season.

The Magpies went on to finish a disappointing 13th in the Premier League, although they did get to the 1999 FA Cup final where they lost 2-0 to Manchester United.

Newcastle striker Duncan Ferguson said: 'Steve was a brilliant coach and a fantastic guy. He was certainly up there in terms of coaches I have worked with. He was a young coach but he was great. To work at the level Steve has, you have to be a top coach and he has gone on to prove that.'

Gullit was to leave Newcastle after just a year. Clarke was initially put in caretaker charge before he departed and returned to Chelsea in an academy role. He made a name for himself in west London, so much so that José Mourinho, who did some of his coaching badges through the SFA, promoted him to his No. 2

when he took over the Blues' hot seat in 2004. It came as a shock to Clarke who feared he might have been surplus to requirements under the Champions League-winning boss.

'The big change was Mourinho,' former Chelsea star Pat Nevin confirmed. 'Steve was working in the Chelsea academy and when Mourinho came in it was a bit of a shock. He thought Mourinho was going to get rid of him. Steve had gone in to speak to Mourinho and said: "Whatever you need me to do I will do and if you don't need me then you don't need me, but I will help wherever I can." The next day Mourinho pulled Steve in and asked him if he wanted to work with him and become his assistant. He was gobsmacked but José had obviously done his homework and knew Steve was a good coach and a good person to have around. He also knew all about Chelsea into the bargain so it was a smart move. Steve remained beside Mourinho for all his time in his first spell at Chelsea, so that shows what a good coach he must be.'

It was to be the start of a golden era for Chelsea. The Blues won two Premier League titles, two League Cups and an FA Cup under The Special One. Clarke was a loyal No. 2 and was given a footballing education. It opened his eyes up to see the game differently. Mourinho quickly became a legendary figure at Chelsea, and although Clarke was loyal, he wasn't afraid to take him on when he felt his boss was in the wrong.

Nevin recalled: 'I remember Steve telling a few stories. He was normally the one who would have to stand up to Mourinho. He had to challenge him and ask him the hard questions when other people in or around the club might have tended to back off. The technical and tactical things. There was one game where Chelsea got thumped by Newcastle. Mourinho had said he was going to make three substitutions at half-time. Steve told him that was stupid because there were only three subs at the time and if they got anyone injured then they would be down to ten men. Mourinho made the three substitutions and I think Jimmy Floyd Hasselbaink then got injured after five minutes and Chelsea had to play with ten men. Clarke told Mourinho after the game he had made a mistake, but his manager insisted in no uncertain terms that he hadn't. Mourinho claimed he had done it ten times and that is the first time it hadn't worked. How was it a mistake? It was still the right thing to do because it has worked nine out of ten times.'

Mourinho left Chelsea in 2007 but Clarke's services were retained by his successor Avram Grant. Clarke, however, became a target for another Chelsea legend. This time Gianfranco Zola wanted him to assist him at West Ham United, as a first-team coach. It was at the start of the 2008–09 campaign.

Alex Dyer explained: 'I was at West Ham when Steve came in with Gianfranco Zola. He was the assistant manager to Zola but he did most things in training. I was working with the youth team on their fitness and I got a job with the reserve team. I always wanted to coach and I had taken my badges so they gave me a chance with the reserves. Steve liked the way I worked. I spent a lot of time with the players and I was always on the training pitch until I thought everything was done behind the scenes. I was, like I am today, completely dedicated.'

The Hammers finished ninth, but the following season narrowly avoided relegation and Zola left after the club had been bought out in June 2010. Clarke departed not long after by mutual consent. He wasn't out of work for long. Just over seven months later, another legend of the game, Kenny Dalglish, called. Dalglish had returned for his second spell at Liverpool and wanted Clarke as his No. 2.

Former Liverpool and Scotland midfielder Charlie Adam said: 'Kenny was the manager and Steve Clarke had come in after Roy Hodgson had left. Steve came in as one of the two coaches, along with Kevin Keen. Clarkie organised and took most of the training though and Kenny would oversee things. Kenny would do a little coaching the day before the game, but Steve would be the main coach. He would take the sessions and dictate them, although Kenny and Kevin could both step in. Steve was the main planner and knew what he wanted to get out of training. The lads, in fairness, loved his sessions because they were great. I really enjoyed the year I had with him.'

Liverpool had top stars like Steven Gerrard, Pepe Reina and Luis Suárez. Clarke was in his element. Adam said: 'Steve does his work. He is engaging. You can talk to him and he is very easygoing. He was great and we knew we could have a laugh and a joke with the players. Sometimes you might not think Steve is like that when he has his public face on and is dealing with the media. He will have a laugh and a joke with the boys when the time is right, but when he works he wants 100 per cent commitment. When you are out on the grass you work hard and you put it all in. Steve will be at his best when he is out on the training pitch because that is where he really feels at home. I remember him at Liverpool and he would do whatever he could to get the best out of his players and the team as a whole.'

Liverpool finished sixth at the end of their first season. The next campaign they were eighth in the Premier League but went on to lift the 2012 League Cup, beating Cardiff City on penalties.

Adam acknowledged: 'The highlight was winning the League Cup, but unfortunately we never did as well in the league as we should have. Steve was a big part of our success. Steve is really strong tactically. He has worked at top clubs, with top players and under top managers, so you have to know the game or you won't last long at the top level. The fact Steve has been at the top level for so long tells you all you need to know. He was at Chelsea, Liverpool and Newcastle United. He has since gone out on his own. What a job he has done with the national team. He has got Scotland in the right place. He has a good group but he has managed to get them to gel and bring a unity. Steve has also found a way and a system that really suits the Scotland players he has at his disposal.'

Clarke left Anfield with Dalglish in 2012 and moved into management in his own right at West Bromwich Albion. He did a solid job at the Hawthorns. He kept West Brom in the Premier League but it wasn't enough for their over-ambitious board who showed him the door in his second season.

BBC Radio 5 Live pundit Pat Nevin was left scratching his head over that decision. He explained: 'Steve has worked under some top managers and nobody ever sacked him. That tells you all you need to know about Steve's coaching credentials. The first time he was sacked was when he was West Brom manager and looking back now how stupid was that of West Brom? If you ask any West Brom fan, they would have told you that then when Steve was sacked and even now. They were in the English Premier League and were steadily building. I mean, look what has happened to West Brom since.'

Clarke's next port of call was with Reading. He was asked to go in mid-season and keep the struggling Royals in the Championship. He did that and also took them to the FA Cup semi-finals where they lost to Arsenal. Clarke left just a few months after with the Royals in the bottom half of the table. His stint at the Madejski Stadium had lasted less than a year.

Clarke returned to assist Roberto Di Matteo, another ex-Chelsea teammate, at Aston Villa and then had a year out before he was finally tempted to return to Scottish football with Kilmarnock.

Former chairman Michael Johnston had tried to persuade him on several occasions to take the Killie helm, but it was his successor, Billy Bowie, who finally got him home to his Ayrshire roots. Killie were sitting bottom of the Scottish Premiership when Clarke was appointed in October 2017. He moved to bring in a familiar face in Alex Dyer.

Dyer said: 'Steve liked my work ethic and told me if he got a job and it was right then he would call. He did that when the Kilmarnock job came up. He made the call and I jumped at the chance. The rest is history as they say.'

Clarke arrived at Rugby Park with a plan and it worked to perfection. He led Killie to fifth in the league with some big results and won the Scottish Football Writers' Association's manager of the year award for the 2017–18 season.

Experienced Kilmarnock defender Kirk Broadfoot recalled: 'When Steve first came in we were bottom of the league and we had hardly won a game. He gave us a way of playing and training. He didn't complicate things; you always played your position and in your shape. We all knew our jobs and his video analysis was second to none. He knew how the opposition would approach games and how we should play against them with and without the ball. Every game was different and he would work on set plays for every game from the Monday, not just the day before. There was no messing – if you didn't do the job he asked you would find yourself out of the team. He told us if we buy into what he was wanting then we would have success. He was spot on. We ended up doing really well and going on to finish the season in fifth, with the club setting a new club record of 59 points in the process.'

Clarke also wasn't afraid to challenge some of the deep-rooted downsides of Scottish football, like the bigotry he endured in a game at Ibrox. Broadfoot said: 'The gaffer says what is on his mind. He does his own thing and what he thinks is right. He stood up for himself after that incident and a lot of people respect him for that.'

Clarke won a lot of plaudits and so did his players with Stephen O'Donnell and Stuart Findlay both forcing themselves into the Scotland squad. The experienced boss didn't do much in the transfer market but in his second season, Kilmarnock really took off and finished third in the league, securing a European return in the process.

Broadfoot worked with Walter Smith at Rangers and puts Clarke in that same top-level management bracket. The centre half claimed: 'He let the senior players get heavily involved but you knew when he came in he was the boss. He had that aura and when he spoke everyone listened. I speak about him in the same way as Walter Smith. They both had that standing. The gaffer also liked a bit of tension and edge in training because it brought the intensity and standards up. He wanted the best and if you didn't pull your weight then he would call you out.'

Clarke was named as SFWA and PFA (Scotland) manager of the year at the end of that second season but that success was to come at a cost. Clarke never got the chance to lead Killie into Europe because the SFA came calling in the summer of 2019.

Broadfoot admitted: 'I think it was inevitable he would go. We all wanted him to stay at Kilmarnock. If he had stayed and been given a bit more of a budget then we felt we could have split the Old Firm. When he left, the club went down a different route and it left us in a low place. The gaffer was unbelievable in the job he did with the budget he had and the way he got us playing. I always say if he had had a budget like Aberdeen or Hearts then we would have challenged Celtic and Rangers for the league. I haven't been surprised to see him go on and do so well for Scotland. He is a top guy and manager and he continues to show it.'

Chapter 4

SETTING SCOTLAND'S STANDARD

STEVE Clarke's first job was to pick a squad for the European Championship 2020 qualifiers at home to Cyprus and away to group favourites Belgium. There was great anticipation to see what that first selection would be and if the new manager would be able to get the team back into contention to qualify out of Euro 2020 qualifying Group I.

The headline pick from that opening 27-man squad was that of Eamonn Brophy. The striker had been Kilmarnock's top scorer in their third-place finish. He had been a major player in Clarke's Rugby Park side and now he was trusting him to come in and try and move up to an entirely new level. Brophy had come through the ranks at Hamilton and in fairness had represented his country at under-19 and under-21 level before this call. Clarke also turned to three of his other Rugby Park tried and trusted stalwarts in Greg Taylor, Stephen O'Donnell and Stuart Findlay. He knew what he was getting from all four. They had served him well in his time in Ayrshire. Experienced Hull City keeper David Marshall and Fulham midfielder Tom Cairney also returned to the squad.

Marshall, who had won his last cap against Slovakia back in 2016, said: 'Steve Clarke phoned me. We were on holiday with Chris Burke and his family. Chris had worked with Steve at

Kilmarnock. A lot of people had thought I had retired from international football but that was never the case. When I was at Hull
I had been injured and Allan McGregor was playing in front of
me so I couldn't really have much complaint. I kept in touch with
Stevie Woods [goalkeeping coach] and Alex McLeish and they
told me they would keep an eye on the situation when I was back
playing. My issue was that I had rolled my ankle and wasn't playing at Hull City so I couldn't expect to be in the Scotland squads.
Steve actually thought I had stepped away from international
football but that was never the case. I explained the situation and
he named me in his first Scotland squad. I also started as his
number one, which was great.'

There were several players who were coming into this camp
full of confidence. Scotland captain Andy Robertson was late in
joining up with the team but he had a legitimate reason – he
was away lifting the Champions League with Jurgen Klopp's
Liverpool.

Aston Villa's John McGinn and Norwich City's Kenny McLean
had also helped their respective sides to win promotion to the
English Premier League, while Scott Bain, Callum McGregor,
James Forrest and Oliver Burke had all helped Celtic to their latest domestic treble.

Clarke's first Scotland squad was:

Goalkeepers: Scott Bain (Celtic), Liam Kelly (Livingston),
David Marshall (Hull City), Jon McLaughlin (Sunderland).

Defenders: Michael Devlin (Aberdeen), Stuart Findlay
(Kilmarnock), Scott McKenna (Aberdeen), Charlie Mulgrew
(Blackburn Rovers), Stephen O'Donnell (Kilmarnock), Liam
Palmer (Sheffield Wednesday), Andrew Robertson (Liverpool),
John Souttar (Heart of Midlothian), Greg Taylor (Kilmarnock).

Midfielders: Stuart Armstrong (Southampton), Tom Cairney
(Fulham), John McGinn (Aston Villa), Callum McGregor

(Celtic), Kenny McLean (Norwich City), Scott McTominay (Manchester United), Graeme Shinnie (Aberdeen).

Forwards: Eamonn Brophy (Kilmarnock), Oliver Burke (Celtic), James Forrest (Celtic), Ryan Fraser (Bournemouth), Marc McNulty (Hibernian), Lewis Morgan (Sunderland), Johnny Russell (Sporting Kansas City).

Clarke had worked at the very top of the English game and it was clear he was used to certain standards and demanded instant respect. He had an aura and probably instilled a little bit of fear into a few of the squad who maybe hadn't come across him before.

Bournemouth winger Ryan Fraser revealed there is a fine line, one players know not to cross, but at the same time if you need Clarke for anything then he is there for you. Fraser claimed: 'You never know if you have played well for him. He's quite scary! But you can also go to him and ask him stuff, which is nice. You don't want to be on the wrong side of him but at the same time his door is always open. If you have anything you need to ask, he is always there. If you have a legitimate question, he'll give you a simple answer.'

Clarke knew he wasn't going to have his Scotland players for long. It was all about maximising those international windows. It was every month or so and for a week to ten days at the most. It was a case of making the most of the limited time he had. It was clear from the outset that Clarke demanded the highest standards on and off the pitch. That started with the little things.

'When I first went in there with Steve we could see it was going to be a tough job,' assistant coach Alex Dyer acknowledged. 'You also knew that given time, Steve would pull it off. You could see from day one that the lads bought into things and what the gaffer was trying to build. The players realised this is not a jolly-up, this is them representing their country, and for a lot of players this could be the pinnacle. Steve had only taken this job on because he wants to be the best. He wants people around him who are ambitious, who think that same way and constantly want to improve. You can see it now. There are some players who might be struggling to get game time at their clubs, but they come back to the Scotland camps and enjoy themselves and look completely different players. They step up to the mark and it is a joy to watch. Every game, every competition, this Scotland team has got better and better.'

The experienced boss also knew if his team and squad was going to be successful, then he was going to need to create a real bond and togetherness. That had been a key ingredient in Scotland teams of the past. It was never about individuals. As they say, there is no I in team. Clarke put rules and stipulations in place for everyone. It was one for all and all for one.

Phones are banned on match days, and all the players have to eat together at mealtimes and aren't allowed to go back to their rooms until everybody is finished.

Dyer explained: 'They are simple things but they are things that represent each other. At mealtimes we would all go down at the same time. It is that discipline and respect for each other. Training is the same. You go out and give 100 per cent. There is no one messing around and going through the motions. Steve makes sure he takes control of things. If you go away with Scotland you know you are working for Steve and your country. You are going to have to train hard and be part of the group, knowing everyone will be asked to do the same thing. It is all about respect. You then grow to love each other and you want to play for that man sitting next to you at the dining table or out on the Hampden pitch beside you. That is what we did at Kilmarnock and it was taken on with Scotland.'

Winger Ryan Fraser admits it was probably the shake-up the squad needed. He said: 'The manager hasn't had long but he made an impact. He imposed rules off the pitch – no phones at the game, eating together every day. No one is allowed to leave the table until everyone is finished eating. No one is having dessert any more – everyone wants to get back to their room! No, listen, I think we needed it. Over the five years I've been involved, you've had people sometimes not even coming down for dinner. So it's nice to have a couple of rules in place.'

Fraser also reckoned it had the desired effect on the Scotland players and squad. He added: 'Sometimes they're hard rules to keep to but, at the same time, the team spirit and togetherness is so much better. It's hard to create that team spirit with a national team because you are so rarely together. The squad can change every time one is announced.'

It isn't just his players that Clarke drives on, but everybody around him. He wants and expects that the Scotland national team will be the best it can be. That means putting everything into every possible session and game.

'He pushes you to your limits and he demands the best every day,' Dyer stated. 'That is what you have to give him. It is intense and you are on it all the time, but it is the best way. It is the best way you can learn and push yourself. You make mistakes but you go at it again. You are always analysing yourself and the team. You are constantly looking at ways to make yourself and the team better. That is the only way you keep improving.'

Experienced defender Charlie Mulgrew had played at the top level with Celtic and Scotland. He was impressed with Clarke and his hard-working ways on the training pitch in those early camps. Mulgrew said: 'The manager has been brilliant. I've been very impressed and we're glad to have him. People say international managers don't have much time with players, but after these double sessions, believe me, he's had time! It's been really difficult but also really enjoyable. We are lucky to have him and it's a good start. It's early days but he's looking top drawer. He keeps things simple. You'd be surprised how often that doesn't happen. It's simple and effective.'

Clarke had put his tactics and game plans into operation and dining rules in place. It was all about serving up results on the pitch. That is what makes or breaks you as a football manager. The omens were good because Cyprus had never beaten Scotland in their previous five encounters. The nation was expecting that to continue and there to be no red faces on Clarke's big opening day. It was more about the intrigue to see that first starting XI and how Clarke would approach it. What changes would he make, if any?

That first game against Cyprus he went with a starting (4-3-3) XI of: Marshall, O'Donnell, Mulgrew, McKenna, Robertson, McGinn, McLean, McGregor, Forrest, Brophy, Fraser. The game plan was there with a defensive shape that allowed the likes of McGinn, Forrest, Brophy and Fraser to get on the front foot.

Fraser confirmed: 'The manager has worked on foundations that are more defensive, making us hard to beat, but at the same time he gives the front four the licence to do their stuff.'

Just over 30,000 of the Tartan Army were at Hampden, but Clarke's arrival had swelled the gate. It was a pretty dull and uninspiring first hour with both sides having chances but neither side taking them. The man of the moment then came to the fore. Captain Robertson was still high on adrenaline after his Champions League final win over Tottenham Hotspur. He took a pass from McGinn, stepped in from the left and fired a shot right across the keeper Urko Pardo and into the top corner of the net just after the hour. It was a thing of beauty and you saw what it meant to Clarke as he celebrated on the touchline. His Scotland tenure was up and running. It was the slenderest of leads and there was still work to be done, as Oliver Burke came on for Brophy and Scott McTominay replaced John McGinn.

Things were going to script until Ioannis Kousoulos got away from his marker to head in an easy equaliser for Cyprus three minutes from the end. It had the makings of a typical Scotland performance of recent times. It offered so much but just failed to deliver. Clarke's side were down but they weren't out. Just 138 seconds later, the Scots stole victory from the jaws of disappointment. Fraser stood up a cross and substitute Burke headed it off the post before he reacted first to knock the rebound into the empty net in the final minute of normal time.

It felt as though the roof was lifted off Hampden. Clarke punched the air, turned and with his fist in the air celebrated in front of the Main Stand. He knew what it meant to get a win and to make an immediate mark as Scotland manager. He needed to get out of the blocks to get the players, fans and the nation onside from the off.

Mulgrew, who won his 40th cap that afternoon, added: 'I didn't see the manager when we scored but I heard he was buzzing. That's good. He was pretty calm in the dressing room but it was a great feeling. That winner felt like one of the great nights at Hampden. We were over the moon with the win. It was important to win, not just for the manager, but in terms of the campaign. We knew it was a massive game and we are delighted to get the manager off to a good start.'

Fraser believed Burke's late goal was an early sign of togetherness that Clarke had started to foster. There was the start of a real spirit. He claimed: 'It's just about trying to get the team together, get the team bonding and get that spirit. You saw that in the way we stuck together and got the winner against Cyprus.'

Mulgrew was sure the hard work in training there had been a major part in Scotland's late, late show. It had been a case of survival of the fittest.

Mulgrew said: 'The hard training at the beginning of the

week showed after 80 minutes on Saturday. We were so close to victory when they made it 1-1 but we didn't let our heads go down and did well. We kept going right to the end.'

The standard had been set and Clarke's Scotland managerial career was up and running.

Chapter 5

BIG GUNS BLAST HOPES OF AUTOMATIC QUALIFICATION TO EURO 2020

SCOTLAND, under Steve Clarke, had got off to a dream start, but there were always far tougher tests ahead in Group I of the 2020 European Championship qualifiers. One of the biggest was to come just three days after that Cyprus win. Clarke had to take his team to Belgium to take on the No. 1 ranked nation in the world. The Belgians, managed by former Motherwell player Roberto Martínez, could call on a galaxy of stars like Eden Hazard, Romelu Lukaku, Kevin De Bruyne, Thibaut Courtois, Vincent Kompany and countless others.

The Scotland players and fans needed no warning of what was to come. Belgium had dismantled Alex McLeish's side 4-0 in a Hampden friendly back in September 2018. Scotland had also lost their previous four games against the Belgians and the general feeling was that this was going to be five. It was just a case of how many and could Clarke and his team limit the damage? It was, after all, a swashbuckling Belgium team who were bang in form and had won their previous seven European Championship qualifying games going into this one.

The yellow-shirted Scots were right up against it in the King

Baudouin Stadium in Brussels. Clarke moved away from the attacking 4-3-3 formation that had kicked off against Cyprus. Belgium were a good few levels above that and so he went for a more traditional 4-4-2 starting line-up, with Stuart Armstrong being asked to get up and support Oliver Burke, who had been rewarded with a start after his late winner against Cyprus.

The Belgians dominated but Clarke's side looked like they were going to come through the first half unscathed, until Belgium sickeningly netted the opener in first half stoppage time, when Lukaku headed home a clever Hazard chip. The big, bustling striker netted his second early in the second period and De Bruyne finished the game off in added time with a low shot from outside the box. Greg Taylor found out at first hand the levels of international football as he made his debut that night.

Clarke had suffered his first defeat as Scotland manager. It left the Scots on six points from four games, in fourth place and three points behind the second-placed Russians. Dreams of automatic Euro 2020 qualification were starting to drift away.

The September double-header was going to make or break Scotland's automatic hopes of making Euro 2020, with Russia and the Belgians travelling to Hampden. Belgium were on a maximum 12 points and looked unstoppable. The best hope, in all honesty, was a win over the Russians, but even that looked a long shot. Clarke needed a big result and performance to try and upset the odds and breathe life into this unconvincing qualifying campaign.

Clarke and his team weren't helped by a social media video that went viral. It showed Oli McBurnie criticising the Scotland national team when he was with Sheffield United. It was hardly what Clarke needed ahead of some big qualifiers. It was an unnecessary distraction, although the Sheffield United striker offered a full and frank explanation and apology to the squad after he met up with them for the Russian game.

McBurnie knew he had to try and do his talking on the pitch, when the chance arose. He said: 'Ever since the manager has come in he has been really good with me. I have not made it easy for him to be good with me with certain situations I've put myself in, but he has always had my back and had confidence in me. My performances for Scotland haven't been where I would have liked them to have been. I haven't carried my club form, when I have been playing well, into my international form which I really want to do. It is time for me to repay some of that confidence.'

McBurnie was given that chance as he was handed the No. 9 shirt for the visit of Russia. Scotland were at home and Clarke knew the Hampden crowd expected more attacking intent. He went with the 4-3-3 formation, with James Forrest and Ryan Fraser providing the width on either side. It was John McGinn who showed an eye for goal as he cashed in on a goalkeeping error from Guilherme Marinato to fire Scotland in front, but in-form striker Artem Dzyuba levelled after Andy Robertson's block had fallen perfectly into his path five minutes before half-time. The Russians turned the game around just before the hour when Aleksandr Golovin crossed and the former Chelsea player Yuri Zhirkov bundled it in, despite Stephen O'Donnell's best efforts to clear, for what proved to be the winner.

O'Donnell was overly self-critical of himself after the game and claimed his lack of discipline on the defensive side had cost Scotland. He said: 'That sums it up. I was back scrambling and it is disappointing but that is football. If I was there again I would try to clear the ball again. That [goal] was on me. I thought we had safe possession but I have worked with the manager long enough and know I need to be inside my man. He doesn't need me to be pushing that high up the pitch and I don't know why

I went that high in the first place. That was early doors in the second half and we didn't need to be chasing it that early. I was caught high and then their quality in the final third has hurt us.'

The Belgians were next to land another crippling blow to Scotland's Euro qualifying ambitions. It was to be a case of Hampden déjà vu as the Belgians handed out another 4-0 thumping. Lukaku and De Bruyne got on the scoresheet again, along with Thomas Vermaelen and Toby Alderweireld.

Scotland could still qualify but it was going to take some turnaround for Clarke and his men. It looked a bridge too far. He and everyone else knew it was all but over. Belgium had a full head of steam and were already out of sight. There was still the very, very remote chance that Russia, in second spot, could be caught. So the trip, next up, to Moscow fell into the must-win category. The October 2019 window was the one where Scotland's direct Euro 2020 hopes were unceremoniously ended. Scotland had the trip to Russia and a home game against San Marino.

Lawrence Shankland was called up after his free-scoring exploits had helped Dundee United go top of the Championship in their charge towards a Premiership return.

The striker was no stranger to Hampden Park as he had come through the youth ranks of Queen's Park before he had moved on to Aberdeen. It was in the lower leagues with Ayr United that his goal-filled career had taken fire and had continued with his move to Tannadice. It was a massive step up from the level where Shankland had been playing, but Clarke didn't exactly have an abundance of striking options and Shankland was very much the man in form in Scotland.

It was the Russians, however, who had the pedigree and the excessive firepower on their home turf. They simply swept the Scots away in a 4-0 victory, thanks to a double from Artem Dzyuba and goals from Magomed Ozdoev and Aleksandr Golovin.

One minor positive for Clarke and the travelling Tartan Army was getting Shankland and Sheffield United midfielder John Fleck on for their debuts.

Shankland proudly said: 'There had been a bit of talk about me getting called up but, playing in the Championship, it was probably still unexpected. When I was told by the Dundee United manager, Robbie Neilson, it was a wee bit of a shock and then it was a feeling of excitement, knowing I would be involved with Scotland. I started on the bench and I went out and got warmed up after Oliver Burke had taken a knock. Then I got the shout that I was going to make my debut. I came on when we were 3-0 down. It was surreal because I came on in the Luzhniki Stadium, where the 2018 World Cup final had been played. It was great for me to have made my debut, but it was at a time when the national team was having a bit of a hard time. The result, however, was the big disappointment for me.'

It saw Clarke come into the firing line for really the first time from pundits, the press and some of the fans. The Scotland manager hadn't even had a full campaign. Points had already been dropped in Kazakhstan before he had stepped into the post, but there was an expectation there, even though it was more than 20 years since Scotland had qualified for a major finals. It didn't matter and for the first time Clarke was to feel the heat.

Striker Stevie Naismith said: 'There was some backlash on the back of that run. I remember way back at the start there were lots of pundits and ex-pros who weren't giving Steve enough time. They were very quickly on to Steve and had their opinions set that it wasn't going to work. It is ironic that a lot of these same critics are now sitting applauding the gaffer and saying how well he has done. It is funny how things change. I am sure it is something the gaffer will have a wee wry smile on his face over those comments now and rightly so.'

Aberdeen defender Mikey Devlin played against the Russians and reckoned it was wrong to judge Clarke on those recent results, knowing he was still finding his feet, getting to know his players and still experimenting with what he had.

Devlin claimed: 'In terms of results, I think there needs to be an element of realism, firstly of the level of opposition we played in those two games in September and the new manager only had two one-week sessions with the players. Steve had been brilliant with his training. There had been an intensity there and he is very clear in what he wants you to do. Albeit the results were disappointing, but I believe we are heading in the right direction and the longer the manager is given to work with the boys, I have no doubt we will get there.'

It was a time for cool heads and not knee-jerk reactions. The Scotland job was never going to come with an overnight fix. It was about showing a bit of patience, a bit of progress and slowly building.

Pat Nevin recalled: 'There was a period when people were calling for Steve [to be sacked]. I was doing a lot of media work and I was telling people: "No, this guy is good and it is not just because he is my mate." Everyone did stick by him.'

For Clarke, he might have been experienced as a coach and a manager, but international football was a different arena. He also had to adjust and find his feet. He also had to take things on the chin and adapt and learn as he went.

His assistant Alex Dyer explained: 'We beat Cyprus in the first game and then we lost a few games. They were tough games but that is football. Steve knew he would have time to put his stamp on things. Good coaches learn all the time and especially from their defeats. Steve is a smart man and he slowly started to make changes. Some players left and others came in and gradually he started to build a team for the longer term. There are some players you can go with in the short term and others for the long haul. It is about finding the right solutions.'

The defeat in Russia was a real low point for Clarke and his team. He made it clear that had to be Scotland's rock bottom and the only way was up. Keeper David Marshall acknowledged it wasn't a happy dressing room.

'Belgium were a different class but Russia away was the one,' the Hibs keeper recalled. 'We lost heavily and in the dressing room after the game there were a few arguments. The clear vibe was that things hadn't been good enough. The manager then came in and told us this is the lowest it can go. We needed to turn the corner from there.'

Motherwell defender Declan Gallagher was new to the squad. He said: 'The first camp, we were over in Russia and it was 4-0 we got beat. The manager made a big speech after it and said: "This is going to be the last time we feel a disappointment like this." Credit to him because that has proved to be the case. I am on nine caps and we went eight games unbeaten at one stage. I think you can see that winning feeling now in the camps and it is starting to build. The boys believe in the manager and what he is doing. Confidence also breeds confidence and that is what is happening.'

O'Donnell knew Clarke prided himself on his teams being solid and hard to beat. He also recognised some of the heavy defeats would have been hard for the manager to stomach. It went against his very principles and coaching beliefs.

'That hurt him,' O'Donnell insisted. 'I know from his time at Kilmarnock that he wanted to be defensively sound and that was the platform from which to build. The Russia performance was something that was unlike one of his teams. He would have been disappointed but Russia is a hard place to go and they were a good team. We used that as a reset to make sure it didn't happen again. I don't think it really has. The worst result after that was the England game [in 2023] but that was a friendly and they are a better side than Russia.'

It brought a bit of reality to where Scotland were and how far they still had to go. It was going to be a long and winding road, with more downs than maybe ups. Nobody had to tell Clarke that. He knew better than anyone. The manager conceded after the Russia game that it was a real low point. Unusually, he turned on his players and demanded more – so much more! The experienced coach was also left doubting himself, as much as his Scotland players.

Shankland said: 'It is quite weird looking back now. The gaffer did state that moment was as low as it was going to get and things had to get better from there. It has been really interesting and positive to see how things developed and progressed in the years that followed.'

Dyer believes the Russia and Belgium games showed the gap Steve and Scotland had to close. His former assistant recalled: 'We went to Belgium and Russia and lost. We had them both home and away. They were tough sides and were another level for Scotland at that point. That time was about building learning blocks to get close to those sorts of levels. Now, when Scotland play the top teams they are much better prepared to match these teams than we were two or three years ago. You can see the improvement is there. The Scotland players feel they can go out and give the big countries a game now. Whether they win or not, the gaffer knows his players will give their all and the opposition will know that they will have been in a game. Scotland have come a long way.'

That Russia game was to be the final international appearance for some of Scotland's more senior squad members, including Charlie Mulgrew and Robert Snodgrass. They were to join a list of top players, like Darren Fletcher, Kenny Miller and Barry

Ferguson, who never got the chance to play for Scotland on the biggest international stages.

Former Liverpool and Rangers midfielder Charlie Adam, who won 26 caps, was one of that lost generation. It remains a major source of frustration. Adam said: 'You always talk about winning the first title or trophy in your career. For us, the longer it went on the harder it got to qualify.'

Goalkeeper David Marshall saw the changing of the guard from inside the camp. He added: 'A few of the boys weren't involved again after that Russia game. The manager decided to go down a different route and it worked, although don't get me wrong, we had some decent fixtures after Belgium and Russia were out of the way.'

From there, it was then a case of using the remaining Euro 2020 qualifiers to try and build up confidence and put points on the board ahead of the Nations League play-off with Israel.

Scotland did get a lift with the 6-0 dismantling of San Marino. John McGinn helped himself to a first-half hat-trick, while Shankland got a goal on his first start, as did debutant Stuart Findlay, and Stuart Armstrong also got in on the act at Hampden.

A delighted Shankland said: 'It was a dream come true just to start for Scotland, never mind to score a goal. I had played at Hampden for Queen's Park, but to play for your country was and remains the ultimate. I felt there were a few chances in the game against San Marino, but John McGinn netted a hat-trick in the first-half – I could have done with a few of his chances. I eventually got one in the second half when the ball came off the bar and I managed to put it away. It was something you dream about. I used to go to Scotland games with my family and support the team, but now I was on the pitch playing for my country. It was so surreal. It was great for my family to be there, to see my goal and to enjoy it with me. It is a night that will live with me forever and I will be forever grateful to Steve Clarke for giving me that opportunity and all my caps and call-ups before and after. I love playing for my country and it is something I would never take for granted.'

The final two matches of the campaign saw a trip to Cyprus and a home clash with Kazakhstan. The remaining games were an opportunity for Clarke to look at new players ahead of the Nations League play-off. Motherwell defender Declan Gallagher made his debut in Nicosia. He had been released by Celtic as a kid and then had spells at Clyde, Dundee and Livingston before his impressive displays at Fir Park had seen his remarkable rise to that first Scotland cap.

Gallagher revealed his first Scotland appearance left him, quite literally, sick. The experienced centre half recalled: 'It was so warm. All I remember was the heat and then the tempo of the game was a level I had never experienced before. I remember coming in at half-time and I don't know if it was nerves, adrenaline or I was absolutely knackered, but I was physically sick at half-time. It might have been a mixture of everything.'

Ryan Christie had put Scotland ahead in the first half, but if Gallagher had been feeling under the weather at the interval, it was nothing to how he felt just into the second half, as Cyprus's Georgios Efrem volleyed in a wonder goal.

He said: 'It was a free kick and I had gone up and won the header and thought it was a decent clearance, high and wide, and then the next thing the boy Efrem, who used to be at Rangers, catches it perfectly on the volley and puts it in the opposite top corner. So I went from thinking I had made a good clearance to suddenly having an assist for Cyprus! A few minutes later John McGinn scored and I thought: "Brilliant." What a relief! I thought if we hadn't won the game then it would have been my first and last cap!'

McGinn's goal in the 53rd minute ended up being decisive. It also meant that it made it a happy milestone for a couple of men in the squad. New boy Gallagher had made his Scotland debut while experienced Hearts striker Stevie Naismith came off the bench to win his 50th cap.

Gallagher recalled: 'It was my first cap and first win, which was good. My family and my in-laws were all at the game, which was also important for me. There were good celebrations in the dressing room and then the manager gave a special mention to me for my first cap and Stevie Naismith for winning his 50th. It was a special moment, making my debut for my country and will be a game I will never forget.'

Scotland were on a two-game winning run and the final Euro 2020 qualifier was a chance to exorcise the ghost of Kazakhstan – which had effectively ended Alex McLeish's time as manager in the Astana Arena. It had been a setback and one that Scotland had never really fully recovered from, in terms of getting themselves back into contention for the top two positions in this Euro qualifying group.

Kazakhstan still had the chance to pile further pain on Scotland when Bakhtiyar Zaynutdinov put them ahead in the first half. The Scots got the momentum after the interval and came out 3-1 winners, thanks to a John McGinn double, sandwiched either side of a goal from Stevie Naismith. It was a hot scoring streak for McGinn who had netted six times in his last three games. It also took the midfielder's tally for the qualifying campaign to an impressive seven goals. It wasn't too shabby a return from the Aston Villa midfielder who was firmly establishing himself as a key component in Clarke's new-look side.

The Kazakhstan win allowed Scotland to seal third place. They were nine points adrift of Russia, who had finished second behind runaway group winners Belgium. It was all about building confidence ahead of the Nations League play-off.

The end of that campaign saw Dyer step down as Clarke's assistant, having been offered the chance to follow in his footsteps as Kilmarnock manager. Dyer left with Clarke's blessing: 'We had won our last three games at the end of the Euro 2020 qualifying campaign and it was after that I came away. The team continued their good run after that and it was nice I was part of that. It was tough because I didn't want to let Steve down although I knew he could more than cope without me. I didn't want to let him down but at the same time I was ambitious and I wanted to manage in my own right. Kilmarnock was a club I knew well and had enormous affection for. It was too good an opportunity to turn down. The gaffer even told me that it was a good job and I should take it on. It did hurt because I loved being away and part of the Scotland set-up. I still watch all the Scotland games now and keep in touch with Steve; if either of us need anything then we know just to pick up the phone.'

Chapter 6

DYKES PROVIDES SOME THUNDER FROM DOWN UNDER

THE pitfalls of international football mean you have what you have. It is not as if you can go out and buy players in the January or summer windows. Steve Clarke knows that better than most. He had a limited but dedicated pool, many of whom were younger players inherited from Alex McLeish's second spell in charge. The good thing was that they had gained experience under McLeish and were looking to kick on and establish themselves on the international stage.

Clarke had been used to operating in the riches of the English Premier League with the likes of Chelsea, Liverpool, Newcastle United and West Ham United, under big-name managers. When he did eventually go out in his own right, he didn't exactly have open cheque books or bottomless pits of money at West Bromwich Albion, Reading and Kilmarnock. Certainly by the time he was at Kilmarnock, he was shopping in the bargain basements, although the Rugby Park board pushed the boat out whenever they could to aid him. It had to be said, Killie were certainly rewarded by Clarke with two big seasons in his time in Ayrshire.

The one area where Scotland managers can add or widen their player options is via the grandparent rule. Other countries have less stringent selection processes but the SFA has always been pretty regimented and a lot more limited than others, like perhaps the Republic of Ireland team of the 1980s and 1990s, where the joke was you could drink a pint of Guinness and be eligible to play for their national team.

The grandparent rule, however, was one that the SFA were happy to adopt. An example of that was a player Clarke had inherited in the shape of Leeds United captain Liam Cooper. He had come through the ranks at Hull City but was eligible as one of his grandparents was born in Scotland. He also nailed his allegiances to the mast pretty early on, representing Scotland at under-17 and under-19 level before he made his full international bow. He was first called up in 2016 but never made his debut until Clarke played him against Russia at Hampden in the Euro 2020 qualifiers.

Clarke may have inherited an abundance of riches at left back but in other positions he lacked options and none more so than at centre forward.

Lyndon Dykes was one who was eligible to play for Scotland and could provide a possible solution to his attacking headache. The 25-year-old was born on Australia's Gold Coast but his parents hailed from Dumfries. He had represented the Australians at schoolboy level but after that had a bit of a nomadic spell. Dykes's early playing career saw him come through the ranks of Mudgeeraba before he moved to Merrimac and had stints at Redlands United, Gold Coast City and Surfers Paradise Apollo sandwiched in between two spells in his parents' homeland with local club Queen of the South. It was there he caught the eye of Livingston who gave the big powerful striker a shot at the Scottish Premier League in 2019. He impressed with 12 goals in just 33 games, including a big goal in a win against Celtic.

Dykes was a battering ram of a centre forward who could

single-handedly bully defences and put them on the back foot with his physique and fearless approach. He was constantly linked with Rangers, Celtic and several English clubs.

The forward had also caught the eye internationally with Australia showing their hand, their assistant manager René Meulensteen sent to watch him in action. Clarke had also seen enough of him and felt Dykes would offer something to his Scotland team. The Scotland boss made his move and sold him on why he should choose Scotland ahead of his homeland. The big selling point was a possible Euro 2020 play-off place. It was a huge decision and one that Dykes, understandably, didn't want to rush into. Clarke and Australia boss Graham Arnold both gave him time. Arnold, however, was confident, having held several discussions with Dykes and exchanged numerous text messages, but Covid-19 might well have cost him. Arnold claimed he was going to call Dykes up for the World Cup qualifiers against Kuwait and Nepal in the March of 2020, but the pandemic and travel restrictions put paid to that.

Clarke remained on the case. Dykes started the 2020–21 season on fire with two goals in three games and that was enough to persuade English Championship side Queens Park Rangers to hand Livingston a seven-figure club record deal for his services. It was at that time that the then QPR boss Mark Warburton let the cat out of the bag by backing his new striker to make a real impact with Scotland. His mystic powers proved to be on the money, as Dykes committed to Scotland. Clarke named him in his squad for the first time in August 2020 for the Nations League encounters with Israel and the Czech Republic.

Dykes said: 'It was flattering to have the choice of Scotland and Australia. It really was. You have to remember I had only just come back from Australia to Queen of the South four years earlier. At that point, it was more about pursuing my dream of being a full-time professional than being an international player. Australia and Scotland had both made approaches before Covid and then the lockdown gave me a bit of time to consider what I was going to do.

'I spoke to a few people close to me like former Scotland internationals James McFadden and Gary Naysmith, whom I had worked with at Queen of the South. They pretty much told me that I should choose Scotland because under Steve Clarke we were on the way up. If I am being honest, that was what my gut feeling was anyway. I was born in Australia but the majority of my family is Scottish. That also played a big part. Yes, Scotland had a Euro 2020 play-off but I was looking more at things long term. Australia are pretty much certs to qualify for the World Cup, but I just felt a connection with the gaffer and what he was looking to achieve with Scotland and that, in the end, made my mind up for me.'

Australia were doing well and probably had the better chance of going to regular World Cups, but Clarke's powers of persuasion had won the day. It was to prove to be a big moment in Clarke's time in charge of the Scotland team. The team now had a focal point to lead the line in the Euro 2020 play-off. There are no international contracts but the new recruit decided to ink his allegiance to Scotland in black and white with a tattoo on his ribs.

Dykes explained: 'I've got a claymore on my ribs with thistles and the date of my Scotland debut [against Israel on 4 September 2020]. Ryan Christie and I have both joked we will get matching Scotland tattoos. We haven't found the right one yet. We might get a Euro 2024 one.'

Dykes may have missed out on a World Cup with Australia, but he is adamant Scotland was the one and only choice for him.

He stated: 'No regrets. It was pretty straightforward. I spoke to both managers before Covid and then the pandemic kicked in. It dragged it out but I knew I was going to Scotland. My time with Scotland has been amazing. I've enjoyed every minute of it. I am playing with world-class players and I feel like I have done well for Scotland and what I can do on the big stage. I haven't looked back and if I was to have the same choice again I would make the same decision.'

Dykes is in no doubt that the dark blue of Scotland is where he really thrives. He said: 'We have built up for a long time to where we are today. It has been a delight to be part of and I'm sure it has been a delight for everyone to watch. Now we are just focused on maintaining the standards we have set and trying to improve again wherever we can. I feel playing for Scotland improves me and it brings the best out of me.'

Chapter 7

FIGHTING A PANDEMIC – AND FOR A PLAY-OFF

IT was now all eyes on the Nations League play-offs. It was the final opportunity to try and make the Euro 2020 finals and the pathway that Alex McLeish had left open. The November draw came in Switzerland just days after Steve Clarke and his men had brought the curtain down on their European Championship qualifying campaign with that 3-1 win over Kazakhstan.

Clarke knew his side would face one of Bulgaria, Hungary, Israel or Romania in the Nations League semi-final draw. It was maybe no surprise when the Scots were paired with old foes Israel. There was a certain inevitability that it was going to be the Israelis. Scotland, under Alex McLeish, had just finished above them to win Nations League Group C1. His side had lost 2-1 away and won 3-2 at home, although both teams had, as a result, made the play-offs.

UEFA confirmed the semi-final and finals would be one-off games. The good news for Scotland was their last four clash with Israel was to be at Hampden, scheduled for 26 March 2020. The winners also knew they would be away to face whoever were victorious between Norway and Serbia in that final step for a Euro 2020 place.

When the cannon was fired from Edinburgh Castle on Hogmanay to signal the start of 2020, it was meant to be a happy new year, with the nation hoping it certainly would be for the national team with Clarke looking to end the 22-year wait to get back to the top table. All eyes were on that Israel semi-final. That was the be all and end all.

There was also the small matter of the 2020–21 Nations League draw before then. It was Clarke's first taste of the tournament proper, which effectively replaced mind-numbing international friendlies and also offered alternative qualifying avenues to major finals, with the national coach and his team looking to become one of the main beneficiaries. The draw was made just over three weeks before the play-off on 3 March 2020 in Amsterdam.

Scotland's promotion in the Nations League saw them placed in Group B2, where Clarke's side were drawn against the Czech Republic, Slovakia and you guessed it, Israel, again! It would mean the two countries would now face the possibility of playing each other five times in two years. There was certainly not going to be any element of surprise when it came to those games.

Steve Clarke, speaking to the SFA's website, said: 'It's an interesting draw for us, and we are looking forward to the UEFA Nations League kicking off again. The competition has already proven its value to us, providing a further opportunity to qualify for UEFA Euro 2020.'

Quickly there became more pressing concerns than football, however. Coronavirus was starting to take a grip of the world. Scotland was far from immune and began to lock down to try and slow the potential spread of what was to become the Covid-19 pandemic. The first impact on Scottish football was seen when it effectively closed down on Friday, 13 March 2020, with Motherwell due to host Aberdeen in the Premiership and Queen of the South taking on Ayr United in the Championship.

Nobody knew what the world had entered. Scottish Professional Football League chiefs were in the dark as much as anyone and controversially, the 2019–20 Scottish football season had seen its last ball kicked. It led to a nasty fallout after the relegations of Hearts, Partick Thistle and Stranraer, which would eventually lead to Scottish football being dragged through the courts and left long-lasting bad blood within the game.

Clarke's one and only concern was the national team. The play-off with Israel was already a sell-out and the boss was due to name his squad, but with every passing day the chances of the fixture being played, as scheduled, looked less and less likely. Needless to say, the press conference for the squad announcement was cancelled as the country went deeper into lockdown with far more pressing concerns. Football was very much secondary. Scotland's play-off with Israel was inevitably postponed and pushed back to a new provisional date of Wednesday, 17 June 2020, but even that looked optimistic with the home nations still in the grip of the deadly virus. The rescheduled June date came and went with neither Scotland nor Israel any closer to knowing when they would play again, never mind in this Euro 2020 play-off.

UEFA confirmed their showcase 2020 European Championships would not be played that summer either because of the pandemic. It would be delayed for a year. So Euro 2020 effectively became Euro 2021, although not in name, which was now set to run from 11 June to 11 July.

Scottish football's top flight did offer a beacon of hope when it resumed for the start of the 2020–21 season, albeit behind closed doors. Through time there was a partial staggered return for supporters as the nation and world tried to battle against the pandemic. Scottish football was a major source of light and escapism for a lot of people during the lockdown, with games being beamed into living rooms and homes up and down the country.

Scotland fans and much-travelled members of the Tartan Army had to wait a little longer before they were to get their much-needed national team fix. UEFA's Executive Committee finally announced resumption of its club and international commitments after the initial Covid shutdown. The only issue was that Scottish government guidelines meant the first batch of games would have to be played behind closed doors.

It was confirmed that Scotland would open up their Nations League group with games against Israel at Hampden and away to the Czech Republic in the September. That would be followed by two huge triple-headers. The Euro 2020 play-off semi-final with Israel would kick off the October games and then there would be home Nations League games with Slovakia and the Czech Republic.

All going well, the November trio would see a Euro 2020 play-off final and the last Nations League games away to Slovakia and Israel.

The good news for Steve Clarke was that he was able to plan for the semi-final with Israel on 8 October at Hampden. The bad news for the Tartan Army was that it was still in the midst of lockdown and there was to be no fans. There were, however, still to be Scotland games, via television, to try and offer a ray of light in some dark times.

It helped when the September games passed with relative ease with Scotland picking up a draw at home to Israel and a win away in the Czech Republic.

So the national team appeared to be going into the semi-final in good health, but there was to be a late twist that threw Steve Clarke's plans into chaos before the game.

The national boss had already picked his team before he had

to rip things up and start again. Covid was still rife. Clarke, his team and his staff had to do regular testing, as part of their international bubble.

Midfielder Stuart Armstrong's test came back positive. It was a blow because he had been involved in the two games the previous month and was likely to play a major part again. That was one setback for the national coach, but there were to be further hammer blows with the news that Kieran Tierney and Ryan Christie had both been in close contact and would also need to self-isolate. As a result, they would miss Scotland's biggest game in years. The pair had not tested positive but it transpired they had been playing the PlayStation as a group and had been in the close vicinity of Armstrong. Like him, they were therefore unavailable – much to the frustration of Clarke, his team and a nation.

That was on top of Scott McKenna, Liam Palmer and James Forrest who were all missing through injury. Declan Gallagher ended up being one of the main benefactors as he got the late shout to come in and take Tierney's place in Clarke's three-man central defence.

'I didn't get time to feel nervous because I was put in at the last minute,' the Motherwell defender said. 'It was meant to be Liam Cooper with KT and Scott McKenna, but KT missed out because of Covid. They were told they couldn't play and I was called in and told I was starting. I didn't get time to get nervous, which probably helped me because I am quite an emotional guy in the build-up.'

The late change was maybe a late curveball to Israel as well. Both sides pretty much knew each other inside out and back to front as they had played each other that often in the Nations League.

Stephen O'Donnell added: 'It was at a time where we seemed to be drawn with Israel in just about every Nations League group at that spell. The good thing was that we knew we were at Hampden. They were a good team who we knew could cause problems but we had a good record against them, especially at home, so we went into the play-off confident.'

Clarke went with David Marshall, Scott McTominay, Cooper and Gallagher as his defence, O'Donnell and Andy Robertson as his wing backs, Ryan Jack, Callum McGregor and John McGinn as his midfield three, with Lyndon Dykes and Oli McBurnie in attack. The manager had shown a lot of faith in McBurnie, as he had got caught up in the social media storm and caused further controversy when he had pulled out of the double-header with Israel and the Czech Republic with a foot injury and then played in a pre-season friendly for Sheffield United. It left McBurnie in another difficult situation.

McBurnie said: 'My manager [Chris Wilder] at Sheffield United and Steve Clarke had sorted that out and it was nothing to do with me. I can understand from the outside how it looks but it is one of these things; it is easy to get on top of me. I hadn't trained in pre-season or since the previous season and I had been out for six weeks. I did one session and then I came off the bench and played 45 minutes of a pre-season game, which I wasn't aware that I was going to be doing.'

McBurnie knew the Israel game was a big opportunity for him to put in a performance and to try and get Scotland into the play-off final.

He said: 'It is the proudest moment for me – international football is the pinnacle and I have always said that. From the under-19s all the way up it is always a proud one to represent Scotland for me and my family. To wear that No. 9 shirt at Hampden is something I dreamt about as a kid. To do that is really special. People are well within their rights to challenge and question my ability or footballing-wise. I am a footballer and that is what I am here to do and if people don't like the way I play then that is fine, but the hard one for me is the commitment. I have been a Scotland fan since I was a kid; I see myself as Scottish and I see myself as a Scotsman. That does hurt and the football stuff hurts my family more than me, but I am used to that sort of stuff.'

Israel boss Willi Ruttensteiner could also keep a bit of an inside track on Scotland via Celtic pair Nir Bitton and Hatem Abd Elhamed and Hibs keeper Ofir Marciano as the trio were playing domestically in Scotland. Everyone knew what was at stake, but there was an eerie silence as both teams took to the pitch. It was played in front of a ghost-like Hampden, with only a few flags tied down amongst a plethora of empty seats, and both countries knew that defeat would leave the losers harbouring an eerie emptiness of their own. A game of this magnitude was always going to be a nervy affair and that was the way it panned out. The Scottish Government's lockdown rules probably did the Scotland and Israeli fans a favour, although it didn't feel like that as nails were bitten and nerves shredded across both hopeful nations.

Israel's Eran Zahavi was the main threat to the Scots. Gallagher knew he was a player the Scotland defence had to get the better of – and he did.

Gallagher said: 'Out of all the games we played against Israel, it was one of the games I felt most comfortable. We dominated for long spells although they had chances because they were a good team with Zahavi, etc. We had played enough against them and knew what to expect. I laugh now because my dad was watching and he said to me: "I knew you were going to have a good game five minutes in when you won the ball in a challenge with Zahavi and you then did a wee turn with the ball and played it away. It was positive and just you." I felt I started well because it was only my third or fourth Scotland cap.'

Scotland had a few chances. John McGinn fired a couple off target and captain Andy Robertson curled a free kick wide. The best chance of the first half came when Scott McTominay found himself free after he got on the end of a Robertson corner, but he headed disappointingly wide. The player and his manager had their heads in their hands, knowing what a big opportunity it had been.

The second half saw both teams create chances, but there was very little to worry either keeper as both defences mopped up easily. Clarke sent on Lawrence Shankland for McBurnie and went even more attacking when he took off Ryan Jack and sent on Ryan Fraser, but both teams were cancelling each other out and unable to break the stalemate.

Dykes said: 'It was great to start that game because we all knew how big it was. It was a tough game which we knew it would be because Israel were a good team. We had a lot of the ball but there weren't really a lot of chances in the game.'

Dykes was replaced by Sheffield Wednesday's Callum Paterson at the start of extra time. It was now getting down to where a moment of magic or madness was going to decide the outcome.

Fraser curled in a cross that was headed out by Bitton to McGregor but his volley was blocked by a defender. O'Donnell made way for Kenny McLean for the final seven minutes. It was another attacking switch but Clarke may have had other considerations in his mind.

O'Donnell joked: 'The gaffer probably didn't want me taking a penalty. In fairness, Kenny McLean is one of the best penalty takers in the squad so I couldn't really complain. I was just hoping that he or one of the other boys could get a goal for us in the last few minutes. It was torture watching the clock tick down from the bench.'

Things were ratcheted up a notch or two when Elhamed

curled an inviting cross into the Scotland box and the Israeli striker Shon Weissman, at full stretch, was millimetres away from connecting. If that was a near thing, the Scots were to go even closer to winning it at the death, in stoppage time of extra time. Andy Robertson took an outswinging corner from the left and Liam Cooper rose highest in front of a packed penalty box to head it towards goal. He beat Marciano but his header cannoned back off the post.

Gallagher recalled with frustration: 'I actually had a chance myself to score. Liam Cooper took it right off my head and hit the post. It was one of my more comfortable games although the scoreline made it look like it was a tight affair.'

Out of a total of 29 shots in the game, only one had been on target. It had actually been the first time Scotland had been involved in a goalless game in 55 matches. It just prolonged the nation's agony and wait. The managers would have been looking for a lot more accuracy when it came to the penalties. Clarke knew this could be an eventuality and made sure his players had got their spot-kick practice in. He knew it could come down to the finest detail and his team were prepared.

Gallagher said: 'I remember we practised penalties all that week and I had scored a couple. The day before I took a penalty and I skied it over the bar! The good thing was the rest of the boys had been taking their penalties so well that I was always confident. I would have taken one if needed to.'

Clarke wasn't the only one who had done his homework. His goalkeeping coach Stevie Woods and the other keepers, Jon McLaughlin and Robby McCrorie, had also put in the hours with No. 1 David Marshall. The group had watched the last ten penalties, where possible, of Israel's possible takers. They had analysed them and had agreed which way Marshall was best to go. The plan was easily devised with Woods's clipboard at the heart of things. Marshall only had to look at the Hampden technical area for advice. If the clipboard was up in the air then Marshall knew he had to go to his right. If it was down he was diving to his left and if Woods turned his back on his goalkeeper then he either didn't know where it was going or it was likely the taker was going to go down the middle.

Marshall explained: 'We set aside a day where the goalkeepers and Stevie would go through the penalties. We came to a consensus where a specific player was going to go. There is a big trust in the group and Stevie. You remember two or three of where you think the penalties will go, but it is hard to remember when you are facing five or six. So Stevie came up with a plan, with his clipboard signal, where I was going to go.'

First up was McGinn against his former Hibs teammate Marciano, which added a bit of added tension. The pink-shirted keeper went the right way and got a hand on it but was unable to stop McGinn's penalty from sneaking under his right hand. It was a let-off but a welcome one.

Scotland keeper Marshall said: 'John McGinn had the penalty that squirmed under the keeper. He knew Marciano because they had been at Hibs together and he was quite nervous about taking his penalty.'

Zahavi was first up for Israel. The data was that Zahavi would put his penalty to Marshall's right and Woods's clipboard was pointed high up into the Hampden sky. Zahavi didn't disappoint as he went to the keeper's right, but didn't put it right in the corner. Marshall read it and was able to push it away. It was first blood to Scotland.

The Scotland keeper knew it was a big one, denying Israel's talisman.

'Zahavi was their first taker,' Marshall explained. 'Saving that first one gave us a bit of breathing space, especially as he was also their best player. It gave us a bit of confidence going into the rest of them.'

It was suddenly a Celtic shoot-out. Callum McGregor put Scotland two up, while Celtic goalkeeping coach Stevie Woods had the inside track on Bitton. They knew the Hoops midfielder was likely to go right or down the middle. Marshall went for the side but the midfielder slotted it down the middle.

McTominay netted his as he found the same side as McGinn, but managed to squeeze it into Marciano's bottom right-hand corner. Weismann went down the middle to give Scotland only the slightest of edges.

Shankland was next up. The Dundee United striker said: 'Yes, there was pressure, but there is pressure in every big game. That is what you play football for. You want to be involved in moments like that. I had taken penalties throughout my career. I was confident and we had also practised that week. I knew where I was going. I stepped up and managed to send the keeper the wrong way. I have to say I was delighted and relieved when I saw the ball hit the net.'

Mohammad Abu Fani knew he had to score to keep Israel in the shoot-out and he didn't buckle. He also sent Marshall the wrong way and it was all on Scotland's fifth penalty. If they could maintain their 100 per cent shoot-out record then they would be in the final. It rested in the hands of another sub in Kenny McLean. The Norwich City midfielder certainly had the complete trust of his teammates.

Gallagher claimed: 'I remember we got to the last penalty and it was Kenny. I knew we had won because he had scored some great penalties in training and I just had so much belief in him.'

That faith wasn't to be misplaced. He was the coolest man inside Hampden. McLean stepped up and sent his penalty to the keeper's right, as Marciano dived to his left. The ball hit the net and a nation celebrated. It is fair to say lockdown rules were being broken, not only on the Hampden pitch, but the length and breadth of the country, as Scotland partied. McLean ran and jumped on keeper David Marshall before the rest of the team ran to celebrate with both national heroes.

Steve Clarke was bursting with pride. He celebrated on the touchline as he was grabbed and held by both John Carver and an equally delighted Steven Reid. There was even time for a quick embrace with doctor John MacLean. Clarke knew there were two sides to every story and while it was utter joy for Scotland it was devastation for Israel. The Israelis might have been ranked 93rd in the world, but they had pushed Scotland all the way. Clarke went across and, following Covid protocol, had a fist bump with Willi Ruttensteiner and offered him words of sympathy before he returned to the pitch to celebrate and enjoy the moment with his players.

Scotland were six games unbeaten but potentially one game away from European Championship qualification.

O'Donnell said: 'It was just such a feeling of relief when Kenny scored. You could see what it meant to us all with the celebrations. We all knew what was at stake. It had been that long since Scotland had been at a major tournament and we wanted to be the team who got us back there. It was typical Scotland that we did it the hard way and I am sure we put our fans through the mill, but we got there in the end. That was all that mattered.'

Scotland's reward was a trip to Serbia the following month. The Serbians had also gone the distance in Norway but had managed to win it in extra time. Sergej Milinković-Savić had been Serbia's hero with a double in their 2-1 win.

Keeper David Marshall added: 'We had expected to play Norway but Serbia beat them away. Serbia is a tough place to go but the good thing is there were limited fans so things weren't as hostile. They were still a very good and dangerous side.'

It was them or Scotland for a place at Euro 2020.

Chapter 8

WE'LL BE COMING – BRILLIANCE IN BELGRADE

THE one thing the Scotland national team has shown is that when it comes to play-offs and over one game, they can get results. The issue has been doing enough over two legs to qualify. That inability had left them short and was a reason why it was 22 years-plus in the waiting.

Yes, there had been the play-off wins over Wales and Australia, who were seen off over two legs, but those were at times when Scotland qualified for big tournaments. We were now in a whole new depressing era, where at times it has been close but no cigar.

Craig Brown's Scotland side famously beat England in the last competitive game at the old Wembley thanks to Don Hutchison's goal, but it hadn't been enough to cancel out the Auld Enemy's 2-0 first-leg win at Hampden. It might have been so different if David Seaman hadn't made that wonder save from Christian Dailly. It was another 'what if' moment in the history of the Scottish national team.

Berti Vogts's side also delivered a famous win over the Netherlands at Hampden thanks to James McFadden's goal in 2003. It gave the Tartan Army brief hope and dreams of making Euro 2004 before they were cruelly hit for six, without reply, in the second game. It wasn't a 'what if?' moment. It was more a 'WTF?' moment as the shocked and stunned Scotland support trudged dejectedly out of the Amsterdam Arena.

This time there was no need to worry about second games or return legs. Serbia was all or nothing. So that was the one positive ahead of the trip to Belgrade on 12 November 2020.

Serbia, as expected, took the game to the infamous Red Star Stadium. It was an intimidating powder-keg venue that the Serbs knew had the capability of striking fear into clubs and countries before a ball was even kicked – even without fans! So it was only natural they were going to use that to try and gain any advantage or edge they could as they looked to qualify for the first time since they had become an independent country.

Serbia had Covid issues ahead of the game which played havoc with head coach Ljubisa Tumbakovic's preparations. The issue was with his Italian-based players. Reports had claimed the local authorities would prohibit clubs from releasing players for international duty because of the pandemic. So there were serious doubts whether captain Aleksandar Kolarov of Inter, Lazio's Sergej Milinković-Savić and Fiorentina pair Dušan Vlahović and Nikola Milenković would even be involved in the play-off. It made headlines but unsurprisingly the quartet all arrived and were available for international duty. Sassuolo's Filip Đuričić did miss out after testing positive. He had been the hammer of the Scots in the past with both goals in a 2-0 World Cup qualifying defeat in Novi Sad back in 2013.

Clarke had pinpointed Ajax's Dušan Tadić and Fulham's goalscoring star Aleksandar Mitrović as Serbia's main threats. He made it clear they were a good team but also insisted so were his Scotland side.

Clarke had gone with a bigger 27-man squad after Covid and injury issues in the previous camp, with the Nations League games against Slovakia and Israel to follow. There were a few old names that were brought back into the fold for the game. Leigh Griffiths was having an indifferent spell at Celtic but he had an eye for a goal, and in this sort of shoot-out Clarke knew he could be a game-changer. Norwich City defender Grant Hanley and in-form Hearts keeper Craig Gordon were both called up by Clarke for the first time.

It had been two years since they had last donned national shirts. Gordon had lost his first-team place at Celtic in Clarke's first year in charge and therefore hadn't been part of the set-up. He moved back to the capital to relaunch his club and international careers.

Hanley's last Scotland call-up had been under Alex McLeish in the end of season trip to Peru and Mexico. Aberdeen's experienced defender Andrew Considine also kept his place after coming in and doing so well in the previous Nations League games. Clarke, as expected, did lose players for these three games. Ryan Fraser and Hanley pulled out with hamstring injuries. Another problem for Clarke was that some of his English-based players had finished a few weeks earlier than those north of the border.

Clarke made it clear that picking his squad was the easy part – picking his XI was the issue. He went with David Marshall, a three-man defence of Scott McTominay, Declan Gallagher and Kieran Tierney. Stephen O'Donnell and Andy Robertson as the wing backs, with Ryan Jack and Callum McGregor and John McGinn making up the midfield behind Ryan Christie and Lyndon Dykes. For some of the squad, it was the biggest game of their lives and they all knew what was riding on it.

Stephen O'Donnell said: 'It was massive. We all knew it had been 23 years since Scotland had qualified for a major finals and we wanted to be the squad who took the country to Euro 2020. Everybody was desperate for Scotland to qualify again. We also knew Serbia were a good team but there was belief in our camp that we could go there and win. We had been on a good unbeaten run and we certainly went to Belgrade full of confidence.'

Gallagher had kept his place and was asked to snuff out Serbia star Mitrović. 'I knew I was starting after doing well in the games before it,' Gallagher claimed. 'I also knew it was a game I was going to enjoy because I was up against Mitrović. It was going to be a physical battle and it was my kind of game. I knew he was a top player and had been scoring goals for fun, but it was a great chance for me to show what I could do. I was a wee bit nervous the week before because I knew the whole nation's hopes were resting on our shoulders. I struggled to sleep a bit but I got into the zone as soon as we got to the stadium.'

Serbia took to the pitch first but that suited Scotland and helped ease the pre-match nerves.

'I remember the Red Star tunnel,' Gallagher recalled. 'It felt like it was about two miles long. It was painted red, white and all different colours to try and intimidate opponents. We were just about to walk out and Serbia went first. I remember shouting, "That will be the only thing they are first to tonight, boys." A few of my teammates started laughing and it lightened the moment. We went out on the pitch and it was wet and raining. This is the type of game that should suit you if you are a Scottish defender.'

Many thought it would take a backs-to-the-wall display from the Scots, but that was never really the case the way Clarke had set out his troops. Serbia, despite knowing what was at stake, were pretty timid and uninspiring in the first period. David Marshall had very little to do and Scotland boasted the best chance when Stephen O'Donnell had been taken out. The advantage was played but John McGinn's shot was saved by Serb keeper Predrag Rajković.

Gallagher stated: 'A lot of people thought we would go to Serbia and sit right back but we were right on it. We went there full of confidence and for the first 45 minutes, we took the match to them.'

The boss would have been delighted with the way the half had gone and confident his team could finish the job.

Keeper David Marshall recalled: 'The first half we were brilliant and we could have been two or three up. The pitch was also horrendous so to play the way we did, we were exceptional. It was just a mud heap.'

Andy Robertson missed a big opportunity. Dykes stepped inside a defender who had slipped and then away from two others before he unselfishly squared it for the captain on the edge of the box but he blazed well over. It was a good chance and the fear was that it could have been a costly one to give up, but within a minute Scotland finally got their goal. Callum McGregor picked up a loose ball from Filip Kostić. He played it to Ryan Christie who had his back to goal on the edge of the Serbian box. He cut inside and turned as McGregor made a decoy run into the box and that gave Christie the time and space to reverse a low shot that flew in off the keeper's left-hand post in the 52nd minute.

Christie slid in the corner to celebrate and was quickly joined by his delighted teammates. Clarke simply turned to the bench and took a bottle of water. Perhaps he would have needed something a bit stronger at that point!

Scotland were in control and Christie had another effort that flew across the face of goal. Serbia were behind and were in danger of going out without as much as a whimper.

Clarke sent on Kenny McLean and Oli McBurnie for the last seven minutes with John McGinn and Lyndon Dykes making way. Callum Paterson then replaced goal hero Christie for the last three minutes as Serbia finally came to life.

Substitute Luka Jović headed a good chance wide and it looked like Scotland had weathered the storm, but with 89 minutes and 34 seconds on the clock, Serbia landed a sickening late blow.

Filip Mladenović's outswinging corner found Jović unmarked in the box. He headed the ball into the ground and it bounced into the turf and looped high over David Marshall and into the net.

The No. 1 said: 'They scored the header. I thought I was getting it when it hit the ground but my momentum was taking me down. It just went in the top corner. When they scored their equaliser, you are the same as every other fan thinking here we go again. The momentum changed and you could hear the roar from their staff when they scored.'

It was typical Scotland. Do they ever do things the easy way? The game and a place at Euro 2020 was back in the balance.

Gallagher admitted: 'It was the most gutted I have felt on a football pitch. It looked like we were there and maybe in the back of our heads we felt we were there and we have done this. They threw so many players into the box and it was chaos. It fell to Jović and he has headed it down and because it has been wet it has skidded up. It was crazy. I remember it going in and thought to myself: "Oh no, don't tell me we have just Scotland-ed this!"'

Now it was about the crestfallen Scotland players trying to pick themselves up and having to go again for another 30-plus minutes in extra time. It was a blow, but nobody could question the character of this Scotland team.

O'Donnell said: 'It was devastating. It was so disappointing but the good thing was that we knew we had played well and there was no reason why we couldn't go again. Yes, it was a sore one to lose the goal in the circumstances, but we knew the game was still there for us. We had to pick ourselves up, knowing there was such a big prize at stake.'

Extra time was a nervy affair with neither side really creating too much. David Marshall produced a decent save to keep out a long shot from Nemanja Gudelj but there was very little to split the sides.

Gallagher added: 'We had to pick ourselves up for another 30 minutes. It was so difficult and Serbia probably got the better of us. It just showed the character that we didn't crumble. We didn't show how some of us were feeling. We got through it and went to penalties.'

It went the distance and once again would come down to who was going to hold their nerve on penalties.

The Scotland team once again stood arm in arm alongside each other on the halfway line. They had prepared for this scenario, pretty much like the Israeli game.

Gallagher said: 'When we got to penalties we always fancied ourselves. We had beaten Israel on penalties, we had good penalty takers and you would always fancy Marsh to save one or two. We had been practising again before it, but it wasn't as positive for me as it had been before Israel. The good thing for me is that the penalty takers basically picked themselves.'

Marshall and the goalkeeping team had again done the groundwork. They had watched videos of the Serbians and had a fair idea of what each player was going to do for each kick. It was a case of trusting the process. This time it needed more than a clipboard in the hulking Red Star Arena. Goalkeeping coach Stevie Woods came up with the plan. If he stood on the far left of the dugout then Marshall would go that way and vice versa or bang in the centre if he didn't know or the taker was going to go down the middle. Both keepers were also warned about the new rule that the penalties would be retaken if they didn't leave a foot on the line when the ball was struck.

Leigh Griffiths had come on for Stephen O'Donnell in the last few minutes, no doubt with penalties in mind. The Celtic striker stepped up and smashed the ball to his right. Rajković got a hand on it but it was too powerful and he couldn't keep it out.

Captain Tadić stepped up to confidently level, although he didn't realise how close he had come to being second-guessed.

Marshall said: 'I went the right way for a couple of them. The one that sticks in my mind was Tadić's penalty. We had kind of agreed amongst the goalkeepers that he would go left. I thought it would go up the middle. When it was 0-0 or 1-0 in games he tended to go up the middle, but if his team were winning he would go to the left. I felt because it was more of a pressure penalty he was going to go up the middle. I was in the goal thinking I wanted to stay in the middle but I had kind of agreed to go to the left. You can hear me screaming when I went left and he went straight because if I had stood there it would have been the easiest save in the world. I probably could have caught the ball. I was gutted because, like the Israel game, if you save the first one it puts you in a good position.'

Callum McGregor then stuck his penalty into the top left-hand corner of the keeper's net. Serbian hero Jović was almost denied as Marshall went to his left and got a hand on his penalty but couldn't keep it out. The heat was on Scott McTominay but he held his nerve as he fired the ball low into the bottom right-hand corner of the net. Gudelj remained calm and calculated as he sent Marshall the wrong way from the spot to make it 3-3.

Oli McBurnie had his ups and downs in a Scotland jersey, but he came up trumps, sending Rajković the opposite way. Aleksandar Katai was just as ruthless as he crashed his penalty down the middle to make it 4-4.

Kenny McLean had been the hero against Israel, and now he knew Scotland were basically in a sudden-death situation. This time his penalty wasn't to win it but it was to give Scotland the advantage and to pile the pressure on Serbia's final taker. The weight of a nation might have been on the shoulders of McLean, but he didn't show it as he netted with ease, sending Rajković the wrong way.

Mitrović was the fifth taker for Serbia. He knew he had to score. Marshall also knew where he would be aiming. The keeper explained: 'I knew in my head where Mitrović was going. He had missed his last penalty for Fulham. He had hit the bar going straight up the middle at Sheffield United. He had previously gone to the keeper's left and scored and gone up the middle and missed. I thought he won't go up the middle again. So I went early and tried to stretch as much as I could because he is a good striker of the ball. It just worked out perfectly.'

The Scotland keeper had done his homework and was ready to take his chances. It worked as Mitrović fired the ball to his right and the keeper dived to his left to save it. You could hear Marshall shout 'Yes' as he stopped it . . . the keeper got himself up and was waiting for the all-clear from the referee that he hadn't come off his line before he could celebrate.

Marshall proudly said: 'That was the first penalty that could have won it. The referee told me not to celebrate. I asked him how long and he said two seconds. If he had pulled that one back then 25 Scotland players would need to be dragged back to the halfway line because they had all charged towards me. I don't look calm because I wasn't, but I knew the process and then when the referee gave me the nod it was just absolute bedlam. It was amazing. It is the best feeling you can have in football. You can win trophies and individual medals, but because it had been that long since Scotland qualified, we knew what it meant to everyone. I had been in Scotland squads since I was 19 and I saved the penalty when I was 35. I had seen so many negatives it was sensational just to get there.'

The rest of the Scotland players weren't sticking around for confirmation. They charged towards their hero and by the time they had got there, Scotland's place at Euro 2020 had been confirmed.

Andrew Considine recalled: 'As soon as David made the save, we all sprinted on the park. It was mayhem because the boys were so emotional.'

Gallagher added: 'The celebrations right at the end when Marsh saved the penalty, there was no better feeling in football, especially as it was for your nation and through all the hard times of Covid, knowing everyone was going to be having a party.'

There was an expectation on the team and they delivered. Lyndon Dykes might have shaved his head, but if he hadn't then he reckons Belgrade left him with one or two grey hairs after that roller coaster.

'The Serbia game was amazing,' the all-action striker said. 'There was so much pressure and so many eyes on us, cheering us on. Going into that game I felt confident and didn't feel pressure. I felt like we were going to win. It was a stressful game.'

Scotland were nine games unbeaten but more importantly after 23 years of pain and misery and a bit of Covid thrown in, they were back in the tournament spotlight.

Clarke said: 'That was a very tough period. The country was deep into lockdown, in the middle of the winter, and there wasn't much to smile about. There didn't seem much hope on the horizon at that stage. The virus was still spreading and the vaccines hadn't yet shown their worth. A lot of people were finding it very tough. To qualify, and give everyone a reason to celebrate, was something we took a lot of satisfaction from. It was just nice to see people smiling again. It was also a reminder of how much football means to the people of Scotland. It means a lot around the world, I know, but there's no doubt it holds a special place here. The fans had been waiting a long time.'

Clarke and his backroom team celebrated with their players knowing what they had achieved. It was summed up by Ryan Christie's emotional Sky Sports television interview where he ended up in tears, stating what it meant to the nation in those difficult times.

The party was only getting started and the players returned to celebrate in their away dressing room and that is where 'Yes Sir, I Can Boogie' shot to prominence. The 1977 chart-topper by Spanish duo Baccara had an unexpected revival.

Kieran Tierney was the man responsible, having a subtle dig and wind-up at Aberdeen defender Andrew Considine. He had been infamously filmed dressed up in women's clothes and dancing to the song on his stag do. It became front-page news and inadvertently an anthem for a national team.

Considine explained: 'When we eventually got back up the tunnel to the dressing room, Kieran Tierney stuck on 'Yes Sir, I Can Boogie'. One of the boys said that if I scored in one of the home games we will stick it on. It didn't happen so KT stuck it on in Serbia and things just took off from there. It was amazing to be part of the squad, history and a night that was so special for Scottish football. To be involved with Scotland at that time will go down as one of the proudest moments of my career.'

It wasn't as if the Scotland players had been complacent. Just as well they were high on adrenaline.

Marshall explained: 'Such was the confidence in the squad we had one bottle of champagne amongst the squad. I think we got one swig each before we went back to the hotel. I missed a lot of the dressing room celebrations but I made up for it back at the hotel. The celebrations were great. It was a brilliant night. My one disappointment was that it was during Covid and there was no Tartan Army there. It was magic.'

The players took the credit but O'Donnell also paid tribute

to the manager and all the backroom staff whose work often goes unnoticed.

O'Donnell said: 'That was an amazing night; everything that goes along with that and Covid. You are in the room and what a celebration it was. I'm not much of a drinker but I had a drink or two that night. Scotland had just got to a finals. We deserved it. It was a real team effort. It is not just the players but the coaches and all the support staff behind it. It is a massive machine at international level. I was delighted for everybody involved.'

It was hugs all round for hero Marshall. He said: 'Steve is very quiet and humble. I had just FaceTimed my dad when he came up and gave me a hug in the tunnel. I had to rush off and do press after it. There were two Scotland fans with kilts on waiting outside to give me a hug.'

The fact that it was during Covid meant the players and staff couldn't share their big moment in person, but they quickly got a flavour of what was going on back home.

Gallagher said: 'You saw the emotions in the team and that didn't change when we got back to the dressing room. I FaceTimed my wife and parents and saw videos of my daughter running up and down the living room, screaming and shouting. It was good to enjoy the moment with everyone close to us and my teammates. We saw people on their roofs in Glasgow out dancing and celebrating. There has been no greater moment in my football career than that.'

The party in the team hotel went long into the night with Clarke, his staff and players. Some of the footage, thanks to social media, has become legendary. Like the Scotland players doing a giant conga to the tune of Whigfield's 'Saturday Night' with the lyrics changed to honour hero of the hour David Marshall.

It left one Scotland player slightly red-faced, however. Gallagher recalled: 'I came out the toilet, saw the conga and thought brilliant and joined the back. I was swinging my T-shirt above my head and Greg Taylor has come up behind me and pulled my tracksuit bottoms down. I was down to my boxer shorts but I just kept going. You see it in the final seconds of the videos.'

Marshall had also become a social media phenomenon and a national hero overnight. The former Celtic keeper revealed: 'It blew up on Twitter and social media. I woke up with a hangover, to 400 messages and thinking: "Oh no!" Seeing the bagpipe player on the roof in Edinburgh and people celebrating all over Scotland was what made it all worth it. Yes, I saved the penalty to get us there, but it was very much a team effort. We had all played our part.'

The national team was going back for a Euro 2020 party, looking ahead to the following summer. They were the toast of a nation – collectively and individually.

O'Donnell said: 'A random neighbour came to my door and gave my wife a bottle of whisky. He said: "That's for your husband; it has been a long time and it is just brilliant we have qualified again." I didn't know him but when I got back I went to his door to thank him. I think he really appreciated me taking the time to go and speak to him. It just showed the impact Scotland's qualification had on people the length and breadth of the country. Now there is a real excitement going into the Euro 2024 finals and the team will be going into the games looking to do the country proud again.'

Chapter 9

FALLING AT THE FINAL NATIONS LEAGUE HURDLE

SCOTLAND'S Nations League fixtures had to be shoehorned in at the same time as the team continued their play-off push to Euro 2020. The national team kicked off their campaign with a double-header in September 2020 with a home game against Israel and away to the Czech Republic. The Nations League clash with Israel came a month before Scotland had skipped past them on penalties in the Euro 2020 play-offs.

The Israeli game was played in front of an empty Hampden and it was fair to say the Tartan Army didn't really miss too much. Steve Clarke, however, finally found a way to field both Andy Robertson and Kieran Tierney in the same team. Robertson played wing back and KT moved into left centre back in a three, beside Scott McKenna and Scott McTominay, who dropped back from his more established position in the centre of the park. James Forrest played on the right with Ryan Jack and Callum McGregor holding, allowing John McGinn and Ryan Christie to play either side of new boy Lyndon Dykes.

Marshall said: 'On paper, it was always going to be tough. If you look at the gaffer's first few squads to what he settled for in the next Nations League campaign, it was a lot different. It took a bit of time to get what he wanted together.'

The real highlight from the Israel game was the international debut of Dykes, but apart from that there wasn't too much that Steve Clarke could take from the game apart from the fact it extended Scotland's unbeaten run to four games. Israel had been the better team and David Marshall had been the busier of the two keepers before Scotland had taken the lead in the final minute of the first half. John McGinn was clumsily floored by Eitan Tibi inside the box. Ryan Christie took the penalty and confidently slammed the ball into the top right-hand corner of Ofir Marciano's net.

Israel had every right to feel aggrieved, but they got the equaliser their play deserved in the 73rd minute through a crisp strike from Eran Zahavi that flew high past David Marshall.

Dykes had been replaced by Oliver Burke just before Israel's goal but was delighted to have made his Scotland bow and to get his international career up and running.

'I loved every minute of it,' Dykes said. 'It was good to start for Scotland and it is a moment I will never forget. It was a proud moment for my family and myself. It was disappointing not to get the win but the most important game was always going to be the play-off with Israel.'

Dykes didn't have to wait long for his first goal. Four days to be precise, in Scotland's next Nations League outing. The Scots weren't the story ahead of their trip to the Czech Republic. The home side asked for the game to be cancelled after their entire international squad was put into self-isolation after a Covid outbreak in their previous encounter against Slovakia. The Czechs, however, weren't granted a postponement and had to go and assemble an entirely new squad, with players who played in their domestic top flight. It left Steve Clarke and his team scrambling to do their homework against a second-string Czech Republic side which included nine debutants. It was the equivalent of Steve Clarke having to pick a squad of players from the Scottish Premiership. It would have been a bit of a stretch.

Clarke made five changes to his own team from the Israel game, with Liam Cooper, Kenny McLean, Liam Palmer, Stuart Armstrong and John Fleck all coming in. It was the Scots who struggled to gel at the start of the game as the Czech Republic took an 11th-minute lead through Jakub Pešek. Dykes opened his Scotland account when he cancelled that strike out just 16 minutes later. Liam Palmer put in a low, inviting cross from the right and Dykes got there first to stab it into the net.

The Czechs kept peppering David Marshall's goal, but Scotland managed to hold firm and got their match-winning moment after Andy Robertson was fouled in the box by Tomas Malinsky. Christie stepped forward and made it two penalties in two games for the Scots in the 52nd minute.

The Czechs piled on the pressure. They hit the woodwork and missed other good opportunities to claim a point. The win left Scotland top of their Nations League group. The Scots didn't win a corner in Olomouc but the only statistic that mattered was the final result.

Dykes was delighted to make his mark but he also didn't forget his roots and sent Scotland tops to his former clubs Livingston and Queen of the South for helping him get to this point.

The Queens Park Rangers frontman said: 'It was great to score my first goal but the most important thing was the win. It is good and it could potentially be an exciting period for the country. I thought it was important to give both teams something back in recognition for helping me get to where I am today as a Scotland international. Queen of the South gave me my chance in Scottish football and Livingston gave me the chance in the

Premiership. That is why I have given an international shirt to both clubs.'

It might not have been the Czech Republic's strongest team, but David Marshall knows that result gave the team a real belief.

The keeper stated: 'People expected us just to turn them over but it was still a tough one. Winning away games is not something Scotland did that often. We had slipped up against the likes of Georgia in the past. To go to the Czech Republic and win was quite a big moment, regardless of the circumstances.'

Scotland would then go on and get the big win in the October window with their play-off penalty shoot-out win over Israel. They continued the feel-good factor with Hampden wins over Slovakia and the Czech Republic. The headline news from those games was a Scotland call-up for the late-blooming Andrew Considine. He came in with Hearts defender John Souttar and Aberdeen teammate Scott McKenna also out injured. Considine got the emotional call after he had been out running at his local park.

Considine recalled: 'It was Adam Stokes [Aberdeen's head physio] who told me. He had also been drafted into the Scotland squad because one of the physios had caught Covid. So he called me and said there is a 99 per cent chance I was going to be called up. Within the hour, Derek McInnes phoned to say that Steve Clarke had been in touch and he wanted me to join up with the squad. I called my wife and we were both in tears. I thought the chance had passed me by at the age of 33. It really was a surprise but a brilliant one. I had to go and get my boots from Cormack Park to head down for training the next morning. It was all a mad rush.'

Former Scotland striker Stevie Naismith knew a few eyebrows were raised by Considine's inclusion, but Clarke's decision was more than vindicated. Naismith noted: 'The manager makes the right calls because he understands and gets it. That comes from working under some of the best managers in the world, to being one of the best coaches under them in the Premier League to going out on his own. On top of that, he is not scared when it comes to decision making and him making the big calls. Andy Considine was the big one. Andy probably never thought he was going to get a Scotland cap as he got into his thirties.

'I came through with Andy in the under-18s and under-21s. He had been a regular for Aberdeen but never really got his international chance. The gaffer, though, saw Andy had a value and could be a real asset to Scotland. He came in and won three caps and did really well. Andy never let Scotland down once. He came in and was effective for the team and the squad. Looking at that, I'm not sure many people would have given Andy his chance at that time if they had been in the manager's shoes.'

Considine had to make a dash down to Glasgow to join up with the squad the following day. He was then told by Clarke that he was being thrown in at the deep end and he was to make his Scotland debut the next night.

The stunned defender recalls: 'I met the manager for the first time on the training pitch. He said he was delighted to see me and said: "Listen, Andy, you are here because of your form at Aberdeen. Go and do what you have been doing at Aberdeen and you will fit in really well." The staff and boys were all really welcoming. The training was short and sharp and then we worked on set plays for the game the next day. Steve then read out the team and before he did that he said: "Andy Considine, you will be getting your first Scotland cap at left centre half." I was like: "Holy fuck." It was a bit of a whirlwind, everything that had happened over the previous 24 hours. I didn't think I would start. The manager then named the team and I couldn't tell you any of the other names because I was so stunned.'

The Aberdeen defender made his international debut at 33,

after a number of injuries and Covid issues led to his call-up. Considine had become the oldest Scotland player to make his Scotland debut since 36-year-old Ronnie Simpson more than half a century earlier.

It was Dykes who was the main man again as he knocked a great cross from Stephen O'Donnell into the net in the 54th minute. Scott McTominay had come in for some criticism for his recent defensive displays, but alongside Considine was able to get the clean sheet and win against Slovakia.

The new cap Considine added: 'Dykes scored. There wasn't an awful lot in the first game. I have to say after we had won 1-0 I probably had the biggest sigh of relief. I had just been so worked up before it and we didn't even have a crowd there. If there had been, it would have been ten times worse. I remember shaking the manager's hand and having a hug with him after the game. It was so emotional and I was so happy to finally have represented my country, helped get the win and a clean sheet into the bargain.'

It ensured that Scotland went an entire 12 months undefeated, since their defeat in Russia in the Euro 2020 qualifiers. It had been just the reaction Clarke had been looking and hoping for.

The national team continued their defensive dominance by claiming another clean sheet at home to the Czech Republic, with a back three of McTominay, Declan Gallagher and Considine.

The Czechs were back to full strength but they couldn't find a way through Clarke's in-form Scots. That ensured an early sixth minute goal from Ryan Fraser was enough to give Scotland another big win in a game where Hibs defender Paul Hanlon also came on to make his international bow.

Considine explained: 'We rode our luck at times, defending well and David Marshall also made a number of saves. We managed to keep the clean sheet and Ryan Fraser got the only goal of the game. It emotionally wiped me out after those two games with everything that had happened. I got in the car with Adam Stokes and he told me to take a minute and let all the emotions out. I was just so happy. I couldn't have asked for a better two games. I can hold my hands up and say I knew I was far from first choice at that point, but to get that call-up, regardless of the circumstances, was amazing and the biggest thing for me was not to let anyone down.'

The win moved the Scots four points clear at the top of their Nations League group. Scotland made it eight unbeaten – their best run in 32 years. It was the perfect way to go out to Serbia in November to dramatically clinch their place at Euro 2020. Scotland were in party central but still had to see out their remaining Nations League fixtures, away to Slovakia and Israel.

Clarke rested eight of the team who had won in Belgrade but they couldn't find a way to extend their unbeaten run beyond nine games – which had been their best sequence of results in 32 years. Lyndon Dykes was suspended and they lacked fire-power. Days after the dramatic play-off win in Serbia, Clarke's men were drained and running on empty in Slovakia. They lost to a deflected Jan Gregus goal in the first half. The only real positive was seeing Craig Gordon resume his Scotland career after more than two years. It also saw the Hearts keeper set a new Scottish record for the longest-spanning international career, at 16 years, five months and 17 days.

Scotland went into the final game in Israel with a one-point lead at the top of Group F from the Czech Republic. Scotland just had to match their rivals' result against Slovakia at the end of that packed, but emotionally draining, triple-header. Manor Solomon got Israel's goal just before half-time and it was enough to see the Scots slump to a second consecutive defeat. That misery was compounded by the Czech Republic's win over Slovakia to win the group.

The late collapse had cost Scotland a major chance to win promotion again in the Nations League. It was tough on the team but a bigger prize had already been delivered.

Considine said: 'It could have been all the emotions after the Serbia game. We just ran out of steam. It was disappointing because we could have topped the group, but I suppose the main objective was achieved – Scotland were going to Euro 2020.'

Chapter 10

THE COUNTDOWN TO EURO 2020

WHEN you have to wait 22 years to qualify for a major finals, another 12 months was never going to make too much of a difference. The Covid pandemic meant that the 2020 European Championships was to be delayed by a year. Euro 2020 would still go ahead and remain in name, but it would be played in the summer of 2021. UEFA was determined that the 60th anniversary of the European Championships was going to be marked in 11 countries across Europe. Hampden Park was going to be one of the host venues and so Scotland's qualification meant they were likely to have home advantage for some of their three group games.

The finals remained the shining light and the one thing that the people of Scotland could look forward to with genuine hope and excitement. It offered a break from the mounting pressures from lockdown, health issues and all the other doom, gloom and general heartbreak that came with Covid. Ryan Christie's emotional celebration after the play-off win in Serbia had summed up what Scotland's qualification meant. It really did come in Scotland's hour of need and it wasn't just in a footballing sense.

The delay to Euro 2020 whetted the appetite, knowing there was a light at the end of a long, dark tunnel. The Scotland team had been a beacon during their gutsy qualifying play-off assault, and now the spotlight was set to fall on them on the big stage. Absence on this occasion did make the heart grow fonder, knowing this was finally Scotland's time.

The draw was made in the Romexpo in Bucharest on Saturday 30 November. So Scotland knew even before their play-off whom they would face if they were to progress along that path. Their successful assault saw Scotland take up the final berth in Group D that also included England, Croatia and the Czech Republic. Clarke's side would face the Czech Republic in the opening game at Hampden, the Auld Enemy at Wembley and finish off their group fixtures with another home game against Croatia.

The one positive from a delayed Euro 2020 also meant that there would be fans in the stadiums. It would be in limited numbers, but it was still better than playing in an empty bowl of a ground as many of our top stars had done at the height of lockdown. Around 12,000 supporters would be allowed into Hampden Park. Having the public in the stands was a big thing for UEFA and the fact that some venues couldn't guarantee that meant they missed out on hosting games.

Clarke was equally delighted that some of the Scotland support would be there in the flesh. The Scotland manager said: 'We'd love it to be a full stadium, but even with only 12,000 fans I know the Tartan Army will create a great atmosphere. It will be important to the players too. It will give them that added bit of fire and motivation to do well.'

Scotland had been on song on the pitch and they were also looking to net chart success off it as well. The Serbia celebrations meant 'Yes Sir, I Can Boogie' also made an unexpected chart return, more than 40 years since it had originally hit number one on the back of Eurovision. It had become a Scotland anthem thanks to Andrew Considine's late international inclusion and had been adopted as the team's unofficial song.

Such was the success that María Mendiola, who was one half of Baccara, offered to re-record a new version for the people of Scotland. A reissue of the original version also went back into the top 60 in the UK charts. Scotland also put its own twist on it. Scottish DJ George Bowie remixed a version of his own on his GBX show. It included new vocals from Baccara and made it all the way to number 11 in the charts.

Clarke was more interested in getting his strongest XI out on the park at Euro 2020. The delayed start gave Clarke more time to consider his 26-man squad. He had also added another striker to his squad in the March pre-Euro 2020 international window.

It was like buses for Clarke. He had been waiting for ages and nothing and then two came along at roughly the same time. Lyndon Dykes was first to get his Scotland ticket stamped and the next one was Southampton striker Che Adams, who had been a long-term target for Clarke's predecessors Gordon Strachan and Alex McLeish.

Adams was Leicester-born and therefore could play for England, but had an abundance of international options. He could also represent Antigua and Barbuda because his dad came from Antigua and he was eligible for Scotland via his grand-mother. Adams had turned down Antigua as a youngster and had the chance to play for England C team when he was at Ilkeston, but lost that when he turned professional with Sheffield United.

He did play for England at under-20 level during his time at Bramall Lane, but that was as far as his international career had gone. Scotland made an approach to cap Adams in 2016, first on the under-21 front and then for a full friendly, but the player declined the invitation at that point. He was making a name for himself at Birmingham City before he moved to Southampton in 2019.

It was on England's south coast where he decided to make himself a saint north of the border when he declared his allegiance to Scotland in March 2021, given a nudge by his club teammate Stuart Armstrong. I got the call from a source close to the English club to confirm Adams's intention. Steve Clarke had opened the door and once again his powers of persuasion had come up with the goods. The following day, Clarke confirmed the move when he named Adams in his squad for the World Cup qualifiers against Austria, Israel and the Faroe Islands.

Scotland had another player who, at the time, was plying his trade at the highest level in the English Premier League with Southampton. It helped that Scotland were heading to a delayed Euro 2020, but the frontman insisted that wasn't the deciding factor.

Adams made his debut coming off the bench to replace Armstrong in the 66th minute at Hampden against Austria. He helped the Scots to fight back from 1-0 behind and then 2-1 down to get a 2-2 draw. Adams then made his first start and played 75 minutes in the 1-1 draw in Israel. It was to be a run of firsts for Adams because in the final game of that triple-header, he got his opening goal for Scotland as he netted the third in a 4-0 Hampden win over the Faroe Islands.

Clarke, by that time, was already a fully paid-up member of the fan club, quipping: 'He is not bad, Che McAdams! He is a good player. Che is not the tallest, but he's a strong bugger.'

Adams might have turned his run to perfection when it came to Euro 2020, but the same cannot have been said for two other key members of the Scotland squad. Midfielders Kenny McLean and Ryan Jack both picked up injuries and were cruelly denied a place at the finals.

Those injuries did open things up and sparked wild debate and speculation as to who Clarke should name in his final squad.

Scotland's next generation was the main benefactor. Chelsea midfielder Billy Gilmour, Rangers full back Nathan Patterson and Celtic's goalscoring midfielder David Turnbull were all handed their first senior Scotland call-ups. They had all shone at underage level and for their clubs. It had also been a major goal of the SFA to have graduates from their performance school programme and Patterson and Gilmour provided that – as well as a fair bit of talent and even more potential into the bargain.

Patterson excitedly recalled: 'Billy and I came down [to England] when we were with the performance school and we played all the rest of the schools. It is a bit weird to come back, especially with the A squad. The performance schools were quite successful and that has been shown with Billy and I coming through into the full squad. It is great coming through with one of your mates.'

It was just as big a thing for some of the more experienced players like Motherwell's Declan Gallagher who was also to get the nod.

He said: 'I did well in the play-offs but I suffered a few niggles at Motherwell. I missed a few games and my contract was up. I wasn't sure what was going to happen but to get the call was a real proud moment for me. It was good for my mum and dad and wife and kids because they had been through thick and thin with me. It is good to give them something back.'

Motherwell teammate Stephen O'Donnell also made it, after joining the Fir Park side at the start of that season to try and nail down his Euro 2020 spot.

O'Donnell recalled: 'I spoke to Steve because he is a manager I have huge respect for and he helped bring out the best in me when I was at Kilmarnock. You need to know what is best for you and your family. I had knocked back a couple of things. I thought, do I hold out for the English Championship and possibly end up waiting until Christmas? Motherwell came in and I told my agent if we can make it work for both parties then let's make it work because I want to get back playing. I knew if I was to have any chance of playing for Scotland I had to get playing at club level. Thankfully, that is the way it worked out.'

The rest of Clarke's squad was pretty much the tried and trusted. Jack Hendry came back in after an impressive season on loan at Belgian side KV Oostende, as did Norwich City's Grant Hanley and Celtic's attacker James Forrest.

Clarke, quoted on the SFA's website after he announced his squad, said: 'It's a privilege to be standing here as the head coach of a national team that is at a major tournament. Well done to the lads who've made the squad and thank you to all of the guys who helped us along the journey. It's been difficult for the players who've been ruled out through injuries and I've spoken to them. While they are disappointed they know it's part and parcel of football. It's also important to look at what is coming through and having a few injured players gives a chance for us to bring some of the young boys in. I tried to keep the core of the squad together which I think is important as we're trying to build a national team spirit and feel good in everyone's company.'

The Scotland Euro 2020 squad was:

Goalkeepers: Craig Gordon (Heart of Midlothian); David Marshall (Derby County); Jon McLaughlin (Rangers).

Defenders: Liam Cooper (Leeds United); Declan Gallagher (Motherwell); Grant Hanley (Norwich City); Jack Hendry (KV Oostende); Scott McKenna (Nottingham Forest); Stephen O'Donnell (Motherwell); Nathan Patterson (Rangers); Andy Robertson (Liverpool); Kieran Tierney (Arsenal); Greg Taylor (Celtic).

Midfielders: Stuart Armstrong (Southampton); Billy Gilmour (Chelsea); John Fleck (Sheffield United); Callum McGregor

(Celtic); Scott McTominay (Manchester United); John McGinn (Aston Villa); David Turnbull (Celtic).

Forwards: Che Adams (Southampton); Ryan Christie (Celtic); Lyndon Dykes (Queens Park Rangers); James Forrest (Celtic); Ryan Fraser (Newcastle United); Kevin Nisbet (Hibernian).

Scotland would warm up for the tournament with two June friendlies against the Netherlands in the Algarve and Luxembourg away. The problem for Clarke, as it was every summer, was that some of his players had stopped playing competitively earlier than others. It meant that several of the English-based players had come up to Scotland to continue training. Derby County's David Marshall was one of them who kept himself ticking over by training at former club Celtic, under Scotland goalkeeping coach Stevie Woods.

When Clarke finally got all his squad together they headed for their Spanish training camp, but even that wasn't as straightforward as he had hoped. Sheffield United midfielder John Fleck returned a positive Covid test ahead of the Netherlands match. Several other Scotland players, including David Marshall, Stephen O'Donnell, Nathan Patterson, Grant Hanley, John McGinn and Che Adams, were also left at the camp headquarters as a precaution.

That opened the door for Turnbull to make his first start against the Dutch, while the likes of Gilmour and Nisbet came off the bench to make Scotland debuts. Jack Hendry fired in the opener from distance before Memphis Depay levelled. New boy Nisbet then made it a night to remember with his first goal before Depay netted again to claim a last-minute draw.

The final game was meant to be an easier one to boost confidence and morale before the tournament, but Luxembourg had other ideas and made the Scots fight all the way. The majority of the players who had missed the Dutch game were back in for the final friendly.

Che Adams's goal in the 27th minute was the difference between the teams after Luxembourg had gone down to ten men following Vahid Selimovic's first-half dismissal. The game also enabled Patterson to make his first start, while Gilmour also impressed as he came off the bench. It was now on to the real stuff. Euro 2020 awaited.

Chapter 11

CHECKED IN, CZECH-ED OUT

STEVE Clarke took the decision to take his team away from the direct Euro 2020 mayhem and madness by setting up their tournament base in North East England. Middlesbrough's Rockliffe Hall Hotel and training ground was the chosen camp. It was there that the national boss put his team through their paces and finalised his plans and where he addressed the media. Scotland were back and it was about trying to make their mark. The country had a lot of catching up to do.

Clarke said: 'When I was younger, it was taken for granted that Scotland would be at major tournaments. What's happened over the past couple of decades shows you how quickly you can lose that and drift away. We lost the knack of qualifying for these competitions. That is why making it to Euro 2020 was so important. Maintaining momentum is massive. We don't want to get back into bad habits, back into that rut of being almost resigned to the fact we're not going to qualify.'

Captain Andy Robertson had moved to make sure none of the Scotland squad would be longing for home, ordering themed gift boxes for all his teammates. It was a great personal touch from the Liverpool player that went down well.

Striker Kevin Nisbet explained: 'When we arrived, Robbo had

bought us a load of gifts off his own back, which were all to do with Scotland. There was a shirt, shortbread, Irn-Bru, a load of stuff. I think it was a great touch from him. It brings the squad together even closer. He's a great guy, a great captain, and he's the one to take us forward. Everyone was very appreciative. He has gone out of his way to do that. When you have got a skipper that does that, then 100 per cent you back him.'

All the hard work and preparations had been done. All the focus was on 14 June 2021, when Scotland would kick off their Euro 2020 campaign at home to the Czech Republic. It was the one game in the group where Clarke's side were most fancied to take three points. Clarke also had a decent record against the opposition with home and away wins in the previous Nations League campaign. The manager had the national team well on the road to recovery but joked in his pre-match press conference that the most treacherous journey hadn't been qualifying but trying to get to Hampden safely.

Clarke said: 'It feels like everyone in the country is excited about the tournament. That's fantastic. With that said, I was a little nervous on the drive from the airport to the hotel when we were on the M8 and all the cars were slowing down to toot their horns. They were swerving to avoid each other but thankfully there were no incidents. Everyone wanted to wish us well . . . and that's great. So we're aware of the magnitude of this game and know what it means to everyone.'

There was a pre-match blow for Scotland. They went into the game without influential defender Kieran Tierney, who missed out with a knock, so Clarke had to rejig his side. He went with a 3-5-2 formation. David Marshall, Jack Hendry, Grant Hanley and Liam Cooper at the back. Stephen O'Donnell, John McGinn, Scott McTominay, Stuart Armstrong and Andy Robertson across the middle, with Lyndon Dykes and Ryan Christie leading the line.

Hampden was at a quarter of capacity because of Covid restrictions, but it was the first time some of this Scotland team had played at home in front of the Tartan Army. For those lucky few in attendance it added to the excitement and the occasion. The players were in the same boat.

Striker Dykes said: 'I have played a few games for Scotland but none of them in front of the fans. I am one of those players who loves the buzz of the crowd and to get that from the Scotland support is something I am really looking forward to. Even the thought of the crowd singing the national anthem with the team is something I am looking forward to.'

Even for the more experienced players in the camp it was still a big game.

Ryan Christie recalled: 'It was an unbelievable experience being at Hampden. That is one of my memories of the Euros. It was great just walking out on Hampden after we had got off the bus, just taking it all in. We were in our civvy gear but all the fans were buzzing and really up for it because it had been so long since Scotland had got to a major finals. For some of them it might even have been the first time they had seen Scotland in a major competition. You could feel the fans and the country had all bought into it.'

Andy Robertson did the honours as the captain led Scotland back out on to the big stage. It was a historic moment and the team was keen to make its mark. Clarke knew the importance of making a positive start, getting the fans up and behind his players. His team took the game to the Czechs although Patrik Schick fired in a warning shot forcing David Marshall to tip behind. The Scots gradually made an impression at the other end. Scott McTominay's low cross from the right was stabbed wide by Dykes and Ryan Christie found Robertson who cracked in a shot forcing keeper Tomáš Vaclík to tip over. Scotland were getting on top when the Czech Republic hit them with a sucker punch before the interval.

Vladimir Coufal burst up the Czechs' right and swung in the perfect cross for Schick to get in front of Grant Hanley and McTominay and to head low into the net. It was a body blow to the majority of the home crowd. This wasn't in the script and it left Clarke back at the drawing board during the interval.

Scotland went in search of a leveller. Vaclík punched another cross clear. O'Donnell gathered it and played it inside to Jack Hendry but his chipped effort came back off the bar. Robertson sent a ball through that just evaded Stuart Armstrong and Coufal tried to intercept and looped the ball over Vaclík's head, but the keeper got back to claw away.

Clarke's side were building some decent pressure and were on the offensive again when disaster struck. Hendry, who had scored from distance in the pre-tournament friendly with the Dutch, stepped forward and let fly. His effort was blocked by a defender and the ball cannoned forward into the path of Schick. He let it run about five yards into the Scotland half before he let fly, sending a shot high over the keeper and into the net. It was described by some as one of the best goals ever seen in the European Championships. To Scotland it was anything but and was a devastating and fatal blow.

Marshall still remembers the misery: 'If somebody was to say to you: "Scotland was to have a shot and a second and a half later the Czech Republic would have a shot," you would think: "How is that possible?" It was the spin of the ball. The position I took as a goalkeeper is one I would take up in every single game. When you analyse it after the game, you think should I have been four yards back or should I have got back quicker? Sometimes you need to hold your hands up and take it on the chin. I am not daft enough to think that wasn't going to be the talking point of the game. It wasn't a nice night and personally, it was one of the hardest moments I have had in the game because I had built up to that tournament. It is what it is and you just need to get on with it because we still had another two group games to play.'

Clarke gave all the credit to Schick. He said: 'Well, if he'd been on his line he would have caught it. But in normal circumstances he's looking to sweep up behind the defence. But it was a fantastic finish. Rather than looking to apportion blame sometimes you've got to credit the goalscorer. David's fine. He's probably faced that type of shot about 50 times in his career and that's the only time it's gone in. It happens. It was a shot from Jack Hendry on the edge of their box and three seconds later it's in the back of our net. It's one of those things.'

Scotland didn't throw in the towel. They tried courageously to get a goal but it just wasn't meant to be. Armstrong saw a shot loop off a defender and on to the roof of the net and Dykes was denied by Vaclík who had come off his line to block at point-blank range. The final chance fell to Dykes. Hendry's cross was flicked on by John McGinn into the path of the striker who tried to slot it past the keeper, but Vaclík denied him with an outstretched leg. It was clear that it wasn't going to be Scotland's day.

Clarke's starting XI was questioned after the game, but he thought the game could have gone either way and the fine margins fell to the Czech Republic.

The manager reflected: 'Hindsight is a wonderful gift. Nobody has got it. We came here to be competitive and we were competitive in the game. Sometimes a football match doesn't go your way and today was that day. I don't think there was much between the two sides if you look at our attempts at goal. The breaks went against us at the wrong time. Obviously losing a goal five minutes before half-time from the second phase of a set play was disappointing for us. We normally defend that quite well so that was a blow. We came out for the second half and tried to get back in it, and Jack Hendry hit the bar. Then Jack had another shot which got blocked and fell straight to their striker and he produced a marvellous finish. We had good invention and chances to get back in the game. Had one gone in it could have been a different ending.'

Clarke's team was also criticised for going too long in certain quarters. The manager insisted that hadn't been a tactic and was down to the Czech Republic squeezing the space than any managerial orders.

He said: 'Sometimes you have to credit the opposition. If you look at the first half, Tomáš Souček was never out of John McGinn's pocket. It was difficult to play through the midfield and get Scott McTominay on the ball. When you play with three centre backs you need one of your midfield players to come off and get the ball and we couldn't get Scott on the ball from the back. If you can't play through the midfield then the next pass has to be longer, up to the forwards. And that's what we did. We created two good chances off Andy Robertson. Robbo crossed one for Dykesy at the near post and he probably got too big a contact on it. Then Robbo had a chance himself.'

Captain Robertson believed it was a game of missed chances. The skipper stated: 'Everyone in the country wanted to get off to a good start. We were confident, excited, and it comes down to not taking our chances. You can't say we've not created. We've had some really, really good chances that we should have done better with. If you do better on that then it's a different game. It's a tough lesson for us that at the highest level, at the best tournaments, you have to take your chances. The Czech Republic did that. Unfortunately we didn't.'

It was a learning curve for Scotland against a Czech Republic team who were hardened and knew what it took at this level.

'It was a first for all the lads,' Marshall insisted. 'It was just disappointing in the first game. I don't think we played particularly well, although their keeper made a good save. I also lost the goal from the halfway line so there were mixed emotions. It was down to the small margins.'

Christie doesn't think the Czech Republic got the credit they deserved at Euro 2020. The Bournemouth star said: 'We were going into the competition for the first time looking to do well. I am not sure anyone realised how good the Czech Republic were. They were a hardened, experienced group and they showed it because they had a good Euro 2020 competition. A lot of people fancied us, with us being at home, to certainly get something from that first game. It was a strange game. It was a freak goal and it wasn't to be and I have to say it set us back in the group. We were left playing catch-up and that is something we need to learn from when we go into Euro 2024 and future competitions.'

Scotland were left bottom of Group D, after England had beaten Croatia 1-0 at Wembley.

O'Donnell said: 'We still had good players and I believed we could have got out of the group. We had done well against a good Serbia side and I really felt we could compete against these guys. The first game against the Czech Republic made it an uphill task. It was a whole new experience, and the Czech team were experienced at that level, as were England and Croatia.'

Chapter 12

A POINT PROVED AT WEMBLEY

SCOTLAND were up against the Auld Enemy and England were amongst the favourites for Euro 2020. Steve Clarke and his side needed to be united to go to Wembley and get a result. The disappointing defeat to the Czech Republic had heaped the pressure on Steve Clarke and his players in terms of their qualification hopes. England had also beaten Croatia 1-0 in the opening game so Scotland needed to go to the English capital and take something back with them. If not, Euro 2020 could be over before it had really begun.

The pre-tournament feel-good factor had quickly evaporated and now Clarke was coming under fire from pundits, fans and the media alike for his team selection against the Czech Republic. Defender Stephen O'Donnell was one of those who had come in for criticism but Clarke jumped to his defence. It had sparked a clamour for Rangers starlet Nathan Patterson or Celtic's James Forrest to replace him at right wing back, but the national boss insists the Motherwell man gets a raw deal.

Clarke said: 'It's the first major tournament we've been in for 23 years and I think after Monday a lot of people forgot that. Analyse the game and tell me what Stephen did wrong. How many chances came off that side? Jakub Jankto, one of their most dangerous players, had a quiet game. Their left back, a really good attacking left back, Jan Bořil, didn't create a chance in the game. So analyse the game before we start killing players, just because of who they are and where they play. Analyse his games when he plays for us. Look at Stephen's performances objectively. Just look at the games. Stephen's first job is to be a defender. So analyse the games. That's all I'll say on that one.'

Striker Lyndon Dykes had also missed a number of chances against the Czech Republic and some of the critics wanted new boy Che Adams to lead the line at Wembley.

Clarke said: 'With strikers it's about getting into the positions. They'll all go through a run of games where they're scoring quite regularly, like Lyndon did at the end of last season. Then they go through little patches when the ball doesn't quite fall for them and hit the back of the net, but Lyndon has a good mentality so he'll keep getting in there. All I'll say to him is, "Just keep getting into those positions, big man, because eventually the goals will start coming." I don't think Che [Adams] would have made too much difference in the first half because we didn't get quality ball into the strikers.'

Most people had an opinion or a view and knew better. The one thing that did unite the nation was the hope that Kieran Tierney would declare himself fit to start against England. The Arsenal defender had missed the Czech Republic defeat and he had remained at the Rockliffe Hall base to work on his fitness, but the game hadn't made good viewing for him and every other Scotland fan.

The former Celtic star confirmed: 'I had to do rehab all day and took an hour or two off to watch the game. I was gutted. I was so down. I was just so flat that day. I stayed back here trying to get fit for Friday and it was probably the longest day. It was a horrible day. Watching the anthem was amazing but what I was feeling inside was terrible. I wanted to be there so much. I wanted to help the boys out, wanted them to do so well, and not being able to help was hard to take.'

Scotland may have been written off by a lot of the critics, especially those south of the border, but Tierney insisted the belief within Clarke's squad was unwavering. He had lifted an FA Cup with Arsenal on his previous Wembley appearance and was looking for another big-time team performance.

He claimed: 'We are here for a reason. We need to believe in ourselves more. It's a big game, no doubt about it. There is no hiding it. England are a world-class team. We are going to do our very best and hopefully we can pull together a good performance. You need to believe. You need to go down there with a game plan to do well and that's what we have been working on in training. We have another day's training to look forward to before the game. It's a derby, a big rivalry in football, and we're really looking forward to this game.'

Clarke also managed to upset his sons, John and Joseph, ahead of the game by calling them English. Yes, they had been born in England but, like their dad and family, they firmly viewed themselves as Scottish.

Clarke joked: 'I said in an interview the other week that my two boys were English – wow, that was a mistake! My eldest, John, was straight on the phone to me after he read that and said: "We're not English, it's just where we were born." He made the point that they've got a Scottish mum and a Scottish dad – that they've all got Scottish blood. So I need to clear that one up.'

Clarke had missed out on an England game as a player and was keen to register a result against them as a manager.

He said: 'Listen, everybody knows the magnitude of the fixture. It's a historic game, a famous game, and there have been lots of moments in the past. If I went back to the moments that meant the most to me, the young boys in the squad wouldn't even remember them. It's a fixture that goes back a long way and everyone is aware of what it means to the people of Scotland. Everyone had written us off in the England game, same against Serbia. We just use that to put a little bit of fire in our bellies and come out and prove a lot of people wrong and make sure people get surprised.'

More than 20,000 of the Tartan Army descended upon London and they included some familiar faces, although there were limited tickets and the Wembley capacity, home and away, was only 22,500!

Striker Lawrence Shankland hadn't made the squad but that wasn't going to stop him heading to Wembley to cheer on the Scotland team. That was another example of the togetherness in and around this Scotland group that Clarke had assembled – even if it put Shankland in the doghouse with his mum.

He revealed: 'I went down to Wembley with my dad – even though it was my mum's birthday. There were a few of the boys who were not involved in this squad who were going down to the game. It just shows the bond that was there. We were all desperate to play for Scotland and to do well, but even if you are not involved you want to be there to give the boys a bit of support and to see them do well. I have always been a big Scotland fan and to get the chance to play for Scotland was a dream come true. It was great to see the team back at a major finals and I hope they can go on and progress.'

Clarke had publicly backed O'Donnell and Dykes after the game and he copper-bottomed that by sticking by them for Wembley starts. The good news was that Kieran Tierney had also declared himself fit and he came back into the backline. In fact Grant Hanley was the only central defender who survived from the Czech Republic game, with Jack Hendry and Liam Cooper dropping out for KT and Scott McTominay. Callum McGregor and Billy Gilmour also came in – a decision that was probably Clarke's biggest call. Andy Robertson and O'Donnell were the wing backs with John McGinn making up the midfield. Dykes led the attack with Che Adams getting the call over Ryan Christie.

Clarke went with this Scotland starting XI: Marshall, McTominay, Hanley, Tierney, O'Donnell, Gilmour, McGregor, Robertson, McGinn, Adams, Dykes.

Both sets of players took to the field and took the knee in a combined show of support against racism.

It was England who tried to take the game to Scotland. Manchester City star Phil Foden – sporting a white tinge reminiscent of when Paul Gascoigne starred in Euro 96 – had the first effort but O'Donnell did well to block. England were looking to sweep their visitors aside. John Stones got free at a Mason Mount corner but his header came back off the near post. Raheem Sterling then set up Mount but he fired wide.

Clarke and the travelling Tartan Army had to be patient for Scotland's first real chance and it was a big one. Tierney raced up the left and crossed for O'Donnell charging in from the opposite flank. The Motherwell full back hit it flush on the volley but England keeper Jordan Pickford put out a strong right hand to push it away. The rebound was just too high for Che Adams and he couldn't get the follow-up on target.

The Scotland manager, speaking after the game, said: 'I was hoping Stephen O'Donnell would score. He was very, very unfairly criticised the other night. His performance tonight was outstanding.'

David Marshall also got in on the act making a good stop to keep out Mount. Scotland grew in belief and Billy Gilmour was the man making them tick. The youngster didn't look out of place as he got on the ball at every opportunity and passed and prodded his way through the England defence. He defied his tender years, playing with purpose and a real passion. The Chelsea midfielder's performance was from the top drawer and a great sign of what Scotland could look forward to in the future. Gilmour was who everybody was talking about, not Harry Kane, Sterling, Foden or Declan Rice. England may have been stunned but not the Scotland manager.

Clarke, when asked about his young playmaker's performance, observed: 'Never in doubt. Billy is a top player. We know what he's got. His legs ran out towards the end but he doesn't get much football at Chelsea.'

Scotland looked more likely to get a winner. Grant Hanley headed back into the box and Dykes curled it towards the top corner of the net but Chelsea defender Reece James got back to clear off the line. It was a close call and there was to be one more. Andy Robertson's deep cross was aimed towards Lyndon Dykes but it came off a defender and fell to Adams but he blazed his shot wide.

The final whistle brought the first ever goalless draw between England and Scotland at Wembley. The boos that went up around the ground at the end from the home fans told its own story. The points were shared but it was Scotland who took all the plaudits. It was in sharp contrast to the first game where Clarke and his team had been standing in Southgate's and England's shoes.

It was the perfect response from Marshall and his Scotland backline. 'It was a big game,' the keeper said. 'The boys did well in front of me. I had a save from Mason Mount and there was a scramble at the end. We were really good that night and Stephen O'Donnell and Che Adams went close. Billy Gilmour was excellent that night. We thoroughly deserved our point.'

Clarke praised his Scotland stars. He said: 'I'm delighted for the players. It was a great performance; we knew we had to come here and suffer a little bit out of possession. I was delighted by the way we played with the ball as well, and we created chances. I've said for a long time, we're a good team. I thought the reaction after the game on Monday was over the top. I've said for a long time we've got a really good group of players and we proved it tonight.'

Scotland skipper Andy Robertson was proud of his team but was left a little frustrated they couldn't find a winner. He said: 'There is a sense of frustration that we didn't win the game because we certainly had the chances.'

England boss Southgate also gave Scotland all the credit. He said: 'It was a frustrating night. You've got to give Scotland credit. They defended valiantly and played well.'

It was suddenly game on in Euro 2020 Group D. It was going down to the last game although England remained favourites to top the section. Clarke and Scotland could also make history by beating Croatia at Hampden in the final match.

Chapter 13

MODRIĆ'S MAGIC SPELLS THE END OF EURO 2020

SCOTLAND only had to beat Croatia at Hampden and the likelihood was that the national team would make the knockout stages of a major tournament for the first time. At home in a tournament proper. What more could you ask for? It was also against a Croatian team that was performing below standard. Scotland had also never lost to Croatia. Yes, they had made the last World Cup final and lost out to France, but they had hardly set Euro 2020 alight. They had lost to England and drawn with the Czech Republic. They still had top talent like Luka Modrić, Ivan Perišić and Mateo Kovačić, but their best days, certainly on the international front, had looked behind them. That was the belief of a lot of the nation as they prepared for their do-or-die final group game on 22 June 2021. In saying that, Modrić was still pulling the strings for Real Madrid, Kovačić was a key player for Chelsea and Perišić was at Inter Milan.

Clarke knew what was in front of his team and was keeping his feet firmly on the ground while the nation dreamed of making history.

The national boss warned: 'We have to find our top performance level and hope it's enough to get us the three points against a team that was in the last World Cup final. This is a big game so let's not lose focus on where we are and what we've done to get here, including the point we got at Wembley. You're talking about a team that played in the last World Cup final. They have quality players, but they are obviously looking for a little spark in the tournament. They are good players. Make no mistake about it, and they are going to cause us a lot of problems. We're going to have to play our best game. We're going to have to play as well as we can to get the result we want. People may say Croatia are past their peak but they are the number one seeds. They always qualify for tournaments, have top, top players in their team and we need to respect them as we do with all our opponents. Then we have to find a way to beat them because, as much as they want to make it to the knockout stages, so do we.'

Scotland had just come off their morale-boosting trip to Wembley and Billy Gilmour looked like a young man that could go on and light up the competition. That was the hope and dream, although that turned into a nightmare for Gilmour, Clarke and the nation. Our flickering light had been cruelly blown out by Covid. He was forced to isolate for ten days.

It floored the Scotland camp as well as Gilmour. A frustrated Clarke confirmed: 'It was obviously a shock to the lad. It wasn't something we expected but it's something we have to deal with and get on with. First and foremost, I'm upset for Billy. I spoke to him and as you'd expect he's very upset. But it's just the times we are in. You have to adapt and deal with it and that's what we'll do. We follow all the protocols. We wear our masks at the right time, we wash our hands all the time and have bottles of sanitiser around the place. We do everything we can within the context of a global pandemic and a virus that you can't see. People all over the world have caught this virus. It's not something you can legislate for.'

The Scotland squad were gutted for the Chelsea midfielder and Clarke urged his players to make sure he got another crack at Euro 2020.

He added: 'We have to make sure Billy's good performance against England doesn't go to waste. The players don't need any added motivation but this is a very tight-knit group. They know if we can progress far enough into the tournament then they can welcome Billy back into the squad. That would be fantastic.'

Leeds United defender Liam Cooper had been a previous Covid case and knew how Gilmour felt. Cooper said: 'I've been in Billy's shoes myself and it's not a nice place to be. I know how rough it can be. I got the symptoms. We're all just really gutted for Billy, first and foremost. He's just announced himself on the world stage with a great performance at Wembley and now this happens. But that's the world we're living in at the moment, the world we've all had to adjust to.'

That left Clarke with a Gilmour-sized hole in his midfield. He had to decide how best to fill it but at the same time try and nullify the threat of Modrić and the rest of his Croatian midfield maestros. He decided not to go man for man.

The Scotland boss explained why: 'Modrić is such a clever player that if you tried to man-mark him, I'm sure he'd find a way round it. So we've got to look for the nearest person to him to be the first man to make the press on him. Hopefully that can keep him under control. I'm sure, with a player of that quality, it's going to be difficult to keep him under control for the full 95 minutes or whatever it is. But we'll do our best. It's a big game. Croatia are professionals and they know better than us what it takes to get into the knockout stages of a major tournament because they've been there before and we haven't. They are wily old foxes but we're ready for them.'

Scotland knew qualification could be a close shave but striker

Lyndon Dykes took it to the extreme. He shaved his head again. Dykes had done it for the play-off final against Serbia and it sent out a firm rallying cry to his Scotland teammates.

Dykes said: 'The boys know that when they see me with a shaved head we mean business. It's a sign, something that shows we're going out to fight. When the boys see I've done this, they know it means we're going to war. So I got a straight zero on the clippers. The boys loved it because they knew it meant we were going to turn up. I first did it for the Serbia game and I did it again before England as it was a big game for us. I do it myself, just get the clippers out. Hopefully it gives us a bit of luck. I did mention the idea of everyone doing the same thing. Imagine the entire starting line-up coming out all with heads shaved down to zero – I think anyone would be scared! A few of the boys have bad hairlines so they weren't too keen!'

Clarke went with the same starting XI that had started at Wembley, with Stuart Armstrong coming in to replace Gilmour. John McGinn was also played in a less advanced role as Clarke played five across the middle to try and stifle the space for the Croats.

Scotland went on the offensive. McGinn curled in an early cross but it was just inches too far from Che Adams. Scotland were finding their feet when the Croats whipped the rug from beneath them in the 17th minute.

Josip Juranović, who would later join Celtic, curled in a cross from the right. Perišić won the ball at the back post and headed it down to Nikola Vlašić, who took a touch and beat David Marshall with a low shot at his near post.

It was a setback. Marshall at full stretch had to tip another long-range effort from Modrić over. Andy Robertson's cross gave McGinn a sight of goal but he couldn't get enough power to trouble Dominik Livaković. There was another issue for Clarke as

Grant Hanley had to go off injured and was replaced by Scott McKenna.

Scotland rallied just before the interval and Hampden erupted in the 42nd minute. Robertson's cross again fell to Che Adams. He couldn't control the ball and a Croatian defender cleared but only as far as Callum McGregor. He took a touch to cushion it and then blasted a shot low into the bottom right-hand corner of the net.

It was Scotland's first goal at a major finals for 23 years. It was worth the wait. Could it now provide the springboard for that all-important win?

The second half, however, saw Croatia step up a gear and Scotland just couldn't live with them. Marshall had to be alert to come off his line and smother at the feet of Vlašić. That was a warning shot and in the 62nd minute they got their second goal.

Some great play in and around the Scotland box saw things open up for Modrić at the edge of the box. With the outside of his boot he curled a beautiful shot into the top right-hand corner of David Marshall's net. For the neutral it was a thing of beauty, but for Scotland it was a heartbreak. Modrić in the process became the oldest scorer at a Euros at 35 years and 286 days.

The classy Croat wasn't finished there. He provided the ammunition as he swung in a corner that saw Perišić rise above Kieran Tierney at the front post to head in. It was also a big personal goal for Perišić as he joined Davor Šuker as his country's top scorer at a finals.

Scotland tried to rally. Adams had a chance but Livaković denied him with a block and Robertson sent in an inviting cross that if McGinn had got a touch on would have netted but it flashed across the goal.

The Tartan Army knew it was over and belted out their anthem 'We'll Be Coming' in the final seconds. It was a defiant final stance as they showed their team and Clarke their appreciation for getting Scotland back to a finals.

Clarke praised the Scotland fans. He said: 'We want to make those supporters proud. They were tremendous, losing 3-1 and all you can hear is the Tartan Army backing the team.'

Scotland's goal hero McGregor claimed it had whetted the squad's appetite to show they weren't a one-tournament wonder. The midfielder said: 'It was a proud moment but ultimately we are disappointed we didn't quite get the result we wanted. It has been an amazing experience. Every single one of us has learned so much. It gives you the hunger to get back there.'

The Scotland boss had no complaints about the defeat to Croatia. Clarke said: 'First of all we got here for the first time in 23 years. It was a big thing for the country and this group of players. I think you saw tonight a team who are tournament-hardened in Croatia against a team who were in their first tournament for a long time. We will go away and learn from it. We started on the back foot and losing in the first game is something we need to address in the next one. We left everything at Wembley against England and couldn't quite get it tonight. We had a good spell at the goal, but Croatia are a top team and they showed that. Hopefully, we can learn our lessons and we don't need to wait as long for the next tournament.'

Croatia had shown they were like a fine wine, getting better with age. The myth that they were past their peak was smashed at Hampden.

O'Donnell said: 'It still irks me that Croatia were an ageing team. Modrić is still strolling about at 38, Perišić is at Tottenham and Kovačić is now at Manchester City. Scotland had taken years to qualify and it shows the challenge when you get to that level against teams who are operating at the later stages of the competitions. Look at Morocco in the last World Cup (2022). They might have been looked upon as whipping boys but they did brilliantly. The key is getting there and after that you never know what could happen.'

Sadly, it was the same old story with Scotland going out at the group stage for the 11th time. It was England, the Czech Republic and Croatia who progressed. The experienced Croatians just had too much for Scotland.

'It was a tough group,' Lyndon Dykes insisted. 'We could have done better but we did our best. The first game was tough and we didn't get the result. We were solid against England and unlucky not to win. We all knew the result we needed against Croatia. They were very good and had world-class players. They had the likes of Modrić and Kovačić, who have big-game experience at that level. It was their night.'

Marshall knew the first game against the Czech Republic had proved to be fatal. 'Croatia were really good in the second half,' the keeper acknowledged. 'I think if we had got something on the board from that first game then things might have turned out differently. Overall, I don't think we could have argued about not getting out of the group.'

Scotland were back but they had missed a real opportunity.

Former Scotland star Charlie Adam said: 'I think there will have been a huge disappointment there. The first game was a huge disappointment. They upped their game and got a very good draw against England, but then we got beat by a very good Croatian team. Games like these are where we have to hold our hands up. We were a little bit short but we are better prepared for the next one. We have more tournament experience, the staff and players, and next time I am certain the team will give a much better account of itself.'

Scotland's final dream was over for this tournament but Clarke was adamant that this team would be more than a flash in the pan.

Ryan Christie observed: 'Everybody loved Euro 2020 and we were disappointed how we performed. Obviously, we had a tough group. We did well against England but in the other two, especially at Hampden, we let ourselves down a little bit. It was strange with the circumstances and the restrictions with Covid. After that, everybody was keen to have another crack at it. I have been to one European Championships with Scotland and if I can get to a second one it would be a dream come true. Listen, I think the Euros gave us a load of experience. Everybody said how long a time it had been for us to be in a tournament. None of us had experienced any time at a tournament, so it was a first for us. I think everybody said on the back of it that we didn't want it to be a one-off, that we wanted to get it again.'

Clarke was confident that this Scotland squad would make their mark over the longer term.

'He said it to us at the start before we had even kicked a ball,' O'Donnell insisted. 'He then said it at the end – that we all want to have this feeling again. We want Scotland to be back in major finals and we want to make it a regular occurrence. The buzz of being at Euro 2020 was amazing. I could only imagine what it would be like if the team qualified out of their group. The manager has set the bar that we weren't a flash in the pan and we are here to stay. He has done that and delivered, as the players have. He set us a realistic target. He wasn't telling us we should be looking to win the next Euros. We achieved the first goal and now it is about seeing what we can achieve next.'

Chapter 14

WORLD CUP HOPES AND DREAMS

THE question now was: could Steve Clarke back up Euro 2020 qualification and get Scotland back to the World Cup finals? Getting back to the European Championships was massive but the World Cup remained the big one.

France 98 had seemed a lifetime ago when the national team opened the tournament up with all the glitz and glamour against Brazil. That was at a time when Scotland had qualified for five consecutive World Cups from 1974 to 1990. It all seemed like a distant memory going into the qualification for Qatar 2022. Could Clarke follow in the footsteps of Craig Brown and take us to another World Cup?

The greatest football show on earth wasn't immune to the pandemic either. The draw had to be delayed until 7 December 2020 and was done virtually in Zurich because of travel restrictions and ongoing Covid issues.

Clarke's side went in as third seeds and were going to need to punch above their weight to win the group or even to claim second place and a potential play-off. There was also no fall-back from the Nations League this time around. It was all on this qualifying campaign.

Scotland were drawn in qualifying Group F where Denmark

WORLD CUP HOPES AND DREAMS

had come out as top seeds. Was that an omen? The last time Scotland had faced them competitively was in the 1986 World Cup in Mexico. Austria were the second seeds while in pot four there was the old faithful Israel and then the Faroe Islands and Moldova. It was a group that was going to be challenging although it could also have been a lot, lot worse.

Clarke, quoted on the SFA website, said: 'When you go into any campaign you want to finish as high as you possibly can and that's what we aim to do. The draw is decent but I'm sure that Denmark, Austria and everyone in the group are looking at it thinking it's a decent group. It's always going to be tough. We have to keep improving, keep working hard and don't get carried away.'

The World Cup qualifying campaign was going to be a challenge anyway, but was even more so when Clarke also had to fit in the delayed Euro 2020 final campaign into the summer of 2021.

Scotland were to kick off at home to Austria, followed by a trip to Israel and another Hampden clash with the Faroes in the March 2021 international window. The World Cup qualifiers would then go into cold storage for Euro 2020 and return in September, where Scotland would head to Denmark, host Moldova and then Austria away. The following month would see Israel in Glasgow and the Faroes away and November would finish off the campaign in Moldova and with everyone hoping for a grandstand finish at home to the Danes.

Clarke made a statement of intent going into the World Cup qualifiers by snaring long-term target Che Adams. Adams was first named in the Scottish squad for the opening qualifiers against Austria, Israel and the Faroe Islands. He was joined by another new boy in the striking department. Kevin Nisbet had been the second-top scorer in the Premiership and was rewarded for his 12 goals for Hibs with his first international inclusion. Norwich defender Grant Hanley and Jack Hendry, who had impressed at

Belgian side KV Oostende in Belgium, both earned recalls and were selected by Clarke for the first time.

Hanley said: 'Steve's given me a chance. I'm grateful for that. I think I had two or three years away from the national team set-up. I think in that time I probably improved a lot as a player. I'd certainly like to think so, anyway. I don't know what other people's opinions are. Especially, the position I play also – you gain that experience through time and through playing games. I'm enjoying my football at the minute. I'm loving coming away and playing for Scotland. For me, every cap's an honour.'

The opener was in front of an empty Hampden. It was just as well because the Roar would well have been substituted with a groan in this rather flat affair. Saša Kalajdžić gave the Austrians a second-half lead. Adams came on for his debut, replacing Stuart Armstrong, before Grant Hanley got his head on a Stephen O'Donnell free kick to equalise. It was his first international goal in eight years. Hanley and Hendry's returns allowed Clarke to move Scott McTominay into his more natural midfield surroundings. Scotland looked to kick on for the win, but Kalajdžić netted his second. Clarke's men went again and levelled. Ryan Christie headed into the box and John McGinn acrobatically scored with an overhead kick, as he dropped into the Hampden turf to rescue an opening night draw. It was also at a point where the Aston Villa star had a goal every two games under Clarke. That took it to eight goals in 16 appearances.

McGinn said: 'I think the way the game panned out, going behind twice, we showed good character and quality to get back into it. We'll take the point. We're progressing. We can believe in ourselves a bit more. When we conceded the first goal, we were on top. We had good control of the game and it was disappointing to lose the goal the way we did. Again we showed good character to get back in the game – then we let ourselves down again. But you can't keep this team down. They want to keep fighting for their country.'

Next up was Israel and a trip to Tel Aviv, a place that hadn't really been a happy hunting ground for the Scots. It remained that way when a long-range shot from Dor Peretz gave Israel the lead just before half-time. Scotland managed to fight back and equalise in the 56th minute when Adams, making his first international start, set up Ryan Fraser. It saw two points dropped and already Denmark were four points clear.

Fraser claimed: 'I think it is decent if I am being honest. We lost both previous games away to Israel so to come away with a draw is a step in the right direction. Obviously, we would like to win, but Austria is a good point as well and it gives us a good platform to go into September to try and progress.'

Scotland finished off their qualifiers, ahead of Euro 2020, with an expected 4-0 dismantling of the Faroe Islands. John McGinn continued his scoring streak with a double before Che Adams opened his Scotland account on the hour and Fraser finished it off with a rare header to make it two goals in two games. The Newcastle United player had also been deployed, unusually, as a wing back.

Fraser joked: 'To be at the back post and score a header, I never thought I would see the day, if I am being honest. I haven't played right wing back for about four years. When the gaffer asked me to do it I said I would play anywhere he wants me to play. That is why we are doing so well; it is because everyone wants to play for the manager. When everyone wants to play for the manager then you will do everything for him and you will run through brick walls for him. I have never said it, but I was buzzing to get the clean sheet as well, it was nice.'

Jack Hendry was pleased with his return to the fold and life under Clarke. He said: 'I learned a lot from them over those ten days. They [Scotland coaching team] gave me great feedback when I was training and after games. They are always looking at ways of improving the team and players individually. It was a great experience over the three games and I just want to keep myself involved. The coaching staff gave me things to go away and look at and to work into my game. The squad and coaching staff were really welcoming and there is a real feel-good factor and team spirit within the Scotland set-up. It was a great learning experience for me. The manager was great and it was good to see his coaching and methods. He and his coaching staff leave no stone unturned both individually and collectively and they set up the team well. You know your job and what is expected as soon as you step on the pitch.'

Clarke and his side were unbeaten in their opening three games and could put World Cup qualifying to bed momentarily to concentrate on Euro 2020. The return to a major finals didn't go the way Scotland had hoped and dreamed, but the SFA certainly had belief in Clarke. They handed him a new deal that would see him lead Scotland not only to the end of these World Cup qualifiers but also through the Euro 2024 qualifying campaign.

The obvious disappointment of failing to get beyond the Euro 2020 group stages added additional fire to the bellies of the Scotland players as they resumed their World Cup qualifiers in the September.

They couldn't allow a Euro 2020 hangover because it was straight into the action with the big one – Denmark away. It reopened the door for in-form Hearts keeper Craig Gordon to reclaim the Scotland No. 1 spot. Clarke's backroom team also changed with John Carver, Austin MacPhee and Chris Woods replacing Steven Reid and Stevie Woods, who had stepped down to concentrate on their club commitments.

Clarke knew how important the trip to Copenhagen was to try and haul Denmark back into the qualifying campaign. It quickly turned into an unenviable task when Covid and travelling regulations hit his squad hard again.

John McGinn, Nathan Patterson and Stephen O'Donnell were all affected and left Scotland without a recognised right back. You could also add James Forrest, Greg Taylor, Scott McTominay, Stuart Armstrong and Kevin Nisbet to the injured list. Every cloud does have a silver lining and it came for the impressive Aberdeen midfielder Lewis Ferguson, who was called up for the first time.

Clarke was also a coach down ahead of the Danish trip, as Austin MacPhee also tested positive for Covid. Former Scotland striker and current Hearts coach Stevie Naismith was drafted in. Scotland were down to the bare bones just about everywhere. It was a makeshift team and squad. The game proved too much of a stretch as two goals in as many first-half minutes from Daniel Wass and Joakim Maehle put Denmark in a commanding position at the top of the group. It looked like a fight for second spot. That was strengthened by the narrow 1-0 home win over Moldova, thanks to a Lyndon Dykes goal. The striker followed that up with an even bigger goal in the next game. His 30th-minute penalty was enough to give Scotland a big win in Austria and moved them back into second above Israel. It set things up nicely for a big showdown with the Israelis at Hampden in October. This game would go a long way to deciding who would finish second. It had certainly caught the imagination of the Scottish public with Hampden looking forward to its first sell-out since 2017, pre-pandemic.

Scott McKenna reckoned it was a sign of the progress that Scotland had made under Clarke that all roads led back to the national stadium. He said: 'I remember when we played there against Israel in the Nations League and how empty it was that night. It's a sign of how far we've come as a squad and a team that Hampden is now sold out for this one.'

Israel, once again, proved more than a match going ahead twice. Eran Zahavi's free kick was cancelled out by John McGinn's brilliant goal. Andy Robertson set it up after taking a ball back from Che Adams, before the Aston Villa midfielder controlled it with his left and swept it home with his right from the edge of the box.

Mu'nas Dabbur bundled in Israel's second before Scotland won a penalty after Billy Gilmour had been taken out on the edge of the box. Dykes retained the responsibility but Ofir Marciano came out on top as he read it and blocked it down the middle.

Dykes thought he had given himself a welcome reprieve when he came in high and managed to get a foot in front of a diving defender to knock Andy Robertson's cross past Marciano in the 55th minute. Polish referee Szymon Marciniak immediately disallowed the goal for a high foot until the VAR officials invited him to take a second look at the incident. He did, returned and awarded a rather relieved Dykes his goal.

Marciano produced more heroics to deny Dykes again and then McGinn. It looked like Israel had done enough to frustrate Scotland – but the home side had other ideas and stole it at the death. John McGinn's deep corner was headed down by Jack Hendry for McTominay to chest it in at the back post in the 94th minute. It comes to those who wait!

The Tartan Army celebrated what they knew was a big and significant win in this qualifying campaign. Amongst those jumping off their seats was the legendary Sir Alex Ferguson. He had taken the team to Mexico in 1986. Was Clarke a step closer to taking Scotland to Qatar 2022? The Scotland manager certainly enjoyed the moment as the final whistle went. He stood in front of Hampden's main stand with his two hands in the air, punching the sky in delight. His team had just landed a big blow of their own on one of their biggest qualifying rivals, in one of the most dramatic games Hampden had seen in many a year.

Hendry said: 'I got a glance on it and just tried to put it into the area at the back post. Thankfully Scott was there to put it in. It was amazing. The scenes at the end – growing up, that's what you want to see from the home support. The fans have waited a long time to see something like that and there's nothing better than a last-minute winner. We made it difficult for ourselves with the first-half performance, but we showed balls of steel the way we came out in the second half and put in that kind of perform-ance for the fans. We deserved it and got our rewards.'

Billy Gilmour, like everyone else at Hampden, went through a roller coaster of emotion in that Israel win. Gilmour claimed: 'That was a crazy game. When they scored early on I was like: "Oh my God, no!" I was constantly thinking we need a result here. I enjoyed the game and we got back in and we got the penalty. I was thinking that Dykes was going to score. He missed and we thought, is it going to be one of those nights? But it was a great team performance after that and Scott scored a last-minute win-ner and Hampden erupted.'

Next up was the potential choppy waters of the Faroe Islands. Berti Vogts and his Scotland side back in the Euro 2004 qualifiers had been left red-faced after a 2-2 draw there. Scotland weren't expected to have such problems although it was all still a bit flat after their Hampden high against Israel.

The Faroes had the better chances and should have gone ahead before Scotland came to the fore and grabbed all three points with four minutes to go. Sub Nathan Patterson's cross from the right came off a defender and hit Dykes who forced it in at the near post, although there was a VAR check for a potential handball before the goal was awarded. It saw Dykes score in four consecu-tive Scotland games, and he had become the first player to do it since Colin Stein in 1969. Scotland also managed to tough it out in Tórshavn for another big qualifying win.

A relieved Hanley claimed: 'We knew it was going to be like that. We knew the Faroes would be organised, disciplined, physical, work their 'you know whats' off and make it very hard for us. No excuses, but the [artificial] pitch plays a part in that as well. We had to dig in and we knew we would have to – it was never going to be easy. So, we stuck in there and got the goal in the end, which is the most important thing. It wasn't our best performance or our prettiest performance.'

It meant Clarke knew his team could seal second place going into the final two qualifiers in November. A win in Moldova would clinch it ahead of the visit of group winners Denmark on the final evening. The issue for Clarke was that goal-getting striker Dykes was suspended for the Chișinău clash.

Clarke took his side to Spain for a training camp ahead of those games, where he lost Scott McTominay through illness along with Ryan Fraser and Grant Hanley because of injury. The Newcastle United star was then filmed doing some work at his club training ground and that grabbed some unwanted headlines at a time when the focus should all have been on grabbing a play-off spot. Hanley's withdrawal opened the door for Hearts defender John Souttar to make his long-awaited return after an injury-plagued three seasons and Stoke City striker Jacob Brown was selected for the first time.

The Halifax-born striker was eligible for Scotland through his Glaswegian mother. He had previously been sounded out for Scotland under-21s but it never materialised. He eventually got his break at full international level.

'When I thought I was going to be picked for the under-21s it was going to be a great moment for me at that time, but when I wasn't in the team I was disappointed,' Brown admitted. 'That was a few years ago. I kept working hard and hoped the opportunity would come again and thankfully it did.'

Brown was called up for the World Cup qualifiers against Moldova and Denmark in November 2021. It was a big day for the family. He explained: 'My agents told me the gaffer was going to ring me and he did to have a chat with me and then it was announced. I only found out the day before the squad was announced that I was going to be in it. My family were the first people I rang when I found out. My mum, being from Glasgow, was over the moon. A lot of the family were in tears when they found out because it was such a big moment for me and my family. Everyone was really proud.'

It was a less likely goal hero that came up trumps in Moldova. Nathan Patterson had been the creator in the Faroes but turned out to be the main man in Moldova. The Everton right back ran forward, took a pass back from John McGinn before he went on and fired a shot through a defender's legs and Scotland into a 38th-minute lead. It was his first international goal.

Patterson then helped Scotland seal the win when he combined with McGinn again and crossed for Che Adams to get Scotland's second in the 65th minute. Patterson was at the heart of everything and there was even a late VAR penalty decision that went against him for handball. Craig Gordon had made a few decent stops on the night and stood up again to deny Vadim Rata from the spot and leave Patterson's big night unblemished.

That was enough to guarantee Scotland a World Cup play-off with one game to go. It was a night to remember for Stoke City striker Jacob Brown, who won his first cap.

Scotland had expected that their last match against the Danes was going to be a big one. Hampden had sold out again but the fact Scotland got the job done in Moldova meant this game was now more of a play-off-clinching party. Clarke, however, wanted his team to be the main event and knew how important a win would be in terms of claiming a home play-off. He was also still irked by their defeat in Denmark earlier in the campaign and this was an opportunity to show what a full-strength Scotland team was all about.

Ryan Christie explained: 'We went into the game on the back of five wins on the trot and we also wanted to put right the away game in Denmark – we didn't think we did ourselves justice over there. The gaffer kind of touched on it as being like the next step. We saw how well Denmark did at the Euros and we want to start competing against these kinds of teams, show what we are capable of.'

Christie remembers the special feeling surrounding the Denmark game, adding: 'Everyone was absolutely buzzing walking out for the start and this place is full, singing the national anthem. I think it's the best the atmosphere's been for a long, long time. It's just those one per cents that are going to help us go a long way.'

It was turned up a notch or two when Scotland took the lead in the 35th minute. John McGinn's inswinging corner dropped deep beyond the far post for Liam Cooper to head back across the goal and Souttar to nod into the net. It was a massive moment and well deserved for the defender, although a lot of credit must also go to Scotland's set-piece specialist Austin MacPhee for his part in its creation.

Denmark were missing a few players but looked dangerous and forced Craig Gordon into a couple of half-decent stops. Stuart Armstrong then sprung the Danish offside trap to let Adams run on and fire a shot low past Kasper Schmeichel in the 86th minute. Clarke had got their tactics spot on to take a big scalp at Hampden.

Christie said: 'It was a great result and we were all excited to be playing at Hampden again in front of a packed crowd. You also know how good a team Denmark is. They showed that in

Denmark and we always had to be wary of that, but I think we executed the game plan down to a tee.'

Scotland were set for the World Cup play-offs. They also had play-off success to get to Euro 2020. Could they do it again and be set to join Denmark at Qatar in 2022? Clarke's message, issued from deep inside Hampden, was clear: 'Nobody will fancy taking us on here.'

Chapter 15

BONDING BRAVEHEARTS

'YOU hear all the Scotland players talk about the manager and they can't speak highly enough about him.' These are the words of Stevie Naismith, who has been on both sides as a player then an assistant coach under Steve Clarke.

That goes from the big English Premier League stars like captain Andy Robertson, John McGinn, Kieran Tierney and Scott McTominay to players like Celtic skipper Callum McGregor and those who are just taking their first steps in their international careers. Clarke quickly got his big players onside and they have formed the basis of this Scotland squad.

Stephen O'Donnell revealed: 'He got to know the players and you need to try and do that as quickly as you can. You don't really do that as quickly as you would like at international level because of the break between games. At club level, it can take a few weeks, but at international level it can take months with how it works. In that time you play five or six games and the pressure could be right on you. I think Steve did great getting to know the players. He built that basis of a team and that has been the core of the squad.'

Clarke is a strict manager. He demands everything when you are training on and off the pitch. The senior players know what he expects but he pretty much lets them run their dressing room, maintaining standards and trying to push everyone on to new heights.

Former assistant coach Alex Dyer said: 'A lot of the players are now in the English Premier League and are top players there. You are not getting players from the bottom English leagues now and that is without being disrespectful. They are top players and they are all making an impact. Steve knows how to treat them with respect but he is still the boss and they know that. He can give them a bit of leeway but the boys will know if they step out of line that Steve will come down on them. He gives them that freedom to go and express themselves on and off the pitch. The camp is a really good place to be in and around. You can see Steve putting his stamp on the whole country and it is a wonderful sight.'

The Scotland manager, however, isn't always Mr Serious, especially when it comes to his players.

'He has been great,' Lyndon Dykes explained. 'He is hard and tough when he needs to be on the group. Other times he can be soft and let us off with stuff when it comes to team bonding and different things. He does that knowing we will be switched on and ready when we need to be. That is the mark of a great manager. He knows what we need and when we need it but he is always looking to improve us and is always putting demands on us, so we don't slip up or fall off from where we are at the moment. It is all credit to the manager.'

Clarke has trust in his senior players. You very rarely see him publicly question or criticise a player unless they have stepped seriously out of line. The players know that Clarke has their backs and won't make them public scapegoats. It works both ways and there is total trust there.

Naismith confirmed: 'Steve lets the senior players, effectively, run the squad. He has given them wee bits and it works really well. It shows in his relationships with Andy Robertson, John McGinn and even guys like Liam Cooper, Grant Hanley, Scott McTominay and Callum McGregor – they all have really good relationships with the gaffer. The gaffer is brilliant at building bonds with the guys, individually and not just as part of a group. That is how he gets the best out of them.'

Ryan Christie believes a lot of that is down to the fact that there are no egos in or around the Scotland set-up. It is all for the country.

He passionately stated: 'Everybody is in the same boat when we go away with Scotland and that is what makes it so special. Everybody wants to play their part wherever or however they can to help the team. Regardless of whether you start, get minutes off the bench or don't get on, all the boys are together, united and with the one goal of doing well for Scotland.'

Andrew Considine had to pinch himself when he joined up with the Scotland squad but found the players and staff couldn't have been more welcoming.

Considine said: 'A lot of the boys I would watch on *Match of the Day*, like Andy Robertson, John McGinn and Scott McTominay. I was in the dressing room and I was thinking I was watching you on Saturday night or on a *Super Sunday*. You build up this persona but they were all so welcoming and really nice people. I remember my first meal I sat next to Scott McTominay and what a nice guy. All the boys were the same. There was a real buzz about the squad but all the boys made things so easy for me, speaking to me and just making me feel a part of things.'

The perception of Clarke is that he is downbeat and pretty serious all the time. Behind closed doors he can be a very different character, but very few people get to see that side publicly.

Charlie Nicholas said: 'I would catch him on a flight when we were both going down to London or coming back up the road.

I have had a few conversations with him. He is an impressive individual. I feel like people are given the wrong impression of him. He looks deadpan and dry but that is not him at all. He is humorous and a really nice guy. People sometimes say the same things about Kenny Dalglish, that he is hard work and serious. I never found that. People look at people and just tag them and that is what has happened with Steve, when it definitely isn't the case.'

Clarke is also a manager who has worked with the best and can get the best out of them. He is motivational and he has set up an international team with a close club-like mentality and togetherness.

Christie said: 'He has been in and around the game for a very long time. He knows what he is doing on and off the park. He is a master of getting the best out of people. That has been his secret over the last few years. He has created a great camaraderie in the squad. Ask any of the boys and they will all tell you that they absolutely love going away with Scotland. We can't wait to join up with the squad. It is the best dressing room I have been involved in. I have been involved in a few good ones but this Scotland one is special. Everyone is buzzing to be there and the feeling in the camp is incredible.'

It is the same for those who meet him for the first time.

Ross Stewart said: 'The manager is to the point. There is an aura there. Everyone listens when he talks and there is also a calmness. He is big on standards and is a winner. You have to treat every game the same and go in to win them all. He is also a very good people person who you want to go out and do well for. He can be motivational as well.'

Clarke has to use the limited time he has available to get his team ready for the games but also knows there has to be balance. The players spend a lot of time in hotels or in camps and it is about trying to keep the players stimulated.

Stewart added: 'It is a really close-knit group. That was the one thing I could sense that everyone got on really well. The second camp was at the end of the season and so we were away a wee bit longer. The manager worked on a few things, like golf days, to break things up. You have the senior players and they lead by example and set the standard. Making sure things are done properly.'

Naismith has also seen first-hand that Clarke's door is always open to any of his squad. Whether that is over football concerns, off-the-field issues or anything at all that is bothering them.

Clarke is well aware that the international team does not pay the wages and he is relying on the goodwill and passion of his players. There are times when he knows that he also has to give a bit of leeway, knowing he will get that back in spades.

Christie saw that when he moved from Celtic to Bournemouth in August 2021 at the end of the transfer window as Clarke was preparing his squad for a vital World Cup qualifier in Denmark.

Christie recalled: 'The manager was great even when I was finalising my move. I signed for Bournemouth during an international break. He was great, really supportive and couldn't have been any more accommodating. He was buzzing, like me, that I was getting the chance to play in England. I had been lucky enough to win a lot of things with Celtic and I felt it was time to try something different. The manager understood my position and why I wanted to go down and test myself in England, like he had during his playing career. The move was all a bit manic in terms of getting the medical and the deal over the line. He let me leave the Scotland camp to finalise my move. He has been amazing with me.'

There have been plenty of similar examples to the Christie situation, outside the public eye, that strengthen that connection and bond between the players and their national coach.

Christie joked: 'I signed my contract on the way to the airport. I then got there, jumped on the flight and had to stick my phone on flight mode until I landed. I didn't even know if my move had gone through until I got to the other side. I had no idea what was going on. I was on the flight with the squad just hoping everything had gone through. If not then I would have still been a Celtic player. When we got to Denmark, I put my phone on and I had confirmation that I had become a Bournemouth player. It was a great moment and I really appreciated the part the manager had played in helping me to get the deal done. We had a big game against Denmark but he knew how big the move was for me. That is just typical of the manager and that is why he has such a close bond with his players, knowing we will run through a brick wall for him and our country.'

It is all about doing the best for Scotland. If it takes short-term fixes or even in the medium term then Clarke will do whatever it takes.

Naismith explained how Declan Gallagher came in and played a big part in helping Scotland to Euro 2020: 'Deccy was a prime example. He earned a right to be in the squad. He was also a valuable member of the squad. Deccy then got a bit older and lost his place in the squad but I am pretty certain that he won't have a bad word to say against the manager. That is because of the way Steve manages the players, building up relationships and trust. The gaffer will have spoken to Deccy, given him his reasons. There is an honesty and an understanding there along with an empathy.'

Gallagher has since fallen out of the squad after spells on the sidelines at Aberdeen and St Mirren before his move to Dundee United, but the defender won't ever close the door on Scotland and Clarke.

Naismith added: 'Look at the way players who are no longer in the squad talk about him. He is just a really good manager. I have not seen one player in the squad feel as if they can't speak to some of the senior players and can you ask the manager this or that. He knows he needs these guys to buy into what he is doing for Scotland to be a success.'

That was backed up by Ryan Christie. He added: 'I am very fortunate because for the majority of the time, since the manager has come in, I have managed to keep my place in the squad. Playing for my country means everything to me. I know I can never be guaranteed my place, but I would have to say the manager has always shown a great loyalty to me and a lot of the boys. I freely admit that in my final season at Celtic I didn't play my best football, but he kept me involved. I played in the Serbia game and I was pleased to repay him with the goal in the play-off. He has been so supportive of me and I appreciate that. I know the other boys feel the same. KT and others have their ups and down on the club front, but the manager has always been really supportive and backed us all. I think that shows.'

That is the key element of management and Clarke knows that better than anyone.

Chapter 16

THE PAIN OF UKRAINE

SCOTLAND finished their World Cup 2022 qualifying group strongly on a high. Their second-placed finish gave the nation hope, on the back of an eight-game unbeaten run, that they could follow Euro 2020 qualification with a return to the World Cup finals in Qatar after a long and dark 24-year hiatus. The World Cup, instead of being a staple of the Scottish diet, had become nothing more than a distant pipe dream with Scotland looking enviously in from the outside, every four years, at one of the greatest sporting events.

Clarke knew what it would mean to awake the Scots out of their World Cup hibernation. They were, potentially, two games away from achieving that. A route to Qatar was within touching distance. This was also the same core of Clarke's squad who had also been over the course in the play-offs; holding their nerve twice in two penalty shoot-outs to see off Israel and Serbia to seal Scotland's long-anticipated finals return at Euro 2020. The nation could almost smell it, it seemed that close.

Clarke and his team never got carried away because they knew there were still two big games and obstacles standing in their way. The Scots went into the play-off draw in Switzerland as one of the seeded teams. They had earned that right and knew they would have a home semi-final tie against Turkey, Poland, North Macedonia, Ukraine, Austria or the Czech Republic. The draw would then be made to see who would play in the final play-off for guaranteed entry to World Cup 2022.

The draw was on the 26 November 2021. It led to the Tartan Army spending days trying to predict the dream draw or the perfect permutation with, of course, all roads leading to Qatar.

Scotland's World Cup fate was in the hands of German legend Lothar Matthäus, a famous name that Sir Alex Ferguson's Scotland side had come up against when Scotland lost to West Germany at Mexico 1986. Gordon Strachan scored his revered goal in a 2-1 defeat. Matthäus was a bit kinder this time when he drew out Ukraine. Clarke knew his team would be at home in the March semi-final.

It was the latter part of the World Cup play-off draw, however, that really caught the imagination. The winners would travel to face whoever came out on top in the Wales v Austria semi-final. There was already talk of a potential Home Nations clash with misty and fond memories going back to Scotland's famous World Cup play-off wins in 1977 and 1985. Clarke's side versus Gareth Bale and Co. Was it written in the stars again?

Not for Clarke. He knew it was on the pitch where his players had to shine and Ukraine was the only nation in his focus.

The Scotland boss said: 'We always treat our immediate opponents with the utmost respect. That's what Ukraine will get, all our respect. We'll approach the game with a bit of humility and do as well as we can. After that, over the months, we'd have to prepare for Wales or Austria. We'll make sure we're well prepared for that if we get through the first game.'

Many of Scotland's stars were walking a yellow card tightrope and were one booking away from a suspension. If they were booked again and the Scots qualified then they would miss the final. Thankfully, UEFA saw common sense and decided to intro-duce a yellow card amnesty cancelling out the cautions from the qualifiers.

It was all eyes on Ukraine. Scotland had played Ukraine just twice before, back in the Euro 2008 qualifying campaign. The Scots had lost 2-0 away and won 3-1 at home. A Hampden repeat was all that was needed or so the nation hoped.

Ukraine, just a month before the game, was left facing an even bigger issue as it was invaded by Russia on 24 February 2022. It turned into a bloody and harrowing war that cost thousands of lives and left the Ukrainian infrastructure and nation devastated.

A World Cup play-off was suddenly the least of Ukraine's wor-ries as the ongoing Russian aggression was ramped up. Many of Ukraine's home-based footballers, like the majority of their men, took to the frontline to defend their proud nation. The Ukrainian Association of Football, just a few weeks before their scheduled trip to Hampden, had to ask for a postponement.

A FIFA statement read: 'FIFA can confirm it has received a request from the Ukrainian Association of Football today to post-pone their matches scheduled for March. FIFA remains in regular contact with UEFA and the SFA to find an appropriate solution. FIFA expresses its deepest solidarity to everybody affected by what is happening in Ukraine. A further update will be provided in due course.'

The Scotland players were left in a state of limbo, but their thoughts were more with the predicament their Ukrainian coun-terparts and people found themselves in.

Ryan Christie said: 'Just going into it, with everything that had happened and was happening between Ukraine and Russia, was really, really difficult. Most people had sympathy for Ukraine and their people. It put us in a strange position because everybody knew they were playing for something more than just football.

The ironic thing was that we were all on their side with what happened in the attacks but then on a football pitch we suddenly had to go up against them.'

Clarke and his team still needed games to keep themselves ticking over and organised a Hampden friendly with Poland to fill the void. It was announced the game would be a fundraiser with all proceeds going to UNICEF's humanitarian efforts in Ukraine.

The Scotland captain Andy Robertson, speaking on the SFA website, said: 'As a father, the images of children in Ukraine has been heartbreaking to watch. When we were informed that the match against Ukraine would be postponed then working in partnership with Robert [Lewandowski, Poland's captain] and the Polish squad to do our bit to help the situation was a no-brainer.'

The games saw Sunderland frontman Ross Stewart rewarded for his impressive 22-goal haul by getting his first call-up and so did Bologna defender Aaron Hickey.

Stewart said: 'It was a bit of a surprise to be fair. I had been doing well and I had been linked with a call-up but until you actually get the call then you are never really sure. I was really excited. As a kid, you always dream about playing for your country and so it was a great feeling when I got the call-up. It was a tremendous honour. There was a bit of nerves as well, going into an environment with top, top players. I went in to be myself to try and learn from these top players and staff and to get used to the environment. In fairness, the squad is a great group of guys and they made it really easy for me to settle in. I didn't play in the games but it was still great to be involved for the first time. It was a bit of a whirlwind.'

Stewart was certainly impressed by his fellow Ayrshireman Clarke and his backroom team. He said: 'The manager is from just a few towns away from me in Ayrshire. I met the manager when I got there. He welcomed me, shook my hand and had a quiet word. He told me to come in and enjoy the experience because I was here on merit. It was the manager, John Carver and Stevie Naismith at the time. Naisy joined in with a few as well. The manager sets up the training and then lets his assistants take training. He speaks to you before and after games and gives you pointers and information. It is hard work.'

Scotland and the Poles drew 1-1. Kieran Tierney had put Clarke's men ahead but a frustrating stoppage time penalty from Krzysztof Piątek had denied them a morale-boosting victory. More than £500,000 was raised for the Ukrainian relief effort through the game.

Wales had also beaten Austria in the other semi-final and therefore the Scots and Ukrainians knew a trip to the Valleys awaited the victors.

It had been agreed from the initial dates that the defeated semi-finalists would play each other and so Scotland with another empty date played another friendly away to Austria to complete their March international double-header. Scotland again got themselves into a promising position through goals from Jack Hendry and John McGinn before late strikes from Michael Gregoritsch and Alessandro Schöpf ensured another frustrating share of the spoils.

The World Cup draw for the finals in Qatar was made on 1 April 2022 in Doha. Scotland still didn't know when or if they would be playing their semi-final, but if they got through that and the final they knew they would be in World Cup Group B alongside England, Iran and the USA. The chance to meet England in another finals, after Euro 2020, whetted the appetite even further, although there was a lot of water to flow under the bridge before that dream scenario. There was Ukraine and another tussle against Wales, which were two major obstacles standing in the way of the national team.

The semi-final play-off was finally given the go-ahead on 14 April 2022, after initial fears that the Ukraine game might go into the September window or might not go ahead at all. Even that date looked a long shot. There was also the sympathetic view that Ukraine should be handed automatic entry to Qatar 2022, but that wasn't logistically possible for UEFA and FIFA to sign off. Discussions took place between UEFA, FIFA and the Pot A semi-finalists. It was agreed the semi-final with Ukraine would be played on 1 June 2022, some three months after it had originally been scheduled. The winners would be travelling to Cardiff four days later for a winner-takes-all clash.

Scotland's Nations League fixtures had to be rescheduled, with games against Armenia home and away and a trip to Ireland to follow at the end of a crammed international window. It meant that Scotland had to play their most important game in years at the end of a back-breaking domestic campaign, although perhaps that was nothing compared to the nightmare preparations Ukraine's players had to face.

Christie recalled: 'Eventually, we got the go-ahead to play the game at the end of the season. The international breaks during the season are good because you are still within your domestic campaign and everybody is firing. The summer camp is different because it comes at the end of the season and players finish their seasons at different times. Boys could be off for a few weeks while others will be coming off cup finals and play-offs. It leaves people at different fitness and sharpness levels. The boys all keep themselves fit and ticking over but it is difficult to try and maintain that match sharpness where you are at the top of your game. The manager and the Association all do well and arrange camps and warm weather training for us. It just has a different feel because it is so late in the summer.'

National coach Oleksandr Petrakov, with the Ukrainian league shutdown because of the ongoing war, took his domestic players to Slovenia for a training camp to keep them primed. They played a number of challenge matches before their foreign-based stars joined them for the final preparations ahead of the game, playing a number of friendlies against club sides including Borussia Mönchengladbach, Empoli and Rijeka.

Ukraine's top players, Manchester City's Oleksandr Zinchenko and West Ham United's Andriy Yarmolenko, both came into sharp focus while in Scotland, St Johnstone's Max Kucheriavyi also made the news over their ongoing concerns on the war in their homeland.

Clarke had to block out all the outpouring of sympathy for Ukraine and put together a squad that would get Scotland through. The delay had also cost him key men in Arsenal's Kieran Tierney and Ryan Jack, meaning a call-up for Luton Town midfielder Allan Campbell.

The Scotland boss picked a 28-man squad to cope with the physical and mental demands of four games in such a short space of time.

There were also players coming into the squad on the ultimate high or the lowest of the low. Scott McKenna came in after being a Wembley play-off hero and helping Nottingham Forest into the English Premier League, while captain Andy Robertson came in nursing the pain of Liverpool's narrow Champions League defeat to Real Madrid.

The good news was that John Souttar and Liam Cooper were back from injury, while Nathan Patterson had also recovered from ankle surgery to take his place in the squad.

Clarke had plenty of time to consider his approach. He went in with a 3-4-1-2 formation. Craig Gordon was in goal with Scott McTominay slotting into a back three alongside Grant Hanley and Cooper. Skipper Andy Robertson and Aaron Hickey took up the wing back roles, with Billy Gilmour and Callum McGregor doing the midfield sitting, with John McGinn allowed licence to get forward to support Che Adams and Lyndon Dykes.

Hampden Park was always going to be a night of raw emotion with the watching world very much in Ukraine's corner. Around 3,500 Ukrainian fans were at Hampden with the SFA playing its part and inviting a number of those affected by the conflict in their homeland. It was cranked up again as the charged-up Ukrainian players took to the Hampden field draped in national flags. Ukraine flags were proudly waved in the away section while it was met with an impressive giant St Andrew's Saltire tifo in the home end. The Ukrainian team knew they had the opportunity to give their nation a welcome lift and hope in an otherwise dark period in its history. The tears had been etched on the face of coach Oleksandr Petrakov in an emotionally charged pre-match press conference.

Ryan Christie said: 'It was just strange. We knew what a good opportunity we had with a play-off semi-final at home. It was just a weird time with the game and everything surrounding it. We also knew that the majority of the world were probably hoping Ukraine made the World Cup after everything that had happened.'

It was Scotland who looked drained as the Ukrainians came out pumped up. If it hadn't been for the early heroics of the ever-reliable Craig Gordon then Scotland could have been a couple behind before they lost the first goal in the 33rd minute. Ruslan Malinovskyi arrowed a long ball over the top to spring the Scottish offside trap and allow Yarmolenko to take a brilliant touch before he deftly lobbed it over Gordon's head. It was a first half where Scotland hadn't been at it and the Tartan Army let them know it as they were booed off at the interval.

Frustrated skipper Andy Robertson acknowledged: 'We didn't

start the game well enough. We didn't settle. They were keeping the ball. We couldn't really get close to them.'

Scotland had shown very little as an attacking force and so Clarke moved to replace Dykes with Christie. Yet within four minutes of the restart it was Ukraine who showed their quality again. Oleksandr Karavaev's cross from the right saw Roman Yaremchuk rise highest, above Hickey and McTominay, to head in, despite Hanley's best efforts to clear on the line.

Scotland rallied and a Callum McGregor block almost brought a goal, then John McGinn missed a great chance with a header and Che Adams saw a shot saved. Clarke sent on Stuart Armstrong for Gilmour and Jack Hendry for Cooper.

Hampden was given hope ten minutes from time when Armstrong swung a long cross into the area. Ukrainian keeper Heorhiy Bushchan came out and only half-cleared it to the edge of the box. McGregor was waiting and fired it back over him, and despite a defender trying to hook it off the line, a goal was given.

Robertson added: 'We threw the kitchen sink at it. We tried everything to get back into the game. We scored a crazy goal really and it gave us a bit of hope, but we didn't really have a chance after that. A couple of long balls, a couple of flick-ons, but not really anything clear-cut, which we needed.'

Scotland kept piling bodies forward and in the fifth minute of stoppage time, Ukraine countered with Artem Dovbyk beating Gordon to crush Scotland's fading World Cup dream. Ukraine celebrated at the final whistle while Scotland and Clarke were left to reflect on a golden opportunity that had passed them by.

'We're disappointed we never really got going in the game until a wee bit of a spell later on,' Hanley said. 'But even then at 2-1 we never really felt like we were building the pressure and really forced them. It's football and that happens and at this level especially – but any level – if you don't really turn up and don't have one of your good nights then you're going to struggle. It felt like that's what happened to us. We never got it right, we weren't quite at it for whatever reason. That's the reason the game went the way it did.'

It had been a highly charged game and Ukraine had channelled it a lot better. Christie conceded: 'Yes, listen, we knew it was going to be an emotional game for them. But credit to them for taking the emotion out of it. Especially at times in the first half you saw how good they were, cutting through us. That's something that we'll be frustrated with because that's something we've prided ourselves on. Our defensive shape is probably one of those things that's got us this far in the last 18 months. It's a tough one to take and everyone felt pretty sore.'

It was a blow that was going to take some time to get over.

Robertson acknowledged: 'We didn't play to the levels that we played at in the last games at Hampden. We didn't play to a level that the full crowd deserved. We didn't really give them anything to shout about. We didn't give them anything to get behind and make it a good atmosphere. We were highly motivated, highly determined. It's highly emotional to get to a World Cup. It's something that this country doesn't do very often. We don't have many play-offs and things like that so we wanted to put in a performance, but we didn't. For their part, you'll need to ask one of their players how emotional they were. With everything going on in their country, they put in a good performance to make their country proud. Sometimes you have to take your hats off to them. I thought they played a really good game and caused us problems in areas where we were weak at that time. Every Scotland fan, everyone watching that game, knew we could play a lot better.'

Clarke not only had to pick up his players but also a country that was left with nothing but a deep depression and a World Cup of broken dreams.

Striker Ross Stewart had been part of the Scotland squad but had been an unstripped sub. Stewart recalled: 'The manager told the players to keep our heads up. The players had done so well to get this far and it is only the start for this group. He wasn't negative at all. We all knew we hadn't performed on the night. He tried to keep our spirits up and to react in the right way by putting things right in the next Euro qualifiers. A lot of the squad were quite young and the manager wanted to stress the positives and what the players could go on and achieve.'

It didn't help as Wales then went on to beat Ukraine in the final to make it to their first World Cup since 1958. That only rubbed salt into the wound of everybody connected with the Scottish national team.

Clarke and his team at the end of every camp go back and review their matches. The national coach did that and his assistant Stevie Naismith reckons his gaffer learned a lot from that campaign and that pain would be to his and to the country's long-term gain.

Naismith claimed: 'When we played Ukraine and we had the optimism of potentially going to a World Cup and that died, we sat and reviewed it. What was good, what was bad and what could we do better? The manager did that and acted upon it.'

There have been ups and downs along the way but for Clarke and his team it has been all about how they react.

'A good team always bounces back,' Lyndon Dykes claimed. 'You are not going to win every game or have the best game. It is how you bounce back and look at the next one, to make sure it doesn't happen again. It is what we have done recently. If things don't go our way we make sure we try and address it in the next game.'

It was to be the end of the road for one international hero. David Marshall decided to call time on his international career after the play-off defeat. He had since returned to play domestically with Hibs and although he had been named in subsequent squads, his last cap had been at Euro 2020 against Croatia. The Serbia play-off hero felt it was time to make way for the next generation. Marshall said: 'It was a two-year process [qualifying for the World Cup] and I felt that was a long time and the time was right when I called time on my Scotland career.'

Chapter 17

RISING ABOVE THE AULD ENEMY

IT was just a month after Scotland had finished their World Cup qualifying campaign with that 2-0 win over Denmark and were looking forward to their play-off semi-final clash with Ukraine (when it was originally scheduled).

The draw was made for the third Nations League. It was a competition that had given us ups and downs. Scotland remained in Pot B and the Nyon draw put them into Group B1 with the Republic of Ireland, Armenia and their World Cup play-off rivals Ukraine. The Nations League offered a potential alternative route to Euro 2024.

Scotland had their fixtures in place but Russia's invasion of Ukraine impacted on that along with their World Cup play-off. Clarke was due to see his side kick off their Nations League campaign at home to Ukraine on 7 June 2022, but that had to be rescheduled to allow the much-delayed World Cup play-off with the same opposition to be played. So that Nations League game was pushed back from June to September 2022 and into an already bursting fixture schedule. It meant that Scotland's players had to open up their Nations League assault on the back of a gruelling domestic season and after the body blow of losing out on a World Cup play-off to Ukraine. Scotland's hurting stars kicked off against Armenia at Hampden and then away to the Republic of Ireland.

Andy Robertson knew they were games that still held import- ance. The captain said: 'We know how important the Nations League can be for us. We proved that in the last Euros when we managed to be successful in it, got the play-off and qualified through it. This camp will always be disappointing regardless of what happens now because of what we've done against Ukraine, but we can try to end it on a small high by trying to get positive results in the next games.'

Scotland had a week to lick their wounds and regroup before they were back out at Hampden against Armenia. Physically, a lot of Clarke's squad were running on empty and emotionally they were probably even more drained. It was hardly the most appeal- ing fixture, especially as the Armenians had shocked the Republic of Ireland with their opening-day win.

The good news was that Armenia weren't so competent on their travels and Scotland went ahead at Hampden in the 28th minute. Stuart Armstrong's perfect diagonal cross from the left picked out Anthony Ralston who headed in his first international goal on his first start.

The proud Celtic defender said: 'My wee girl and my family were here. It was a proud moment that will live with me forever, standing singing the national anthem. It felt amazing to make my first start and to get my first goal. It's a lot to take in but I enjoyed every minute of it.'

Scotland had the points and their pick-me-up was sealed by the 40th minute when Scott McKenna also netted his first Scotland goal as he got his head on a curling back-post corner from John McGinn to power into the net.

McGinn had a chance to add to Scotland's lead in the second period but his powerful strike came back off the bar.

It was also a day Sunderland striker Ross Stewart would never forget. He came off the bench for Ryan Christie in the final few minutes. It capped a remarkable rise for the frontman who started off in the juniors with Ardeer Thistle and Kilwinning Rangers before he moved on to Albion Rovers, St Mirren, Ross County and was playing in League One when he got the call.

Now at Southampton, he recalled: 'I have never got my training kit off so quickly. The manager told me to go on and enjoy it. We were winning the game and it was great to get on at the end. To make my Scotland debut was a huge honour. My family and friends were in the stand at Hampden and it was a moment I will never forget. The manager and staff congratulated me and said they hoped it would be the first of many. Six or seven years ago, when I was in the juniors, playing for Scotland seemed a million light years away. It was all a bit surreal. I couldn't wipe the smile off my face up until the Ireland game.'

The trip to the Emerald Isle three days later put the tin lid on a miserable international window. The Irish looked to be there for the taking after losing in Armenia and then at home to Ukraine. Irish boss Stephen Kenny was under serious pressure and his players had been stung by the criticism that had come their way. That sparked an angry reaction and the Scots bore the brunt of it. Alan Browne gave Ireland a 20th-minute lead and Troy Parrott doubled that before the half-hour. Scotland were on the ropes and Michael Obafemi landed the third and a second-half knockout. It looked a game too far for Clarke and his men after a long, hard season and off the back of losing the World Cup play-off to Ukraine. Clarke himself declared the performance in the Aviva Stadium a head-scratcher and even he struggled to put his finger on what had gone wrong against Ireland.

Stewart had come off the bench for Che Adams with Scotland

already 3-0 down. The frontman admitted: 'It was a poor performance on the day. We went behind and we chased it but it was difficult in front of a big Irish support. You have to give Ireland credit; they were the better team and deserved to win. We went across there with confidence. We had a good few days' training but we just couldn't reach the levels we knew we were capable of. It was a long camp and we had come off the back of a long, hard season with the Ukraine game right at the start of it.'

Things looked like they would go from bad to worse when they went behind away to Armenia to a Vahan Bichakhchyan goal. It took Scotland, without injured captain Andy Robertson, just eight minutes later to level as Che Adams's overhead kick fell to Stuart Armstrong who fired low into the net.

Arman Hovhannisyan was booked for a challenge on Nathan Patterson and then got a second and a red for going head to head with John McGinn. It gave Scotland the advantage and they took the lead just before the interval. Callum McGregor – wearing a mask to protect a fractured cheekbone – found McGinn who flicked it into the path of Armstrong again. The Southampton midfielder stepped inside a defender and arrowed his shot low into the bottom corner to allow Scotland to turn this game around. They were in an even stronger position when Greg Taylor's deep cross was volleyed back in by Nathan Patterson to McGinn, who took a touch, turned and fired in the third. Armstrong played it through for Adams who went on his own and curled in the fourth.

The result gave the Scots a bit of positivity at the end of a long, hard season to regroup and get ready for the final Nations League push in September, where a few old wounds could be addressed in the double-header with Ukraine and the Republic of Ireland's trip across the water.

Andy Robertson acknowledged: 'Everyone looked at the losses

to Ukraine and Ireland last year when we went for a pre-camp last week and it was tough work to be fair to us!'

Ukraine were first up at Hampden on 21 September 2021. It was a chance to exorcise the ghost of the World Cup play-off defeat. It certainly wouldn't cure the nation's broken dreams, but Clarke and his men could show that Ukraine had caught them on an off night.

Clarke wasn't helped by the fact that Andy Robertson, Liam Cooper, Grant Hanley and John Souttar were all out, limiting his defensive options. He sent his Scotland team out on the front foot. They created a number of chances with Che Adams hitting the bar with a header and then being denied by keeper Andriy Lunin. Scotland kept knocking and would eventually open the door. Kieran Tierney forced it into the box and captain for the night John McGinn used his strength to shrug off his marker and fire in a low shot in the 70th minute.

Lyndon Dykes was sent on for the final ten minutes, replacing Adams. It worked a treat as the Queens Park Rangers striker headed a Ryan Fraser corner low into the net.

The Scotland star then grabbed a brace as he got on the end of another Fraser cross to force into the same corner again with the aid of his shoulder. It was a convincing win for Scotland against a Ukrainian team who didn't have a shot on goal.

The Republic of Ireland were up next and it looked like it was going to be the same old movie when John Egan fired in a low shot that gave the visitors the lead.

Jack Hendry, though, had other ideas. He raced out of defence and continued his run as Ryan Christie put in a cross that saw Hendry level with a header. It proved to be lucky for Scotland's No. 13.

Scotland got a bit more luck after some Craig Gordon heroics. They were awarded a penalty when Alan Browne's hand stopped the ball from getting to Scott McTominay. Ryan Christie stepped up and fired it down the middle to give Scotland a 2-1 win and sweet revenge.

All Steve Clarke's men needed was a point when they travelled to take on Ukraine in Krakow to win Group B1. Scotland would have to do it without a number of key men as Scott McKenna, Andy Robertson, Nathan Patterson and Kieran Tierney missed out through injury. That opened the door for Hibs defender Ryan Porteous to make his Scotland debut, with Scott McTominay also suspended.

Ukraine were keen to show they were a different animal than at Hampden earlier in the Nations League and it was a rearguard performance from Scotland for long spells.

Andriy Yarmolenko blazed a good early chance, while Craig Gordon had to be alert to deny Artem Dovbyk and Mykhailo Mudryk. Sandwiched between had been a penalty award when Ryan Fraser's cross was adjudged to have been handled by Taras Stepanenko, but the decision was reversed after a VAR review. Ukraine kept peppering Gordon's goal, but he and the Scotland team stood firm to protect their clean sheet and grab the point that was needed to win the group. Clarke hugged John Carver, Austin MacPhee and Chris Woods on the touchline.

Scotland had won their group and there were added extras for that. They went into Pot 2 for the Euro 2024 qualifying draw, they had a play-off fall-back for the same qualification campaign and they had also won promotion to the top tier – League A. It came at a time when England had been relegated to League B, with Scotland passing them on the way up.

Ryan Christie said: 'Pot A? I know, it is mental. Three years on and I don't really know how the competition worked. I know we have done well, won a few groups and it was also big in getting us a play-off for Euro 2020. We just kept our heads down and kept winning. We know if we do that then all is good. Being in the top section is also some achievement. If anyone would have said we would be in Pot A when the manager first took over then nobody would probably have believed them. It shows the progress that has been made and just how far we have come. If we can stay up there, playing and competing with the big teams, then it will only be better for us. It should help us to improve and get stronger, testing ourselves against the best. We all just want to push on.'

Striker Ross Stewart suffered a serious injury later that season at Sunderland but watched on from afar and reckons Clarke and his team showed their true character to go and pick themselves up after looking down and out in Ireland the previous summer.

Stewart said: 'No one likes to get beat but fair play to the boys, they went on to bounce back and to win the group. The Nations League is big for the Euro qualifiers and got Scotland a play-off and promotion to League A. You always have to learn from these defeats and the players definitely have. It is all credit to them.'

Chapter 18

RAISING THE SALTIRE

WHEN you look at Steve Clarke's squads, you know there is always an experienced core there. His captain, leaders and guys who set the standard on and off the park. Clarke's tried and trusted. Players who have been there and done it and worn the T-shirt. They know what it takes to get results and get over the line on the international front. That simply can't be underestimated in this Scotland team.

This squad has clearly evolved and improved massively under Clarke's guidance. There is strength and depth for every position and more and more of the country's top players are now playing domestically at the highest level, which has added another dimension and important strength to the national team.

If you look at Clarke's most recent international squads, the majority of the players pick themselves. More and more top stars are now making a name for themselves in the English Premier League, with Celtic and Rangers or in one of Europe's top leagues. It all starts at the very top with Scotland captain Andy Robertson. He has Champions League and Premier League winners' medals from his time at Liverpool. Robbo had already been given the captain's armband by Alex McLeish and it has been a simple continuation under Clarke.

Left. Steve Clarke unveiled at Hampden by Scottish Football Association chief executive Ian Maxwell (Kenny Ramsay)

Below. Oliver Burke celebrates his last-minute winner against Cyprus, with Stephen O'Donnell and James Forrest, as he gets Clarke's Scotland managerial career off to a flying start (Kenny Ramsay)

Bottom. Have you heard the one about the Scotsman, the Englishman and the Irishman? Steve Clarke's initial Scotland coaching team of Steve Clarke, Alex Dyer (left) and Steven Reid (right) (Kenny Ramsay)

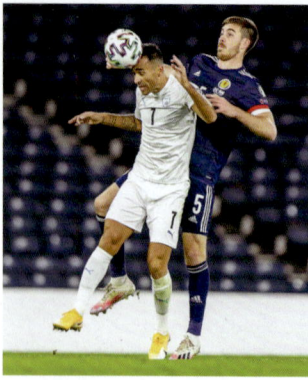

Declan Gallagher takes care of Eran Zahavi in the Euro 2020 play-off semi-final win over Israel (Kenny Ramsay)

Ryan Christie scores the goal that puts Scotland ahead in the Euro 2020 play-off final in Serbia (Novak Djurovic/ PA / Alamy Stock Photo)

David Marshall makes the penalty save from Serbia's Aleksandar Mitrović that sends Scotland to Euro 2020 (Novak Djurovic/ PA / Alamy Stock Photo)

The jubilant Scotland players run towards hero David Marshall after his penalty save (Xinhua / Alamy Stock Photo)

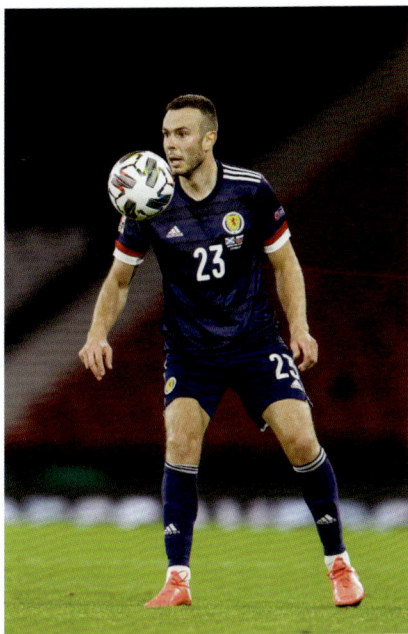

Above left. Andrew Considine makes his Scotland debut at 33 against Slovakia in the Nations League (Kenny Ramsay)

Above right. That feeling of a late winner, as Steve Clarke celebrates Scott McTominay's stoppage-time strike against Israel in the World Cup qualifiers at Hampden (Kenny Ramsay)

Left. Steve Clarke consoles Andy Robertson and John McGinn after the World Cup play-off semi-final defeat to Ukraine (Kenny Ramsay)

Right. Steve Clarke goes to give David Marshall words of support after the Euro 2020 opening game defeat to Czech Republic (Kenny Ramsay)

Below. Steve Clarke looks on as Stephen O'Donnell bravely battles with England's Tyrone Mings in the goal-less Wembley draw at Euro 2020 (Kenny Ramsay)

Bottom. Callum McGregor nets Scotland's only goal at Euro 2020 in the final-day defeat to Croatia at Hampden. (Kenny Ramsay)

Above. The victorious Scotland team that started the famous Euro 2020 qualifying win over Spain at Hampden Park. (*Back row*: Lyndon Dykes, Angus Gunn, Grant Hanley, Ryan Porteous, John McGinn, Scott McTominay; *Front row*: Ryan Christie, Andrew Robertson, Kieran Tierney, Callum McGregor, Aaron Hickey) (Kenny Ramsay)

Left. Goal hero Scott McTominay celebrates his opening goal in Scotland's Euro 2024 qualifying win over Spain (Kenny Ramsay)

Below. Steve Clarke, John Carver and Stevie Naismith considering a tactical switch in the Euro 2024 win over Spain at Hampden (Kenny Ramsay)

Lyndon Dykes scores Scotland's goal to spark their amazing Euro 2024 qualifying win in Norway (Kenny Ramsay)

Lyndon Dykes, Billy Gilmour and Stuart Armstrong celebrate with Kenny McLean after his dramatic, late winner in Norway (Kenny Ramsay)

Right. Ryan Christie in the opening Euro 2024 Hampden win against Cyprus
(Kenny Ramsay)

Below. Callum McGregor scores the opener in the Hampden rain against Georgia
(Kenny Ramsay)

Scotland's John McGinn and Alex Gogić tussle for the ball in Cyprus (Kenny Ramsay)

Scott McTominay's goal celebrations about to be killed by VAR in Spain (Kenny Ramsay)

Super sub Lawrence Shankland scores Scotland's injury time equaliser against Georgia (Kenny Ramsay)

Steve Clarke and his Scotland squad take a well-deserved Hampden lap of honour after the Norway game to celebrate their Euro 2024 qualification (Kenny Ramsay)

It has been some rise for Robertson after being released by Celtic as a youngster and going on to play amateur at Queen's Park. He went on to win a Premiership move to Dundee United and his impressive displays at Tannadice were enough to win him a move to Hull City and from there Jürgen Klopp took him to Anfield in 2017. It is fair to say that one of Scotland's favourite sons has never looked back. Robertson had 67 caps by the end of Scotland's Euro 2024 qualifying campaign. There is no doubt if he hadn't suffered the shoulder injury that forced him to sit out the France friendly and the final games against Georgia and Norway he would be on 70 caps.

John McGinn, or Super John McGinn as he is more commonly known by the Tartan Army, isn't far behind. The all-action midfielder hit the 60-cap mark in the October friendly in France in 2023. He is another who has impressed in the Premier League as the Aston Villa captain. McGinn has been an integral part of the Scottish squad and his goals have been a big factor in Clarke's success. McGinn currently has 18 goals and currently sits sixth in Scotland's all-time scoring charts with Kenny Miller, and just one behind Ally McCoist.

Celtic captain Callum McGregor is well through the 50-cap barrier, Southampton's Stuart Armstrong has 48 and Scott McTominay is just one behind that. Ryan Christie is also in a similar range when it comes to Scotland appearances.

Even when you look behind that there are players coming with real solid international experience. By the end of 2023, Kenny McLean had 36 caps, Lyndon Dykes 35, Scott McKenna 33, Jack Hendry was on 28, Che Adams had 27 and Billy Gilmour 23.

There were times in the past where Scotland caps were tossed around like confetti. That is no longer the case. It is probably as hard to get in the squad as it ever has been in terms of modern-day football.

Declan Gallagher believes the bar has continually been raised under Clarke. The defender said: 'I had no doubt about that, with the players coming through, how young the squad is and a lot more of the players are now down playing in the English Premier League. You can see that there is a togetherness now. When the gaffer first took the job, when I was in the camp, he wanted a togetherness and the same core of players all the time. He also wanted players with a lot more caps under their belts and that is something he is getting now. More of the players are in double figures in terms of caps. They are winning games with that confidence. It breeds confidence through the entire camp and in most matches it looks like they are going to win the game.'

Stephen O'Donnell is another who is still playing in the Scottish Premiership with Motherwell but has slipped out of the international set-up. He knows it is down to the progression of Clarke's squad and the emergence of young talent playing at the top level in England.

O'Donnell admitted: 'There have been a couple of low points and there has been a big turnaround in players, but that needs to happen for progression. There needed to be change and you need to get a better calibre of player in. Thankfully, the likes of Patterson, Hickey and Gilmour coming through have answered that. It gives Steve a different problem. He has so many players in the English Premier League now. The squad is a lot stronger now. I am in no doubt that Steve coming in and managing the way he does have helped the team and players individually as well. I think we have all seen that and would agree.'

Look at Lewis Ferguson. He has been a standout in Serie A with Bologna but has been unable to nail down a regular starting place because of the abundance of riches that Clarke has available to him in his midfield engine room.

Ferguson came through the ranks at Hamilton but really made his name in his four years at Aberdeen, where in his final season at Pittodrie he netted an impressive 16 goals. That saw him win his first cap under Clarke in the 2-0 World Cup qualifying defeat away to Denmark. The young midfielder was linked with a number of clubs in England and Scotland but decided to follow in the footsteps of his Scotland teammate Aaron Hickey and made the switch to Bologna. Hickey had made the move from Hearts to the Stadio Renato Dall'Ara and that helped the versatile full back to break into Steve Clarke's squad and then win his move to the English Premier League with Brentford.

Bologna certainly seems to be a city that brings out the best in Scots and that has continued to be the case for Ferguson. Such has been the impact Ferguson made in his first season in Italy he was linked to the likes of Juventus, rewarded with a new contract and is now the highest scoring Scot in Serie A history.

Ferguson, however, has struggled to make the same impact internationally and that is down to the strength and depth of Clarke's midfield options. The likes of John McGinn, Callum McGregor and Scott McTominay are all pretty much a given and after that you have the likes of Billy Gilmour, Ryan Jack, Stuart Armstrong and Kenny McLean who have all been in the Scotland squad longer and had to show even more patience to get their Scotland opportunities. The majority of the time, the guys coming from the fringes have also taken their chances adding to Clarke's selection headaches.

Ferguson knows it is all about doing the best you can at club level, keeping yourself in the squad and then impressing Clarke and his backroom team in training and looking to grab any playing opportunity you get with both hands.

Ferguson said: 'It is difficult but that is what you want if you are Scotland manager. Having strength in depth all over the squad is only good for the team and it is showing in our results and performances. It was the same when I first broke in – the midfield is so strong. We have the likes of McGinn, McGregor, McTominay and Billy is back playing well. We have so many top players like Ryan Jack and Kenny. We have top quality players in there but all I can do is train as best I can and show I am prepared and ready to play. We have such a good, strong team and we have competition all over the park. For myself, the midfield is strong. I can't sit here and say these boys shouldn't be playing because they should. They have done really well for Scotland over the past few years. They deserve to be in the manager's team. They have been excellent and it is difficult for me not to get as many minutes. But I just need to be patient. Hopefully then my time will come.'

Fringe players like Jacob Brown have had limited action but he insisted there is a real togetherness and everyone wants to do the best they can for Scotland.

Brown said: 'Everyone knows it is a big thing that if you are not starting then you need to come on and play your part, so everyone is ready, whether they are starting or not. Everyone gets on with each other so well too, so everyone wants to do their best for each other whether you are starting, on the bench or if you don't come on; we all want the same thing and are pushing for it. Everyone is pulling in the one direction and that is the main thing; that is why we have done so well in this campaign. You've seen it in previous games; players that have come off the bench have made big impacts and that has got us points, so it's important that everyone is ready. It is like a club atmosphere; that is exactly what it feels like, and I think that has been one of the main keys to the success.'

When Clarke took over there were glaring holes in his Scotland team. He had world-class left backs in Robertson and Kieran

Tierney. The biggest issue was how to get them both into his team and get the best out of them. The same quality wasn't there on the other side. Stephen O'Donnell had been a steady and solid right back for Kilmarnock and Liam Palmer had played the majority of his football at Sheffield Wednesday.

Now Clarke has Nathan Patterson and Aaron Hickey, who are both playing in the English Premier League with Everton and Brentford, respectively.

Another area where Scotland were short of options when Clarke took over was in the striking area. His first squad saw him call up Eamonn Brophy for his first cap. Brophy had done well for him at Kilmarnock and he went with what he knew. If you look at the other options from that first squad there were Oliver Burke, who was on loan at Celtic, and Marc McNulty, who was also on loan at Hibs. None were really natural goalscorers and the forward list also included wingers James Forrest of Celtic, Bournemouth's Ryan Fraser, Lewis Morgan of Sunderland and Sporting Kansas City's Johnny Russell.

Clarke tried a few frontline options and even Lawrence Shankland after his free-scoring stint in firing Dundee United to the Championship title in 2020. It was then left to the likes of Ryan Christie, Stevie Naismith and Oli McBurnie to pick up the baton before Clarke was able to convince the likes of Lyndon Dykes and Che Adams to join the Scottish cause. Jacob Brown has since been added, Millwall striker Kevin Nisbet has forced his way in and Shankland has always been back in there or therca-bouts. Shankland hit 28 goals for Hearts in the 2022–23 season but still had to be patient before the Scotland door reopened.

Southampton's Ross Stewart also found it hard to force his way in. He hit 26 goals for Sunderland in League One but had to be patient with the majority of Clarke's team playing in the min-imum of the English Championship. Since joining Southampton his time has been blighted by injury and that has limited his Scotland call-ups.

It has now become equally difficult for players in the Scottish Premiership, unless you are at Celtic and Rangers challenging in Europe and for the top domestic honours. If you look at Clarke's squads there aren't many players from other Scottish clubs. That is also a two-way street at times with more and more overseas talents taking up slots at a lot of our top clubs and therefore Scottish players aren't always getting the same first-team exposure.

Clarke has turned to the likes of Motherwell defender Declan Gallagher, O'Donnell and Aberdeen's Andrew Considine at times to fill voids, but now it is very much about the longer term and building for the future. That hasn't stopped others from giving up hope.

Gallagher insisted: 'I would love to get back because I would love to get that tenth cap and into double figures. Maybe my age is playing a part because there are a lot of good young centre halves coming through in Jack Hendry, John Souttar and Ryan Porteous. It would be a very tough ask for me in there but I would never say no to my country. I would never retire and if I was ever needed then Steve Clarke knows he could rely on me because I have been there and done it. I would love that tenth cap if he wants to throw me one in a friendly or something like that.'

Stephen O'Donnell has seen a real upward surge in the Scotland squad: 'At the start, the squad maybe wasn't as strong and it was a lot more defensive-minded. I know there are games, like Spain and Norway away, where we needed to be a bit more defensive. Some of the football played in the Euro 2024 qualifiers has been amazing and really good to watch. That is where I see the progression. That is because Steve is a top manager and when you put square pegs in square holes then you start to get better results and outcomes. We now have the more talented players and we are now reaping the rewards.'

Covid also pretty much spelled the end for the Scottish players plying their trade on the other side of the Atlantic. Sporting Kansas City's Johnny Russell had been pretty much a regular for Scotland and Lewis Morgan, who went out to Inter Miami and is now at Red Bull New York, was also in and around the squad before the pandemic hit. There were, of course, major travel issues at that point, with the players having to isolate for some time on their return to their clubs. Clarke felt that was unfair and limited his options to Scotland, England and European-based options.

Russell is now at the veteran stage of his career. Winger Morgan certainly hasn't given up on his Scotland hopes but has found it hard to force his way back into the Scotland fold. Morgan said: 'I was in pretty much all of the squads before Covid and then the boys who got called up came in and did well. I would like to think I can play myself back into the squad. Johnny Russell and I were called up for one of the Israeli games but we were unable to travel. It has been great to see the national team boys do so well over the last few years. It was unfortunate that I haven't been part of it but I just need to keep pushing and hoping I get the call-up. Playing for your country is the biggest honour a player can have.'

The big talking point, though, when it comes to Major League Soccer in recent years has been Ryan Gauld. The playmaker has grabbed major headlines playing for Vancouver Whitecaps but it has never been enough for him to really catch the eye of Clarke. So much so that the former Scotland under-21 cap could potentially make the switch to play for Canada in the future if he is successful in his bid for Canadian citizenship.

Other players in Clarke's squad have had the option to move to the MLS but have turned them down because they have known that making such a move could put their international careers on the line.

In fairness to Clarke, he does have the ability to throw in the occasional curveball or reward a player who has done well or caught the eye domestically, as he did by promoting young Max Johnston from the Scotland under-21s for the friendly in France. Clarke knows more than anybody it will keep players hungry and driven knowing they could be the next one through the door.

Chapter 19

CLARKE'S NEW CONTRACT – BUT McTOMINAY IS THE BIG DEAL

STEVE Clarke told SFA chiefs privately that he was confident Scotland would qualify automatically for the finals of the 2024 European Championships. The Hampden hierarchy might have got the heads-up to book their early flights to Germany, but publicly the manager was far more reserved.

The draw in Frankfurt saw Scotland land in qualifying Group A. They had gone in as second seeds and were alongside Norway, Georgia, Cyprus and favourites Spain.

Clarke, quoted on the SFA's website, said: 'It's going to be competitive. There are five good teams, and hopefully, we can be the best. Cyprus was my first game as head coach, so I've got good memories of that one. The games aren't won yet. You have to go there and you have to be competitive. We think that we're confident enough to try and continue that through to the groups. We work day to day, week to week. We try to improve all the time; we feel as though we're improving, and we want to continue that improvement. To continue that improvement we need to qualify for Euro 2024: that's the aim.'

There had been the disappointment of losing the World Cup semi-final play-off to Ukraine that had been offset slightly by the success in the Nations League.

The SFA's decision makers were convinced they were on the right track, under the right manager in Steve Clarke.

They announced just days before the Euro 2024 qualifiers were to kick off that Clarke had signed a new deal that would keep him in the Scotland job until, at least, 2026.

Scottish FA chief executive Ian Maxwell, quoted on the SFA website, said: 'This has been one of the easiest decisions and conversations during my time as chief executive. Steve has united the nation behind a successful men's national team and as we look forward to a new UEFA Euro 2024 campaign, it was important we demonstrated our commitment to Steve and his backroom team, and acknowledged the continuity that has been key to our improvement in the past four years.'

Clarke was not only getting a vote of confidence for this campaign but also the 2026 World Cup as well, which is due to be held in Canada, Mexico and the USA.

Clarke, in the same SFA statement, said: 'I am proud that my coaching team and I will continue to lead the team through the next two qualifying campaigns, as well as Nations League Group A, but being able to do so is a testament to the squad of players who have been central to our improvement. The immediate focus is ensuring a positive start to our Euro campaign against Cyprus, who were the opposition for my first match in charge in 2019.

'When we named our squad for the double-header, I spoke with my coaches about how the quality and depth of the squad has evolved in those four years. We now have an experienced core who have been constants throughout, but we have also added quality and competition in every area of the team.

'We also played that game in front of around 30,000 fans and will walk out on Saturday, and Tuesday against Spain, to a full house at Hampden Park. It's imperative that we keep the fans and the nations engaged and entertained and that is something we are all committed to achieving through winning games and qualifying for more major tournaments, starting with Germany next year.'

Clarke and his national team were looking to get off to a fast start with two Hampden games to open the campaign, kicking off with Cyprus at home and then the mighty Spanish. If Scotland had genuine ambitions of finishing in the top two, then the head-to-heads against Spain and Norway were going to be vital, but the games against Cyprus and Georgia were must-wins, especially at Hampden. Home games are always key and the fact that Scotland had three of their first four games in Glasgow meant they needed to pile points on the board.

There was a real desire within the squad to claim a top two spot and an automatic qualifying slot from Euro qualifying Group A. They had seen the risk and rewards of the play-offs in recent qualifying campaigns. The Nations League had brought entry to Euro 2020 but a play-off defeat against Ukraine had cost them their shot at the 2022 World Cup. That pain was still burning deep within the Scotland squad.

Billy Gilmour said: 'We have built on the Euros and we were gutted to miss out on the World Cup – we know we let ourselves down. We want to prove we can make another finals and that's the aim. The summer was tough as we let everyone down against Ukraine. We should have been at the World Cup. We were good enough to be there but we never turned up in that game. Now we want to prove a point and show we should be at the Euros. We know we are a good enough team to be there with the players and staff we have. Hopefully we can do it.'

Ryan Christie highlighted the Scotland team were going into this campaign looking to control the controllable and to get the job done under their own steam. They had another play-off slot via the Nations League but that was not a trick they were looking to repeat.

The Bournemouth attacker explained: 'We had the World Cup play-off with Ukraine and everything that went with that, so we all went into the Euro 2024 qualifying campaign determined to make sure we got over the line. We knew if we finished in the top two we would qualify and that was a big motivation. We didn't need to rely on a Nations League play-off or anything else. So that was the goal.'

It was a new start for Scotland and there was a new look as the national team took to the field wearing their 150th anniversary kit. It might have been around £90 for an adult shirt, but such was its success that the first batch sold out within 48 hours.

It meant the Scotland team certainly looked the part when they stepped out on the Hampden turf. However, Scotland had one glaring issue which was the goalkeeping department. Craig Gordon's leg break while playing for Hearts left Clarke desperately short of experience between the sticks. The old guard, one by one, had decided to call it a day. Gordon was the last survivor and his injury left a major void.

Clarke and his goalkeeping coach Chris Woods had to come up with a solution. They turned to the son of a former Scotland keeper in Bryan Gunn. Scotland had tried on several occasions to get Angus Gunn to follow in his dad's footsteps when he had been coming through the ranks at Manchester City and had made his big-money move to Southampton.

Gunn, however, was Norwich-born and had spent most of his life south of the border, where his father had made himself a Carrow Road legend. Gunn had also been capped from England's under-16s to under-21 level and probably felt the door could have opened to the full England squad. It also looked like it could have been the case as Gareth Southgate called him up to train with his England team ahead of the 2018 World Cup. The move had been made after Alex McLeish had tried to get Gunn to make the switch from the Auld Enemy.

Then Gunn found himself in a bit of an international limbo and that allowed Clarke to grab the initiative and succeed where McLeish and others had failed. He met with the player and assured him the door was open for him. If he came to Scotland, he would get the opportunity and after that it was up to him. There were no guarantees, unless you perform, which is the norm in Clarke's Scotland squad.

It was enough to convince Gunn to pledge his allegiance to Scotland and to give Clarke another solid goalkeeping option going into the Euro 2024 qualifiers. Clarke had seen his side put together an unbeaten run bar a friendly 2-1 defeat to Turkey in the November.

The Scotland boss had made it clear that Gunn wasn't a certainty to start the first game at home to Cyprus – but he was handed his cherished debut.

Defender Jack Hendry missed out through injury and that opened the door for Blackburn defender Dominic Hyam to win his first cap, while Celtic's Anthony Ralston also received a late call-up before the game.

Ryan Porteous had impressed in the previous games and was given the ideal 24th birthday present as he kept his place in the Scotland defence, alongside Grant Hanley and Kieran Tierney, with Aaron Hickey and captain Andy Robertson either side of them.

Celtic captain Callum McGregor and Ryan Jack of Rangers provided the midfield base with Stuart Armstrong and John McGinn providing the legs and attacking runs to get up and support Che Adams.

Clarke clearly believed runs from deep could cause more

damage than going for two up front against a team who he knew would try to sit and stifle the space in behind.

It was a big afternoon for McGregor as he was winning his 50th cap. It had been quite the journey for the classy midfielder since he had made his debut for Scotland in a friendly against the Netherlands at Pittodrie back in 2017 under Malky Mackay.

Scotland came out and knocked the ball about well. They were in control although Gunn caused a second or two of alarm around the Hampden stands as he slipped. He got lucky as he fell back into his 18-yard box and was able to gather.

After that moment of slight panic, it was more about what was happening in and around the Cyprus box. Jack found Hickey who turned into an old-fashioned winger as he jinked into the Cyprus box, beating a number of defenders before he forced Demetris Demetriou into a near-post stop.

Scotland were building things up nicely and took the lead in the 21st minute. Tierney gave it to Armstrong and he played a ball through for Robertson. The captain swung in a cross that came off Cyprus defender Alex Gogic and the ball fell perfectly into the path of John McGinn who had one of the easiest volleys at the back stick to put Scotland in front.

The unfortunate Gogic said: 'I went to block it and it hit my shin and spun up to the back post for John McGinn. I was unlucky but from a Scotland point of view you make your own luck and they did. There is no doubt getting that goal helped Scotland and settled them into the game. Getting the goal meant we couldn't frustrate Scotland and you could see it gave Hampden a real lift. When I first went to Scotland, Hampden wasn't always full. Since Steve Clarke has got the job there is a real buzz and excitement about the national team again. It helped they had qualified for Euro 2020 and now they are hoping and expecting to qualify. As soon as you start doing well, for club or country, then more supporters come out and follow you. That is the way it is. Hampden certainly can be an intimidating atmosphere when it is sold out and the Scotland fans get right behind the team.'

There was a VAR check before McGinn was officially credited with his 16th international goal and the Tartan Army could really celebrate.

Midfielder Stuart Armstrong said: 'I really enjoy playing in that little triangle, with Callum McGregor on that side as well. Robbo's a joy to play with. He's so energetic that he creates a lot of different things with his movement. KT is so dynamic as well that things just open up naturally. It's a joy to play with them, to make those little passes and get crosses in. It's three players I'm very comfortable with. I know how they play. This feels like we have a very good connection. Hopefully it looks like that too and we can create some nice things. I very much enjoy playing in the advanced role, off Che [Adams] as well.'

Adams was subject to a few hefty challenges and had to be replaced just before the hour by Lyndon Dykes, who was making his first appearance since being floored by pneumonia just two months before. It was an admirable achievement to be back playing football so quickly, never mind wearing a Scotland shirt again. Dykes said: 'It has been a crazy year. I was lucky to get back playing as quickly as I did. I love playing with Scotland, getting away with all the boys and giving my all. Playing for my country and on the big stage means everything to me and I always want to do as well as I can. I just want to keep the team getting results and to keep my place in the team.'

Scotland remained in control but Clarke knew there was always the element of risk with just a one-goal advantage.

McGregor acknowledged: 'I thought the first half-hour was really good. We pressed high, kept it well and created a good few opportunities. The last part of the first half was okay and I thought we reset quite well. As the game grew, they had a little bit more of the ball and naturally, at 1-0 up, we wanted to protect that. The game continued that way until we got the second goal, then it opened up a bit and they had to chase.'

The Scotland boss then sent on Scott McTominay and Ryan Christie for Stuart Armstrong and Ryan Jack in the 67th minute. It was to be a big moment in terms of the campaign. Nathan Patterson also came on for Hickey for the final ten minutes of normal time.

The Tartan Army's nerves were eased as one of Clarke's substitutes came to the fore, grabbing more goals.

Sub Christie won the ball and crossed for fellow replacement Dykes to head down and McTominay came on to it, controlled it with his knee and smashed the ball high into the net in the 87th minute. It was a superb finish and only his second international goal. Eight minutes later and five minutes into stoppage time, the Manchester United midfielder had two goals in the one game.

Scotland tried to take a quick free kick but Christie's cross was half-cleared. It fell to Robertson and he squared for McTominay and with his right foot he passed it into the left-hand corner.

There was one final insult for Cyprus as Nicholas Ioannou kicked the ball away and was sent off for a second yellow card. McGregor was full of praise for goal hero McTominay.

The Celtic captain explained: 'The structure of the team probably allows one of the midfielders to go, the other one to sit and be secure with the three. Scotty has great athleticism, he can get forward, he can join in, and he has shown the quality as well to go and finish. He's a brilliant weapon to have for any team, and especially for us to try to utilise that as we can. You have to be able to score goals in your team to be successful at this level, and if you can spread them around then you're not relying on the strikers or wingers. You need goals in your team to win matches and to qualify for tournaments, so it's brilliant for Scotty and what a night for him individually.'

It was the perfect Scotland debut for Gunn as he kept a clean sheet. Armstrong was not surprised to see the Norwich keeper sail through it as he had played alongside him at Southampton.

He said: 'I know his qualities. He's fitted into the squad really well and he knows some of the boys from his time at Norwich too. It was a quiet game as far as debuts go and he'll be quite happy with how it went. He's got a clean sheet and I'm sure he had a good time.'

It was pretty much the theme for the Scotland team. It was job done, three points, three goals and a clean sheet, knowing that far tougher challenges were just days away.

Stuart Armstrong added: 'What we wanted from the first game was a good performance, but what we needed was a win. We got that so we're all very happy. A 1-0 would have been good for the group – 3-0 is convincing so we're very happy with the start.'

Chapter 20

A STATEMENT OF INTENT

THE mere mention of Spain used to automatically spark memories of that history-making Kenny Dalglish goal from 14 November 1984. Those who are old enough, who could forget?

A throw-in from Steve Nicol was laid back by Davie Cooper into the path of Dalglish, who had come in off the right to take a touch, then a second and from about 18 yards arrowed a left-foot shot high into the top right-hand corner of a helpless looking Luis Arconada's net. The rest, as they say, is history as Dalglish wheeled away in delight with his trademark two arms in the air before he punched the jubilant Hampden sky.

Dalglish had put the icing on the cake for Jock Stein's side as they claimed a famous scalp on their way to qualifying for the 1986 World Cup finals. The goal was massive in terms of Scottish football landmarks as it saw Dalglish draw level with Denis Law at the top of the Scotland men's international scoring charts with 30 goals.

Maurice Johnston had netted twice for Scotland in that 3-1 win but those have paled into insignificance now because everybody talks about the Dalglish goal.

For the older generations of the Tartan Army it was like a JFK moment. If they weren't at Hampden they will be able to tell you where they watched it.

For the new guard of Scotland supporters, they are more likely to have seen reruns of King Kenny's golden goal via uploads on X or TikTok.

Steve Clarke was still in the early stages of his own playing career, making his mark with St Mirren and Scotland's under-21s when Dalglish produced his crowning Scotland moment. Clarke made his international bow the year after Dalglish had called time on his Scotland career to focus on his player-manager role at Liverpool.

The youngster made his Scotland debut a year later, in 1987, although they had come across each other in England, and on the coaching side they would eventually work together in Dalglish's second managerial stint at Liverpool.

Clarke took his team into the second game in Group A looking to famously sink the Spanish Armada again.

Scotland's record since 1984 had been more about the pain against Spain. The Spaniards took their revenge on Jock Stein's side on home soil thanks to a goal from Francisco Javier Clos and in the five games since, Scotland had claimed a couple of friendly draws but had lost all their qualifiers, including home and away in the European Championship 2012 qualifiers, 3-2 at Hampden and 3-1 in Alicante.

It maybe wasn't a surprise because Spain were 2010 World Cup winners and were about to go and make it a dream double by going all the way to Euro 2012 glory. It was the golden generation of Xavi, Andrés Iniesta and Sergio Busquets.

Spain had failed to hit those dizzy heights again but remained a world power. They, however, had flattered to deceive at the 2022 World Cup and a shock exit at the hands of Morocco in the last 16 on penalties had effectively cost Luis Enrique his job.

Luis de la Fuente was the man charged with taking them through the Euro 2024 qualifying campaign. He had inherited a talent-packed squad and that was shown in their Group A opener as they swept past Norway 3-0 at home thanks to a goal from Dani Olmo and a double from Joselu. The Norwegians along with Scotland were to be the biggest threats in the group, but the general acceptance was that they were both playing for second place, behind Spain. Scotland might have equalled Spain's opening-day win against Cyprus but everyone knew the second game was going to be a massive step up.

Yet, under Clarke, the one thing they had brought back to the nation was hope. All right, there wouldn't have been many crazy predictions about Scotland winning, but there was certainly a belief that Clarke and his men could make things difficult for Spain. The one place where there was total belief was within Clarke's squad. Yes, Scotland were clear underdogs, but underdogs can bite. That was the crystal-clear message from the players.

A fired-up Lyndon Dykes said: 'Before the game against Spain I said: "I believe in this team and I believe we can do really well." I believe we can turn teams over, especially when we are underdogs and teams don't expect us to do things.'

Clarke's preparations weren't helped as Southampton striker Che Adams suffered an injury in the Cyprus win and he and Celtic's Anthony Ralston had to pull out. Clarke turned to an old familiar face in in-form Hearts striker Lawrence Shankland, who many felt was unfortunate not to be in there in the first instance. He had broken the 20-goal barrier domestically.

Shankland's last Scotland appearance had been in the 1-0 defeat to Slovakia back in 2020. His career had stalled after he had left Dundee United for Belgian side Beerschot, but his move back to Edinburgh that summer had seen him reignite his career under his former Tannadice boss Robbie Neilson. He had helped get him back to his free-scoring best. Shankland had been on holiday when he took the call to join up with Clarke's squad. He didn't need to be asked twice.

Shankland recalled: 'It was on Saturday night when I took the call. I was in Spain on holiday. I got the call about 9 p.m. and I had to fly back at 7.50 a.m. the next morning. I had to get back for training at midday on Sunday. In fairness, it is Scotland and I would do anything to play for my country.'

It was very much a change from our darkest days when we were struggling to qualify and players would make the slightest excuse to drop out of squads, much to the anguish, frustration and disgust of former managers. That wasn't something that could be thrown at the players under Clarke. Such is the competition that players, refreshingly, were chapping at the door looking to force their way into Clarke's thoughts.

Yet it wasn't Clarke's team selection but that of Spanish coach Luis de la Fuente that raised the pre-match eyebrows. He decided to make wholesale changes to the team who had beaten the Norwegians. Only three players remained in his starting XI: keeper Kepa Arrizabalaga, Rodri and Mikel Merino. Maybe it was a show of faith in the abundance of riches he had at his disposal within his squad. Some of the locals saw it as a lack of respect, albeit knowing the selected Spanish side still had the quality to come out on top.

Whatever was said in the inner sanctum of Clarke's home dressing room will forever remain there, but there would have been no doubt that the manager and his Scotland players would have been lifted by the sight of the Spanish team lines. Not that they would have said anything or even given the opposition the slightest bit of ammunition. That was not part of Clarke's make-up. Some joke it is more of a mask as very rarely does the Scotland boss look too up or down. Clarke was too long in the tooth and had worked at the highest level to give opponents even an inch. He was more interested in injecting a self-belief amongst his own players.

Clarke knew it was going to be as much a mental challenge as well as a physical one facing up to Spain. Discipline was going to be key.

The Scotland manager was more interested in his side making their own headlines after the game. Trying to follow in the footsteps of 'King Kenny' and Co. To secure their own piece of Scottish football history at Spain's expense again.

Scotland midfielder Scott McTominay, speaking to broadcaster Viaplay Sports, said: 'That was what the manager said in his talk before we went on to the bus and then into the stadium. He told us it was our own chance to create our own legacy as Scotland players.'

The weekend clash with Cyprus might have been flat, but there was no danger that was going to be the case for this game. Tickets were like gold dust and the sell-out signs were up. It had become a recurring theme as things exploded under Clarke's reign. I would wager that some of the Tartan Army might not even have been in their seats when Ryan Christie put a ball up the line for Andy Robertson to put Pedro Porro under pressure. The Tottenham defender slipped, the Scotland captain stepped in and pulled it back for Scott McTominay to fire a low shot through the grasp of the unconvincing Kepa Arrizabalaga in just the seventh minute. It was right on cue as Clarke had made it clear that his team had to go for the jugular.

McTominay added: 'We did really, really well. We knew they would have a lot of the ball. The manager told us to be clinical with our opportunities. I thought we had more than a few opportunities to really hurt them and score some goals.'

It wasn't the expected backs-to-the-wall approach from Clarke and his men after that. They continued to create chances and a darting Ryan Christie break saw him poke a shot just wide.

The Spanish team, with their quality, were always going to pose a threat and it was the Espanyol striker Joselu who had the majority of the Hampden crowd breathing a huge sigh of relief when his header came back off Angus Gunn's bar. Spain followed that up when Rodri flashed a header wide from a corner and Porro's long-range shot forced Gunn to tip over. It was a time when Clarke needed his own big players and personalities to stand up and be counted – as they so often do! His leadership group was to come to the fore.

Celtic midfielder Callum McGregor explained: 'If you want to be successful then you need four, five or six leaders in your team. It's good we've got that mix. We've got big Granty [Hanley], Kieran [Tierney] is a leader, you've got guys right through who are big leaders and big personalities as well. You need five or six of those in your team to drag you over the line in the moments where you have to defend. There was probably a five- or six-minute spell just before the end of the first half where we were under the cosh a little bit. That's the moment when you need the big players with the personalities to stand up and ride you through it. I thought we did that excellently.'

Yet, Scotland could have gone in 2-0 up at the interval. A long Robertson clearance sent Lyndon Dykes clear but he fired just over in stoppage time as he was chased down.

Dykes said: 'We started really well, didn't concede and it was a real team performance. We were the underdogs against Spain and that worked in our favour because in that position you can always shock people. We are a lot stronger than people think. That is what we are trying to change and to build. We know if we are at our best we can do amazing things.'

It gave Clarke the chance to get his players in at the interval, to get them calmed down, regrouped and ready to go again. The job was only half-done and there was a lot more work ahead with Spain making a double substitution. I'm not sure even Clarke would have believed how things were turning out when Scotland netted a second just six minutes into the second period and McTominay was again the main man.

Kieran Tierney charged down the left and past Real Madrid defender Dani Carvajal like he wasn't there. He burst into the box and fired in a low cross that was half-cleared by David Garcia but it fell perfectly to the incoming Manchester United star who came in and drilled a low left-foot shot through the legs of the Spanish defender and past the despairing dive of Arrizabalaga.

McTominay jumped in the air to celebrate then ran up the touchline and made straight for his manager on the half-way line, where he gave Clarke a quick shake of the hand and a celebratory hug. It was four goals in two games for the midfielder, who had struggled to get in Erik ten Hag's Manchester United team and wasn't exactly renowned for his scoring streaks.

Bournemouth star Ryan Christie said: 'Scott came off the bench on Saturday to score two great goals and he did it again against Spain. We were probably looking at him and Callum McGregor to be more of a defensive block in front of the back five, but it just shows the standard and threat we have.'

Clarke had to combat more Spanish changes but the Scots were in control and able to see the game out quite comfortably.

The Scotland manager was also able to bring on fresh legs, making five substitutions over three spells to see out the game and the seven minutes of stoppage time with considerable ease. Scotland actually had the better chances, notably when John McGinn smashed the bar with a free kick.

Shankland was one of those replacements as he made his

long-awaited return in the final minute of normal time as Dykes got a well-deserved applause from the delighted Tartan Army.

The Hearts striker had a chance to net but it came off a defender. Shankland said: 'My cousin sent me [a clip of] my chance after the game. I've watched it back about ten times hoping that it would eventually go in – but it never did. Callum McGregor did brilliantly on the counter-attack and put a ball through. I got my shot away but it took a deflection. On any other night it might have sneaked under the keeper but he made a save and it wasn't to be.'

The final whistle brought wild Hampden celebrations as the supporters marked a big win and a statement of intent from Clarke and his players. They had the nation believing again.

'We went into the game confident and it was an amazing feeling when the final whistle went,' Dykes recalled. 'You could see the joy it brought to everyone and the crowd especially. There have been a lot of these big nights at Hampden. The big thing was to change the feeling of the fans, to get them supporting us and right behind the team at Hampden. We have been doing that recently and the atmosphere has been great. The fans played their part against Spain because from the very first whistle they were fantastic. The atmosphere just keeps getting better and better at Hampden.'

It was a special night and was right up there with the sinking of Spain that famous night back in 1984.

Shankland had been in the crowd when Scotland had beaten France back in 2006, thanks to Gary Caldwell's goal. Now he was delighted to play a small part in another landmark Scotland victory.

The frontman said: 'To be on the pitch and to see the supporters from the other side was absolutely brilliant. Spain were going through a bit of a transitional period but they still have top-quality players. I know people still talk about Scotland's victory over Spain back in 1984. It is nice for the lads now to make history this time around. I have been there as a supporter in the past. I was there when we beat France with my mum and all my cousins. My dad was away working at the time and my mum had to queue up twice for all our tickets. They are the sort of games you remember all your life and the Spain game will be another one the fans will remember.'

It might not have involved King Kenny this time, but Clarke and his squad had their own crowning moment against Spain.

The Scotland boss, speaking to the written press, said: 'What I said to the lads before the game was that the media wanted to speak about the game against Spain in 1984 before this game. So that tells you that in 39 years' time, when you are all the same age as me and have kids and grandkids, that people could still speak about you.'

Goal hero McTominay had ensured he was to be the latest modern-day hero. McTominay, speaking to Viaplay Sports, said: 'Look at Hampden – I have never seen anything like it. It is incredible. These are the nights in 20 or 30 years that people will remember. They'll watch back the games and say they were there or had children who were. It is what the game is about.'

The enormity of the achievement was also added to by the fact that just four months later that same Spain squad lifted the Nations League.

Clarke was quite happy to let the nation dream and get swept away on the crest of a Euro 2024 wave, but he personally was never going to get carried away. He was as grounded as ever. The same message was conveyed from his Scotland dressing room.

'It was important not to get too ahead of ourselves,' attacker Ryan Christie stressed. 'The gaffer touched on that. It is an amazing night and a massive win against a big team, but we are only two games into it. We need to go away to Spain, Georgia and Norway; these are tough places to get results. If we do that we can do well. That is the main ambition. It would be nice to do it through proper qualification rather than the play-offs this time. We couldn't have asked for a better start to this group.'

For Clarke's Scotland, this was a big win in terms of qualification, but also in terms of everything else that came with it. Yes, his side had won big games, like the play-off in Serbia, and beaten Denmark in the World Cup qualifying, albeit the latter had already qualified. Spain, however, was a genuine bona fide big scalp, when the heat had been turned up and the manager and his team had shown they were up for the challenge and delivered. There is no doubt the win added to the growing confidence and belief within his squad.

Dykes said: 'To get that result when it really mattered and when we needed it, it just shows the character and squad we have built up since I have been in it. That is what makes us so strong. When teams come up against us they get a bit surprised because of the determination we show to try and bring success. That comes from the feeling of being at the Euros in 2020 and being involved in that. We want to keep doing that and being successful. When it comes down to the games we know we need to perform and we did that. Credit to all the boys involved because we worked hard across the camp to get both these results.'

Ryan Christie praised the Scotland support and reckoned they were the 12th man that famous evening.

Christie stated: 'It was amazing, what a night. The feeling you get now going into big games at Hampden is something else. The crowd played a big part. The games are sold out and there is a real togetherness and connection with the team. It is special when we play at Hampden. We just go into these games feeling we can take anyone on at home, in front of our own fans. It felt that way going into the Spain game. Norway had played Georgia before us and we had seen that they had drawn and dropped points. We knew that if we could take something from Spain it would put us in a right good place. It ended up being the perfect night.'

Scotland have had some big performances under Clarke – but Dykes reckons that probably topped the lot. He proudly claimed: 'The Serbia night is one that will stay with me because it was a massive game, winning that game and the achievement of getting to the finals. The Spain result and performance is up there. Just look at their ranking because they are one of the top ten teams and the calibre of players they have, so it was a massive win. There are a lot of big games that come to mind. The one at home to Israel and drawing with England at the Euros – but Spain is definitely one that sticks out.'

Chapter 21

RODRI'S RUBBISH

THE Spanish national team's nickname is La Furia Roja. Roughly translated as The Red Fury. It is fair to say there was a fair bit of that in the away dressing room at Hampden after Spain had slumped to their 2-0 shock defeat. There could have been very little argument that Steve Clarke had done a job on Luis de la Fuente's men. Scotland deserved their win. It was hardly a hit and run. The Scotland team had been disciplined, stuck to the tactics, taken their chances and got the job done.

There were the usual post-match interviews from both sides and it was there where Spanish captain Rodri let his frustrations get the better of him. The midfielder had won just about every major tournament with Manchester City and clearly wasn't used to losing. Rather than biting his lip and dishing out the usual hollow platitudes, he went on the offensive. He had clearly overlooked his own team's shortcomings and decided to dig out Clarke and his team for their pragmatic approach.

Rodri, speaking to Viaplay Sports, controversially claimed: 'Always when you lose you are disappointed. I think we did many good things to win and in the end we weren't sufficient to score and we conceded easy goals. This is football and if you concede easy goals then you are penalised at the end. It is the way they play and you have to respect that, but in the end, for me, it is a bit rubbish because they were always wasting time and they provoke you and they always fall. For me, this is not football. The referee has to take control but he said nothing. It is what it is; they have the weapons and we will have to use our weapons and try for the next time.'

Rodri's undignified response was about to spark major headlines and something of a backlash from Scotland. The bottom line is that on the pitch Spain had been second best.

Scotland don't have the wealth of riches that Spain have available to them. Clarke has a good, honest, reliable and professional group of players who give their all when they pull on a dark-blue jersey. They are never going to be able to go toe to toe and play the Spaniards at their own game.

Callum McGregor said: 'We obviously needed to do it in a slightly different way and when teams come here, we want to make it difficult for them. We upset the rhythm of their game and they probably got sucked into it a little bit as well, trying to argue with the referee and things like that. They probably didn't play the game as slick as they like to play it.'

It wasn't as if Spanish sides, domestically and internationally, haven't used the other side of the game to frustrate and upset Scottish opposition in the past. This time the tables had been turned.

Scotland had got the first goal, through Scott McTominay, and that gave them something to hold on to and protect. They tried to let the clock run down whenever they could and were economical in their play. Yes, they took soft free kicks and didn't break their back to get the ball back into play quickly, but how many winning teams do?

Scotland were hardly employing the dark arts of a prime José Mourinho. Clarke may have worked and learned with him, but his team certainly didn't go to those full extents.

McTominay insisted that Scotland didn't do anything worse than what their Spanish counterparts had tried to do to gain the edge.

The Scotland midfielder, speaking to Viaplay Sports, claimed: 'I feel everyone on the pitch was at it, diving around, making the game slow. It wasn't really a clean game. Everyone was making the most of everything. It is difficult but sometimes that is the way it has got to be. When you are winning and you want to keep a hold of a lead then you have to do things like that.'

Captain Robertson reckons Scotland won the mental and physical battle and the Spanish were far from perfect.

Robertson, talking to Viaplay Sports, said: 'I think they were going down a little too easily. We were always going to be physical and to try and get in their faces, to win our headers and challenges. I think we did that and I don't think we crossed the line. They were, especially in the first half, rolling about a wee bit much, but they used their experience and got a couple of us booked, which is fair enough to them. I think we won that battle and got under their skin a wee bit.'

Rodri's comments certainly did irk the Scotland dressing room. Defender Liam Cooper, one of the elder members of Clarke's squad, said: 'We're not a horrible team. That was a good, solid performance from us, one where we created a fair amount of chances and in the end we thoroughly deserved the win. It's sometimes unfair to ask someone from the losing team how they feel straight after a game and, who knows, maybe now that he's won the treble and scored the winner in the Champions League he might say something different! But emotions at the time were high and there's no doubt a lot of the lads – including myself – took it the wrong way. Beating Spain gave us proof that you can compete, that you can beat the best nations in the world. What it gives you most of all is confidence – because a hungry, motivated and confident team is a dangerous team and we need to use all those qualities here.'

The Scotland win created headlines across Europe. Lewis Ferguson had come on to help Scotland see out the win. When he got back to Italy a lot of his Bologna teammates were asking him about Rodri's comments. Ferguson said: 'When I went back in, some of the boys had seen the result and had asked me how the game had gone. Rodri made his comments and my team-mates were basically laughing at what he had said. I told them we played well but, of course, we time-wasted. Who wouldn't when you are 2-0 up against Spain? It is normal. It's not as if we sat in and robbed them because we played really well and that adds to it. The performance was brilliant.'

As they say, sometimes actions speak louder than words. Rodri and his team found that out the hard way. The City player was to retract his comments further down the line, blaming his poor English. At that point, it was all about Escocia for Rodri.

Chapter 22

SCOTLAND'S HAVING A PARTY AND HAALAND'S IN HIS BED!

SCOTLAND may have been on maximum points, but all talk going into the third qualifying fixture was about a certain footballing superstar in Erling Haaland. In Norway, it was all about Haaland's homecoming. The superstar was heading back after helping all-conquering Manchester City to their first Champions League title. Haaland had helped City win the ultimate prize with their 1-0 win over Inter Milan. Some seven days later he was asked to shoulder the burden of Norway's Euro 2024 dreams.

Haaland hadn't played for Norway for nine months because of injury and was being asked to try and spark his country's Euro qualifying hopes, although he was given extra time off to enjoy Manchester City's celebrations. Norwegian coach Stale Solbakken was more than happy to accommodate, knowing there was a fair chance he would bring his goal-den touch to the party. Steve Clarke and Scotland were hoping he had been living it up Jack Grealish-style, who looked to have taken things to the extreme before he left Manchester City's celebrations for the England camp.

Haaland being the centre of attention is nothing new and it was the same from Clarke. As soon as the dust had settled on the Spanish win, the majority of the questions he and his players faced were about how he was going to halt Haaland. The big Norwegian had fond memories from his first taste of Scottish football. He was a fresh-faced youngster at Molde as he scored a double in a 3-0 aggregate win over Hibs in the Europa League back in 2018. It was something of a glimpse into the future.

Now after his moves to Borussia Dortmund and City he was very much a modern-day footballing icon. So much so that the *Daily Mail* had sent a reporter out to Oslo just to cover Haaland and his build-up to the Scotland game. The pre-match Norwegian press conference was held in a mix of Norwegian and English. The majority of the talk was about Haaland. There was more of a Scottish feel when Norwegian attacker Mohamed Elyounoussi took to the stage. The former Celtic loanee did speak about Haaland but was also asked about some of the key players in Clarke's squad whom he had played alongside, the likes of Callum McGregor and Greg Taylor.

Scotland's press conference was held in the Ullevaal Stadium later that same evening. Before they had arrived, the news broke that former Scotland star Gordon McQueen had lost his brave battle against dementia. The early pre-match Norwegian press conference had only just finished when Scottish football was plunged into mourning.

The dominating centre half was, quite rightly, handed his place in Scottish football's Hall of Fame in 2012. The former St Mirren, Leeds and Manchester United star was a larger-than-life character and an icon of Scottish football.

Cruel and some rather ill-timed injuries meant McQueen's international career had been limited to 30 caps and five goals. Maybe it was fate. His last goal for Scotland came against Norway in the same stadium, albeit it had been heavily modernised and brought into the 21st century since Jock Stein's side registered their famous 1979 European Championship qualifying win. Joe Jordan, Kenny Dalglish and John Robertson all netted before McQueen put the gloss on that 4-0 win.

Steve Clarke's team would gladly have accepted something similar. The team had prepared with a training camp in Spain before they returned home for their final preparations. Che Adams and Grant Hanley both missed out through injury. Steve Clarke's side might have been high-flying in this group but not on this particular outbound journey. It was delayed and pushed the late evening press conference back, forcing the manager and defender Liam Cooper to make a mad dash in a car from the airport. Clarke paid his respects to McQueen and gave his pre-match thoughts on the Norwegians.

It was another Leeds United and Scotland centre half, in Cooper, who paid his own emotional tribute to McQueen. Cooper said: 'It was sad news and a really sentimental one for me because of the Leeds United connection. I know he played for a few clubs but for me he'll always be Leeds United and for me that means he'll always be a legend. Whenever you walk into Elland Road you're reminded of the club's history, it's plastered all over the walls – and the Scottish part of it runs right through the place. My late grand-father was Scottish and he died when I was young, so I always had this idea in the back of my mind that I might play for the country one day and it means so much that it has happened. To do it in the same position for Leeds and Scotland as someone like Gordon is a huge privilege. I know he scored his last goal for his country here in Oslo so who knows – maybe if I get on it might happen for me too? I haven't scored for a while so I'm due one. I tell you this, you'd want him in the trenches with you any day of the week.'

Scottish football paid its respects and the team wore black armbands on the sleeves of their white away kits as a show of solidarity for the McQueen family in its time of need.

Clarke and his team had put his squad through their main preparations before they headed for Norway. They were set for a hot reception, regardless. A summer heatwave had hit the Norwegian capital. On match day the temperatures hit more than 30 degrees and the hosts were handing out water to the 1,300-plus travelling Tartan Army.

It was on the park that Clarke had to come up with a plan to douse the potential fiery threat of Haaland and Co. There was no doubt the conditions had come into Clarke's thinking. This was more about the long game and not a 100-mile-an-hour start, knowing they could quite easily burn themselves out.

Captain Andy Robertson pointed out: 'It's the warmest we've probably played in in a long time – it was so hot. We knew we had to be careful. We knew we had to use our whole bench, we knew that was going to come into play. The lads who came off the bench did so well. We had a game plan and obviously giving away a penalty and going behind against a good team was difficult.'

Clarke sent his team out with his usual defensively sound structure of a 3-4-3, with John McGinn and Ryan Christie asked to get up and down to support Lyndon Dykes as the sole striker. Scotland, as always, were disciplined, kept their shape and invited the Norwegians to make the opening advances.

The good thing for Clarke's team was that when they stepped off the Norway defenders, they knew the majority of the time they maybe didn't have the quality they had in other areas of the park. Passes would regularly go astray or even out of the park.

There was still a strong anticipation amongst the home fans. Haaland had them off their seats, but fortunately for Scotland his header was straight down the throat of Angus Gunn. It was very much a rearguard performance from Clarke whose team rarely looked threatened. At the same time, they hardly troubled the Norway goal in the first half apart from a blocked John McGinn shot.

The Norwegians were more in need of the points and you would have expected more urgency from them, especially at the start of the second half, but they remained passive and that suited Clarke and his team. The home side eventually came to life when they appealed for a penalty after Jack Hendry challenged Haaland in the box, but referee Matej Jug waved those appeals away.

Just a few minutes later, the Slovenian official wasn't so lenient. A cross came in and Ryan Porteous and Haaland grappled inside the box. The big striker defied his hulking physique to go down all too easily. Jug pointed to the spot and booked Porteous for his actions.

Haaland stepped forward to take the penalty. It was the moment the majority of the crowd had come to see and he wasn't about to disappoint. Gunn had done his homework and tried his best on his line, pointing to his right in the battle of the mind games. Haaland duly obliged, sticking it to that side but low, and despite Gunn's best efforts it nestled in his bottom corner.

Gunn, in a nod to the type preparation that had served predecessor David Marshall so well, said: 'Liam Kelly, Zander Clark and I all do a lot of work analysing a lot of penalties. We thought we knew where he was going – and we did. It was just down to whether or not he hits it cleanly enough, and in this game he did.'

It was the first goal that the keeper had conceded in his international career. It was a setback and a body blow for Scotland and Clarke. Things were to get ever more challenging as key defender Kieran Tierney slumped to the turf. He limped off and was replaced by Liam Cooper. Norway remained on top before Clarke turned to his bench to try and inject some life and energy into his flagging side. It started with a formation change. Kenny McLean came on for Porteous and Stuart Armstrong and Billy Gilmour replaced Ryan Christie and Callum McGregor.

Brighton midfielder Gilmour knew they had to try and make an immediate impact. He said: 'Of course, when you come on as a sub you need to try and change the game. I thought we did a good job of that. Everybody gave their all and we have great players to come on and help the team. We have got a great squad with real strength and depth. Everyone from the boys who start to the boys on the bench and even those in the squad are all in this together.'

Clarke's Norwegian counterpart Stale Solbakken also made changes and that included taking Haaland off for the final six minutes of normal time. Maybe he thought the game was won and wanted to give his star man the adulation he deserved from his adoring public. The exit of the Norwegian superstar seemed to give Clarke and his men the adrenaline shot they needed.

John McGinn confirmed: 'It gave us a boost to see one of the best players in the world being taken off, because although they have good players on the bench there's no one else as good as him. When it went to one each and they needed to chase the win again, him not being on the pitch really helped us.'

Robertson reckons Clarke was the game changer.

He said: 'I think we got a lift from starting to dominate possession a bit more. We created a couple of chances, fresh legs on, changed the formation. When we went 1-0 down they started sitting back and protecting what they had. That suited us. We started to get a bit more time on the ball. We brought on fresh legs and we just started pushing.'

McGinn also insisted Clarke's decision to introduce McLean, Armstrong and Gilmour cannot be underestimated.

He said: 'We need to give a big shout-out to the substitutes, because they were phenomenal. Before then, it was a really poor performance from us on the ball, on as hot a night as I can ever remember playing in. We went behind and had to respond, but it wasn't really happening until Kenny, Billy and Stu all came on and changed the game.'

Jack Hendry and McLean combined to get it to McGinn and he tried to slip in McLean as he continued his run into the box. Leo Østigård made a mess of his clearance and it fell to the incoming Lyndon Dykes who knocked it past the keeper with just three minutes to play.

Goal hero Dykes admitted: 'We didn't really do the things we wanted to do, to play the way we'd planned to. It was a tough night for me up front, battling for balls in the air and taking a few knocks. All I kept hoping for was that one sniff. When it came I just toe-poked it and I've never seen a ball trickle so slowly towards the line. It was just so good to see it finally go over the line. The momentum changed from then on. Our subs had come on and done really well and suddenly you wondered if we could go on and win it.'

The Tartan Army couldn't believe their eyes although Clarke wasn't getting carried away with the same furore. Amidst the euphoria of the celebrations, on and off the pitch, he was getting a hold of captain Andy Robertson on the touchline to get his troops organised and ready to go again.

Whatever he said or did it worked, because two minutes later Scotland were in dreamland. Scott McTominay put in a long cross from the right. It was over the head of Dykes but fell to McGinn who pulled it back for Dykes to cushion it into the path of McLean and he coolly guided a low right foot shot into the bottom left-hand corner.

McGinn recalled: 'It was a really good goal. I don't know how big Scott McTominay saw me from out on the right, but he pinged a great ball, Dykesy blocked off their defender and to be honest I was going to have a shot before I saw him out of the corner of my eye and decided to square it instead.

'The big man laid it off lovely, and Kenny's run was perfect. It couldn't have been a better end to the night for us.'

Scotland had grabbed victory from the jaws of defeat in two mad Oslo minutes. Agony had turned to ecstasy and this time even Clarke couldn't hide his emotions. There was a pile-on between the staff and players while the Scotland boss had two hands in the air before he headed towards the fans and punched the air in delight. Who says Clarke never shows his emotions?

Norway didn't know what had hit them and the Ullevaal was left in a stunned silence apart from the partying away section behind Gunn's goal. The big keeper was even in amongst them.

The keeper knew it was survival of the fittest and Norway were out on their feet. Gunn insisted: 'Norway emptied the tank more than they thought. When we got the first goal we were in the ascendancy, and it showed with the second goal. Even after that there were six minutes left, and they didn't threaten us at all. We defended well and showed we were stronger physically.'

There was even time for Clarke to send on Blackburn defender Dominic Hyam for his debut and to see out the stoppage time in place of McGinn.

Skipper Robertson added: 'By that stage we were working off adrenaline a bit. Then it was probably the longest six minutes of our lives after the 90 had passed. I thought we defended superbly. We defended the goal and they didn't have any chances in that period of time.'

The Scotland support partied late into the Oslo night and the next morning but the celebrations in the away dressing room were more reserved. Mainly because they had given their all in searing conditions, but there was also the small factor of the upcoming home game against Georgia.

Scotland were sitting pretty with nine points from nine and on cloud nine as they flew out of Norway. McGinn believes this win was bigger than the Hampden victory over Spain: 'It was definitely bigger in terms of the group. The group [table] came up on the big screens when they were 1-0 up and at that point it was wide open, so for us to turn that around the way we did is huge.'

McLean and Dykes were the goal heroes, but captain Robertson insisted that Norway was as much about Clarke and his coaching staff and what they had achieved, as much as anyone.

Robertson acknowledged: 'It didn't look likely at times, of course it didn't. But I think the main folk in the stadium who believed were the players and the staff. We knew we had to come away to a top team and try to get a win and we've managed to do that. Credit to the manager and the staff. They've created such a great bond between us all in this squad. You start to see that because we're so much closer off the pitch. That's where the manager earns his money off the pitch. He makes sure we're all singing from the same hymn sheet.'

At that point, it was very much Scotland the Brave – but the last words must go to some of the more mischievous and buoyant Tartan Army.

Dykes claimed that win was the Euro 2024 qualifying highlight for him. He said: It was great the way the whole game played out. It wasn't our best game but it showed how determined we were throughout the whole competition. We scored two quick goals to win it. Before, it was likely that Scotland would have ended up on the wrong side of a result like that. You saw the feeling after I scored and then when Kenny scored. It was a major point in the qualifying campaign.'

The doors of the post-match mixed zone were left open because of the heat. The Scotland fans were heard singing, 'Scotland's having a party and Haaland's in his bed!'

It was also a night of celebration for Scotland as they flew back home. Dykes added: 'Most of us have been together since the last

Euros. We have built up and nights like in Norway and Spain at home produced great nights as a team. We all enjoy spending time together, playing cards or whatever. The bonding, friendships and morale is always strong. It was a night to remember for all the squad after that Norway win.'

Chapter 23

SCOTLAND RIDE THE CREST OF A WAVE AFTER HAMPDEN DELUGE

IT was, quite literally, the calm before the storm. Walking up to Hampden Park it was a typical June day in Scotland. It wasn't exactly sunny, more a little grey and overcast. The outlook for Steve Clarke's squad certainly looked a lot brighter, coming in on the back of three straight Euro 2024 wins. Scotland had seen off Cyprus and Spain at home and Norway away and now it was all about maintaining that momentum and not slipping up against one of Group A's lesser seeds. The 50,000-plus crowd were certainly heading to the national stadium with genuine belief.

It hasn't always been Georgia with love for Scotland in previous encounters. It is very much a fixture that has gone with home advantage. Scotland had beaten the Georgians at home 2-1 in the Euro 2008 qualifiers and 1-0 in the same competition seven years later in 2014.

Scotland had a perfect record against the Georgians here, but on their travels it was a different story. They had lost on both visits to Georgia under Alex McLeish and Gordon Strachan.

For Clarke's class of 2023, they looked a different proposition. It was about being professional, focused and giving their all. Pretty much the essential requirement needed when you join up with Clarke's squad. They wanted to extend their unbeaten run and didn't want to give their qualification rivals a glimmer of hope.

Captain Andy Robertson said: 'If we don't [win] then it probably blows it open again because Georgia will all of a sudden be lifted and the gap won't be as big as it could be. It's rubbish saying it but the next game's always the biggest. You beat Spain and Norway then it's so important you go and back it up. It's pointless everyone singing and dancing about us beating Spain and Norway then you back it up with a defeat or dropping points. You have to make that result important to you achieving what you want to achieve. We've obviously backed up that Spain result with another massive win against a really strong Norway team. Georgia becomes the biggest game, knowing if we win that then we're in a pretty good spot.'

Georgia had made a positive start to the group and were also unbeaten in Group A after their opening home draw with Norway and a 2-1 win away in Cyprus. Their star man Khvicha Kvaratskhelia had come off the high of helping Napoli to the Serie A title. There was one man in Clarke's squad who had an inside knowledge of the winger and that was Lewis Ferguson, who had come up against him regularly in his own time in the Italian top flight with Bologna.

Ferguson warned: 'He had been a key player for Napoli in the Champions League and in helping them win Serie A. He is so dangerous and is somebody we will need to look at because he is a real threat. I would say he is one of the best players I have faced up to in Serie A this season. He is a winger but he has a similar build to Diego Maradona. He is quite small and stocky. He is fearless with the ball and just goes and tries to create things.'

Clarke had done his preparations. Finalised his plans and tactics and selected his team, but there are just some things that no

SFA coaching courses or manuals can prepare you for. Scottish rain for one!

There are times when your fate is in the lap of the gods and that is what happened as the heavens opened. It was almost biblical and got heavier and heavier as both sets of players and the officials finalised their warm-ups on the Hampden pitch.

It was clear from the subs who remained out on the pitch that the ball was holding up in the water. A pre-match postponement looked to have been avoided when the teams appeared and Hungarian referee István Vad whistled for kick-off, even though the overhead conditions weren't showing any signs of relenting. The rain continued to batter down. The surface was absolutely drenched as players slipped and aquaplaned across it. The pitch looked unplayable.

Georgian coach Willy Sagnol made his feelings known to the fourth official but Scotland were to make a big splash minutes later.

John McGinn took a corner from the right and curled a ball into the near post. It came off Lyndon Dykes and a Georgian defender and fell to the feet of Callum McGregor. He fired in a right foot shot, through the water, that was too powerful for keeper Giorgi Mamardashvili to keep out in the sixth minute.

Celebrations quickly turned to groans of discontent as the referee decided work needed to be done on the drenched Hampden surface if this qualifier had any chance of finishing. He sent the players back to the dressing rooms in the tenth minute but the visitors wanted the plug pulled on the game.

John McGinn recalled: 'No, it shouldn't have started given the conditions. We could have maybe waited for 30 minutes. Listen, I can in a way understand why they [the Georgians] were wanting it off. They had just conceded and we would probably have done the same thing. It became clear the game was going on, but even then they were at it.'

The Hampden ground staff were sent out with giant squeegees to try and push the surface water off the pitch. They were aided by the ball boys who went out armed with upside brushes to try and fight the elements. All the while, the Travis track 'Why Does It Always Rain On Me?' was played over the Hampden PA system.

The pitch was inspected 20 minutes later and, although the ground staff had done everything in their power, it was still sticky and in some areas unplayable. The rain had finally eased off.

Some of the Scotland players were keen to get back out on the pitch to play their part. McGinn said: 'The ground staff and everyone involved did an amazing job clearing the pitch. It hadn't rained for about two weeks and I don't think anyone was expecting the downpour. I don't know if it [the pitch] should have been able to handle that amount of rain, I'm not an expert. But they all did an incredible job. I was wanting to give them a hand but we weren't allowed. It might have helped because it was painful to watch, but I was told it might tire me out.'

For Clarke, it was about keeping his players focused, reiterating the tactics and game plan, making sure his team were ready – whenever they were asked to finish off this fixture.

'The manager was just telling us to stay focused,' former Hibs defender Ryan Porteous revealed: 'Credit to all the staff, from the physios to the sports scientists, for keeping us ticking over. They got us food at the right times, and things like that are important as well. We eat three hours and 15 minutes before kick-off, and when that gets disrupted for an hour, it can have a massive knock-on effect. So credit to all the staff and I'm just glad that we delivered for them. They were just getting carbs into us, carb drinks, bananas, carb bars etc. We're professionals, so we know what should go into our bodies.'

The referee asked for more work to be done on one of the goalmouths and it was announced over the loudspeakers that the game would restart at 8.55 p.m. The longer it went on there was still that element of doubt. The players reappeared for another warm-up but the heavens opened again and it had become more and more of a thankless task, trying to fight the elements.

It was announced that the match would kick off again at 9.15 p.m., but the reluctant Georgians hadn't come back out and there was genuine concern whether the match would be finished. There were unfounded rumours that if the match was to be called off then it would need to be completed at St Mirren's ground behind closed doors. That, however, was never going to be the case, even in the worst outcome.

Captain Andy Robertson clearly wanted the show to go on. He knew Clarke's men had the Georgians where they wanted them. McGinn joked that Robertson had another reason for the game going ahead. There were short-term fears that we could face another 'One team in Tallinn' nightmare scenario, when Estonia didn't turn up for their Euro 1996 qualifier. Thankfully the Tartan Army were spared another no-show.

The Aston Villa star explained: 'Funnily enough, that was one thing we were told [playing at St Mirren]. It wouldn't have been ideal, that's for sure. We had Robbo's charity golf day on Wednesday and at one point it looked as though that might have been off. In the end, common sense prevailed. It would have been tricky had we been asked to go again behind closed doors.'

Georgia were eventually coerced back out but many of their players looked like they would rather be anywhere else than in Mount Florida's water park for the evening.

Scotland were determined this wasn't going to turn into a damp squib. John McGinn and Lyndon Dykes splashed efforts just wide while Scott McTominay saw a low shot saved in a first half that was nervy and tense. Clarke knew the one thing his team couldn't do was slip up. He called on his players to keep doing what they had been doing. Clarke and the nation made the perfect start to the second half. They doubled their advantage within two minutes and got a grip of the Georgians.

Kieran Tierney sent it up the left for Andy Robertson but it came off a defender and fell to McTominay outside the box. He took a touch and pushed it to the edge of the 18-yard box before firing a low left-foot shot into the corner of the net. Clarke, on the touchline, applauded the goal but then pointed to his head to tell his players to remain switched on.

McGregor cracked in another shot but that was well off target and Scotland looked like they would see out the game without any hiccups until VAR intervened and awarded Georgia a late penalty after a cross had come off the hand of Aaron Hickey in stoppage time.

Their main man Khvicha Kvaratskhelia stepped up but only gave the Tartan Army more reason to celebrate as he blazed his penalty kick high over the bar.

The final seconds were seen out and another Hampden party was in full swing. Scotland were singing in the rain.

Goal hero McTominay praised the Tartan Army for helping Scotland out of what could have been a sticky situation. McTominay, speaking to Viaplay Sports, said: 'Full credit to the boys. We were warm in there and kept our heads. It was more keeping warm and keeping your mind focused. I don't think it is about getting distracted because everyone in the dressing room felt the game would get played; they would clear the pitch and it would be fine. I thought they looked a little bit rattled and didn't want to play. We kept our concentration, to the game plan and we did really well. The crowd kept us going. It was tough because they had quite a lot of the ball and more than we expected, but we stuck in there.'

Clarke headed to shake hands with Sagnol and there was a

mutual respect and empathy of what they had both been involved in.

A match that had started at 7.45 p.m. and finished at 11.20 p.m. but also saw Scotland make history. It was the first time the country had won their first four qualifying games. It was something to be proud off.

Ryan Porteous added: 'This team continues to make its own history; every time we go away there seems to be something. Listen, we enjoy every night as it comes but we probably don't look at the bigger picture as much as others do – that's your job. You've got to get the fans excited and quite right too. It's very important that we are grounded, because throughout history – as the gaffer said in the press – when you think you are doing well that's when football can bite you. So, we're just taking it a game at a time.'

John McGinn noted the after-match celebrations were in tune with the match – pretty much a washout. It was after midnight before they started to appear out of the home dressing room and in the interview mixed zone.

McGinn said: 'It all felt a little bit subdued if I am honest. We've had a massive win but the supporters needed to get their buses and trains home. Fair play to every single one of them; it was them I felt for. It was fine for us, we were getting shelter and everything we needed.'

Queen's 'Another One Bites the Dust' could be heard booming out of the home dressing room. A pretty accurate assessment!

Chapter 24

REMEMBERING CRAIG BROWN

WHEN Steve Clarke stepped into the Scotland job he was looking to follow in the footsteps of Craig Brown. He had been the last man to take the country to a major finals. The legendary boss had led Scotland to Euro 96 and followed that up by leading the national team to the World Cup in France two years later.

It had seemed like a lifetime until Clarke had taken the helm and ended 23 years of pain and disappointment by taking the Scots to Euro 2020. Clarke was now looking to join Brown in taking Scotland to two finals, as manager, with Euro 2024 qualification.

The country was still basking in the glory of four straight wins and sitting proudly on top of qualifying Group A but, just six days after that win over Georgia, Scottish football was plunged into mourning again when it was confirmed Brown had sadly passed away, at the grand old age of 82, on 26 June 2023.

The game's top names lined up to pay tribute to one of Scottish football's most popular figures. He had managed Clyde, Preston, Motherwell and Aberdeen, where he remained an ambassador until his death, but it was his achievements with the national team that had given him a place in the hearts and minds of the Scottish people.

Clarke was amongst the most famous and distinguished names from the world of football to pay their tributes. Clarke, quoted on the SFA's website, said: 'Craig led the way in bringing sustained qualification to the men's national team, first as assistant to Andy Roxburgh and then in his own right. He was a student of the game and I am proud to say that I followed in his footsteps by taking a Scotland team back to a major tournament. The thoughts of the players and my backroom staff go to Craig's family and friends at this difficult time.'

SFA chairman Mike Mulraney paid his own respects to a true Scottish managerial great, putting him up there alongside greats like Sir Alex Ferguson, Jock Stein, Jim McLean and Walter Smith.

Mulraney, in the SFA statement, added: 'Words cannot do justice to the impact Craig Brown has had on Scottish football and on behalf of the Scottish FA, and his friends and former colleagues at Hampden Park, I send our deepest condolences to his family. As Scotland men's national team coach, he took us to Euro 96 in England – a tournament that only recently he described as one he and the players simply could not allow the fans to miss out on. He also took us to the World Cup in 1998 where we opened the tournament against Brazil with the iconic kilt walk pre-match. But he was much more than that – he was meticulous in his coaching preparation and passionate in his support of Scottish football.

'The greatest tribute that can be paid to his professional capabilities is the respect in which he was held by his peers, who also happened to be our all-time great coaches: among them Jock Stein, Sir Alex Ferguson, Walter Smith, Jim McLean and Andy Roxburgh. Craig deserves his place in the pantheon of great coaches. He will be missed – but never forgotten – by those who had the pleasure of his company, or by the fans and players who shared in his successes as Scotland manager.'

Brown had battled bravely in his final months. I had been standing at Edinburgh Airport about to check in to my flight to Norway for Scotland's visit when my mobile went. It was a colleague who called to inform me that the former Scotland manager wasn't in a good way. He was a gentleman whom I had known well as the national coach and then latterly at Motherwell and at Aberdeen. It was still a shock, even though I knew he hadn't been well and had recently undergone treatment.

Brown remained a passionate Scotland supporter until the very end. There was nobody more delighted when Clarke took Scotland to Euro 2020. He was a big supporter of Clarke but an even bigger supporter of the Scottish national team. When you spoke to him about the current manager he always joked that when it came to Clarke, he had every right to feel aggrieved because he has only won six caps. He had played under Andy Roxburgh and then Brown when he had become Scotland boss in 1993.

It was all part of an amazing 60-year association that the former teacher had with Scottish football. The former Rangers youngster went on to play and be part of Dundee's title-winning team before he moved to Falkirk, but his career was cruelly cut short by a knee injury.

Brown kicked off his long and successful managerial career at Clyde before he was headhunted by the SFA, where he was appointed assistant manager and assistant technical director, under Andy Roxburgh in 1986.

The popular figure was part of Sir Alex Ferguson's coaching staff for the World Cup finals in 1986 and was named as Roxburgh's No. 2 when he was appointed manager after qualifying for the World Cup four years later.

Brown's success with the Scotland's age group teams also stands up against the best, including taking Scotland to the under-16

World Cup final, where they lost on penalties to Saudi Arabia. He then led the under-21s to the semi-finals of the 1992 UEFA European Championship.

Brown, from there, was appointed caretaker after Roxburgh stepped down in 1993 and he did enough to keep the job leading Scotland to Euro 96 and World Cup 98. He also remains the last Scotland manager to beat England. Don Hutchison's goal was enough to defeat the Auld Enemy in their last European qualifier play-off at the old Wembley.

Brown remains Scotland's longest-serving national manager, eventually stepping down in 2001. He remained a popular character within Scottish football and quite rightly was inducted into Scottish Football's Hall of Fame in 2010.

Scotland's national team held a minute's silence for Brown before the 150th anniversary match with England on 12 September. It was broken by England fans booing.

A colleague, speaking after the minute's silence, said: 'Wee Brown would have loved that, knowing he was the last Scotland manager to get one over on England.' He was bang on the money. Scottish football is a lot poorer without Craig Brown.

Chapter 25

A FAMOUS FIVE TAKES SCOTLAND TO THE BRINK OF EURO 2024

SCOTLAND were at the halfway point of their Group A Euro 2024 qualifying campaign and things couldn't have gone any better. An impressive 12 points from 12 put the team in a commanding position at the top of their section. The team was full of confidence, fuelled by their 100 per cent start and the fact that they were also unbeaten in ten competitive games, spanning back before the qualifiers. Three of the first four opening Euro games had been at Hampden so Clarke and his players knew the second half was going to be more of a challenge with trips to Cyprus, Spain and Georgia to come before the campaign came to a climax with Norway at Hampden.

The Scotland fans knew on paper that Cyprus was probably the easiest of the three away trips. It was up next. If Clarke's team could extend the winning run in Larnaca then it would leave the national team with one foot in Germany! It would also pile the pressure on the chasing Spaniards and Norwegians, who were always trying to play catch-up.

Qualification was the big talking point but when Clarke named his Scotland squad for the double-header against Cyprus and the 150th Hampden anniversary clash with England, there was a new name on the list. Newcastle United's Elliot Anderson had been included in the Scotland squad for the first time. It was a major boost because the talented attacker had played for Scotland up to under-21 level although he had temporarily switched to play for England under-19s. Anderson was born in Whitley Bay but qualifies for Scotland through the grandparent rule. He had been doing well and making his mark in big-spending Newcastle United's team, and so it was a coup that Clarke had convinced him to commit to Scotland. Anderson was still only 21 and his best years were very much ahead of him. It certainly was a welcome surprise and another example of how box office the Scottish national team had become.

The Scotland camp got together and Anderson joined and met up with his new international teammates. He was photographed as he trained, and everything in the garden looked rosy until news began to leak out that Anderson had decided to leave the squad. The SFA confirmed the departure and claimed that Anderson had an injury. Others close to the player alleged he didn't feel 100 per cent that Scotland was right for him at that stage of his career, so he returned to Newcastle United to consider his options. England remained a live alternative.

That became the hot topic of conversation in Clarke's pre-match press conference. It was a prickly subject for the national coach and one he probably didn't have all the answers for. The national coach, however, answered everything with a straight bat, stating the player needed time and it was up to Anderson to decide whether or not he wanted to play for Scotland. Clarke, at that time, had more immediate and pressing matters to address. Cyprus away.

Anderson's abrupt departure had also been softened by the fact Clarke's attacking options had been boosted by the return from injury of Che Adams. The Southampton striker was pitched straight into Clarke's starting XI. He replaced Lyndon Dykes who dropped to the bench in the only change from the Scotland team that had started against Georgia.

The temperature in Larnaca was hot but the chasing Spaniards turned up the heat even more before kick-off with a 7-1 drubbing of their hosts, Georgia. The 4,000 or so Tartan Army members soaked up the sun in the AEK Arena and hoped they would soon be another step closer to getting their passports out again for the following summer.

If there were nerves in the Scotland squad they masked it well as they took a sixth-minute lead. Skipper Andy Robertson's cross was flicked goalwards by John McGinn and Scott McTominay came in to head in at the back stick.

It took his red-hot scoring streak to six and with another assist he sat proudly at the top of the Euro 2024 scoring charts.

McTominay, speaking to Viaplay Sports, said. 'The manager gives me a lot of freedom to get into the box and potentially make things happen. He has shown a lot of faith in me and I just want to repay him. You always speak to your family before the game and they wish you good luck and stuff. You just want to make them proud. You want to make the people of Scotland happy. That's my job and the team's job. I think we are doing it well at the minute.'

He had become the new pin-up boy of the national team. The Manchester United player had scored six goals in five games and it all kicked off with his opening-day double against Cyprus. He had come back to haunt them again.

Cypriot defender Alex Gogic recalled: 'He was getting a bit of stick for his performances at Manchester United at the start of the season. He wasn't always in their team but I think his Scotland performances have helped him. He came off the bench and scored twice against us and since then he hasn't looked back. Scott shut people up in that game and then even more so with his goals against Spain. Doing your talking on the pitch, as a footballer, is the best way to prove people wrong and Scott has done exactly that. He is now a big player for Scotland and Manchester United.'

Cyprus might have struggled in the group but they were defiant and weren't just going to sit back and let Scotland steamroller over them. They produced some neat and tidy moves of their own, worked Angus Gunn and caused one or two moments of minor panic before Scotland scored their second in the 16th minute. It had the Scots in dreamland. Robertson's free kick was headed down by Jack Hendry into the path of fellow defender Ryan Porteous, who controlled it then beat the keeper. It was a moment to remember as the Watford star netted his first Scotland goal on his sixth appearance. This was a young player who had potential at Hibs but under Clarke had shown a real maturity and was turning into the top defender that so many had predicted.

Things were going to script for Scotland and within half an hour the game was done and dusted. Billy Gilmour's great piercing pass was laid back by Aaron Hickey to McTominay, who charged up the right and pulled a ball back for John McGinn to fire a shot inside the keeper's right post from the edge of the box.

The Cypriots had been far too accommodating and it was little consolation to Gogic that one of his former Hibs teammates Porteous had put himself on the scoresheet.

'Scotland scored three quick goals and if I'm being honest it was a bit sloppy from a Cypriot point of view,' Gogic claimed. 'We switched off for the first goal and then they got the second five minutes in. There was a bit of pressure on Scotland because they had won their first four games but getting those early goals relaxed them and took the pressure right off them. They were 2-0 up and could enjoy their football. They got another one on the half-hour and the game was finished. I congratulated Porto after the game because it is always a nice moment to score your first international goal. It was against Cyprus but I will forgive him.'

The stunning Scots saw out the game with relative ease and allowed Clarke to send on Dykes and Kenny McLean for Adams and Gilmour. McTominay almost grabbed a fourth but his shot came back off the post, and Stuart Armstrong, Nathan Patterson and Ryan Christie all came on near the end as Scotland shone in the sun.

It was another clean sheet from the Scotland defence. Goalkeeper Angus Gunn had made a stunning start to his Scotland career. He had won every game he had been involved in and the only goal he had conceded in five games had been from the penalty spot to Erling Haaland. It was an impressive record that wasn't to be sniffed at.

Gunn revealed his Scotland teammates had joked he had brought them luck. He, however, was more modest, insisting it was very much a team game: 'The boys told me I should have come earlier because I'm their lucky charm! But it's really all about the work the manager and the squad have put in, even before I came in.'

It helped to make the Scots the top nation, in terms of form, in Europe at that point. Clarke and his men had made it 11 games unbeaten. The job was still a work in progress and Clarke warned his players they were still far from finished.

'We have won five out of five and 11 unbeaten in one of the longest unbeaten streaks in Europe at the minute,' McTominay, speaking to Viaplay Sports, proudly noted. 'I feel we are in a good spot and the manager is telling us to keep our feet on the ground.'

The perfect run moved Scotland into the top 30 in the world rankings.

Gogic could see Scotland was coming together and were on the verge of something special. The St Mirren player said: 'The first game they beat us 3-0 and then they won at home against Spain. It shows what a good team they are and the levels they hit in the qualifying. The start Scotland made was amazing. They beat Spain at home and then the win away in Norway was amazing. They have shown good character. Scotland were losing in Norway but got the late equaliser and most people would have settled for the draw but they then went on to win it. There were some amazing scenes from that game. You could see what it meant to everybody with all the players, staff and fans celebrating together. That was a big moment for the team in that campaign.

'Scotland have a lot of good players but their real strength is the group and the team. You can see they are all united as one; it is not about the individuals. They are good defensively and all the players know their jobs and they also know how to take their chances. A lot of the Scotland team are playing in the English Premier League or the Championship. You can see that with Porto going to Watford and then stepping into the Scotland team. It is a hard squad to get into now. You need to be doing well for your club and playing at a very high level.'

Scotland were almost at the Euros. Their spot would be sealed if Norway and Georgia were to draw in Oslo the following Tuesday, as Scotland prepared to take on the Auld Enemy in their 150th anniversary match. If not, then Scotland would need just two points from their remaining fixtures away to Spain and Georgia and home to Norway. It was a matter of time – surely?

The focus for the time being was on the England game. It had been a long time since a Scotland v England game hadn't been the be-all and end-all for the Tartan Army. Clarke had since raised the bar and Scotland now had bigger fish to fry. Euro 2024 qualification was far more important than a one-off friendly. Not that any member of the Tartan Army would ever turn up their nose to the bragging rights over the Auld Enemy. It was 150 years since the two countries had first met at the West of Scotland Cricket Club back in 1872.

It is fair to say that England has held the upper hand but there have been some big wins like the Wembley Wizards and their 3-2 win over the world champions in 1967, the celebrations from a Joe Jordan strike and a Colin Todd own goal in 1974, Kenny Dalglish's goals in '76 and '77. The John Robertson penalty from 1981 or Richard Gough's winner in 1985. Since then it has been slim pickings. A 1-0 play-off win, thanks to a Don Hutchison goal, in the final game at the old Wembley got Scotland a result but wasn't enough to overturn their 2-0 defeat at Hampden. England won 2-1 on aggregate and took their place at Euro 2000. Since then, the closest Scotland had come was a couple of Leigh Griffiths free kicks at Hampden but a late strike from Harry Kane cost the Scots a famous win.

England were also on the rise under Gareth Southgate and had narrowly lost the Euro 2020 final to Italy. They had an embarrassment of riches and Premier League stars that Clarke could only dream about. Yet more often than not it was about raising the bar for 90 minutes to try and bridge the gap. Scotland had always been the underdog to their neighbours but that hadn't stopped them giving their rivals a bloody nose both in terms of football and historically.

England were also on top of their Euro 2024 qualifying group and that was their main focus, but Scotland wasn't a proposition that they were going to take lightly. Southgate added a bit of edge to things by declaring his interest in capping Newcastle United's Elliot Anderson – days after he had walked out on the Scotland squad. Clarke refused to be drawn and again insisted the midfielder needed time and space to decide where his international future lay.

Anderson was one for the future. It was about the here and

now. Clarke wanted to keep the feel-good factor going and Scotland on their unbeaten run, which would stand them in good stead to get over those final Euro 2024 hurdles.

They were facing an England team of extreme quality and which travelled north with the bit between their teeth. They were just too strong for the Scots, who looked jaded and just off it. They were a shadow of the team who had lit up the Euro 2024 qualifiers.

The visitors bossed things from start to finish. Their young stars Phil Foden and Jude Bellingham put them into a convincing 2-0 lead. Scotland gave the home fans hope when Harry Maguire put through his own net, but a late Harry Kane goal extinguished any hopes of a glorious comeback. It had been a one-off night where Scotland just hadn't been at it.

'It was a disappointing night but overall the camp has been positive,' Bologna midfielder Lewis Ferguson claimed. 'The main focus when we came away was three points in Cyprus and taking another step towards qualification. Cyprus was massive and we managed to come through it with three points and a positive performance.'

The Euro 2024 campaign was also going to go to the October international fixture window because Norway had beaten Georgia to keep their outside qualification hopes of gatecrashing the top two alive. Scotland were going to Spain and knew a positive result could spark their own fiesta.

Chapter 26

BLOODY VAR

FIVE wins out of five. Let that sink in! Scotland's best ever start to a qualifying campaign. Steve Clarke and his men were on the verge after their 3-0 win in Cyprus. Had qualifying ever been more straightforward for Scotland? Okay a place in the finals hadn't been officially sealed, but it always looked like a case of when rather than if. The chants had already been bellowing from the stands in Cyprus: 'We're the famous Tartan Army and we're off to Germany.' I suspect quite a few of them would have already started to gamble and bag an early 2024 summer bargain for hotel rooms and flights.

Scotland's position at the top of Group A left them sitting pretty. It was the talk of the sports pages in the national press, across social media and group chats the length and breadth of the country. Yes, Scottish society has, at times, had a tendency to fear the worst or to look for the negative. Surely from their current position, Steve Clarke's men would finish the job they had started so imperiously? As always, there would have still been a few Doubting Thomases – it is never over until it is over and Scotland never does things the easy way!

Publicly, that was exactly the stance Clarke and his players would take. Who could blame them? Privately, he would have felt confident his team would finish the job but there was no way he was going to come out and tell the world. The gaffer had been around the block and was far too experienced to fall into that trap. Clarke would have drilled that same message into his players. Yes, some of them would speak about the possibility of qualifying for the Euros, but for a lot of them it was straight into the Clarke mindset of one game at a time. They also didn't want to give any of their rivals that extra motivation they needed to leave the team and the country with egg on their face.

The reality was that the team had not only one foot in Germany but two feet and nine toes if you listened to the statisticians. We Global Football (@We_Global) on the X platform delves deeply into football numbers and stats. Before the trip to Seville, it had noted Scotland had a 99.36 per cent chance of qualifying. That meant there was still a bit of doubt and a 0.64 per cent chance that the Scots could do the unthinkable and not make Euro 2024 via the qualifiers, although the Nations League would always be there as a fall-back.

The upcoming opponents, Spain, were also at a lofty 98.2 per cent chance to qualify automatically, although at that point, statistically, Scotland were the favourites to finish top of Group A. The Scotland team were rated as a 65.5 per cent chance to top the section while the Spaniards were a mere 34.4 per cent.

Clarke and his backroom team didn't have to crunch the numbers. The reality for them was a lot more simplistic. It was down in black and white. If Scotland could avoid defeat in Spain, albeit a big ask, then they would become the first nation to make it through the qualifiers to Euro 2024. A win would be utopia, a draw wouldn't be far off that! Even then, if group strugglers Cyprus were to spring a surprise at home and take points off Norway then the job would be done. It wasn't a bad position to be in. Even then, Scotland still had two more qualifying matches to do things under their own steam.

Spain were still hurting from Hampden. They weren't used to losing and certainly not in a qualifying campaign. Clarke knew it was going to be a whole different ball game going away from home. Spain, starting with Luis Enrique as national coach and going on to his successor, Luis de la Fuente, had won their previous 24 games on home soil.

The Royal Spanish Football Federation (RFEF) likes to take their national team across the country when they host fixtures. Seville, however, remains a firm favourite when La Furia Roja need a big result. It was no surprise to see the 60,000 capacity La Cartuja Stadium selected as the venue for the Scotland game. Spain had beaten Sweden there in the World Cup qualifiers to seal their place at the 2022 World Cup.

It was also a stadium that had broken a few Scottish hearts In the past. Celtic, under Martin O'Neill, had lost the 2003 UEFA Cup final there to Porto. It was a victory that was masterminded by a certain José Mourinho. The Special One who was to go on and become Clarke's boss and a big influence on him at Chelsea.

In fact, the city of Seville had been something of a graveyard for Scottish club teams in European finals. Rangers had also lost the Europa League final in 2022. Giovanni van Bronckhorst's side missed out on penalties to Eintracht Frankfurt, although they had been across the city in Seville's Ramón Sánchez Pizjuán Stadium.

Seville had also been the home of David Narey's Scotland wonder strike against Brazil back in 1982. The Dundee United legend had smashed Jock Stein's side ahead in the group game against the South American superstars. Unfortunately, it only upset them and the Brazilians eventually ran out 4-1 winners in Real Betis's Estadio Benito Villamarín stadium.

There was also the added dimension to this game as Scotland were to play Spain on 12 October. It was the National Day of Spain – a massive celebration and they hoped it would be another one in footballing terms. The RFEF weren't exactly shy in ramping things up before the game. The confirmation that the match was going to be played at La Cartuja came complete with a special message after what had happened at Hampden back in March.

It read: 'La Cartuja Stadium in Seville, on Hispanic Day. The Venue Selection Committee of the RFEF has thus approved La Cartuja Stadium in Seville to host the Spain–Scotland match on Hispanic Day. A match that will be an opportunity for the national team to seek revenge after the 2-0 defeat in Glasgow in the first leg, in this Group A qualification for the Eurocup.'

Scotland and Clarke had to shut out such talk and concentrate on the things they could control. Outside noise was not one of them. Spain were playing catch-up and had to use everything at their disposal to try and wipe out Scotland's Group A advantage.

Clarke named a strong squad and one that was along usual lines, although there was one big omission in Kieran Tierney. The influential defender had just made a loan switch to Spanish football with Real Sociedad. It was there in a match against Athletic Bilbao he suffered a hamstring injury that had ruled him out.

Jacob Brown, who had just moved to Premier League new boys Luton Town, Liam Cooper and Greg Taylor all came into the squad. Hearts striker Lawrence Shankland dropped out as did Elliot Anderson after his brief and infamous cameo appearance in the previous training camp.

Clarke was to lose two more players in Ryan Jack and Kevin Nisbet through injury before his squad met up for the Spain match and a friendly against France. There was time for Scotland to get a major European Championship result before they boarded the flight to Spain. Okay, it wouldn't help them in their immediate quest for a place at Euro 2024, but it was confirmed that Scotland would be joint hosts for the Euro 2028 finals, along with England, Northern Ireland, Wales and the Republic of Ireland. It maybe wasn't the biggest of surprises as the other rival bidder, Turkey, had previously pulled out, preferring to bid for Euro 2032 as co-hosts with Italy.

The news would see Hampden as one of the host venues again, as it was at Euro 2020. It was also confirmed that all the host nations would go through qualifying and the highest two nations who don't make it would be given the two automatic host nation spots. It was something to look forward to but it was still five years away. Clarke acknowledged it was great for the country but joked he might not be around as Scotland boss at that point.

The Tartan Army would be quite happy if he was still in the hot seat in 2028 because it would mean he was continuing to have success and taking Scotland firmly on an upward trajectory. Clarke, however, is a man who operates in the here and now and that now was Spain in Seville in match day six of the Euro 2024 qualifying campaign.

It was also against a Spanish team who had been crowned as Nations League champions, beating Croatia in the final, just three months after they had lost in Glasgow. Clarke acknowledged before the game that they were a top, top team and Scotland had got them at the perfect time at Hampden, after their World Cup hangover and with Luis de la Fuente still trying to implement his new ideas and style on to his charges.

It was fair to say, with the Nations League in the bag and hitting 13 goals in two qualifying games against Georgia and Cyprus, that Spain now looked a far more formidable proposition. It was to be a game where the heat was to be turned up on Clarke and his men. It was 28 degrees in Seville as the Tartan Army soaked up the sun and the local beer.

Clarke had to come up with another master plan. Scott McKenna came in and filled the void on the left-hand side created by Tierney's absence, while Ryan Christie replaced Billy Gilmour and Lyndon Dykes was preferred to Che Adams. Clarke went for a 4-5-1 formation, but wanted John McGinn and Ryan Christie to get up and support Dykes whenever they could. Spain fielded just three players who had started at Hampden. Rodri, Mikel Merino and Mikel Oyarzabal. They needed the win and went out with an adventurous 4-3-3 formation.

Clarke knew the importance of making a solid start, trying to nullify Spain's early threats and to quieten the expectant home crowd. The Scotland squad normally follow out his instructions to the letter, but within two minutes they were almost undone as Álvaro Morata put Ferran Torres clear, but with only Angus Gunn to beat he fluffed his lines and fired wide. It was a sign of things to come.

Scotland's players struggled to get up the park and Spain created a number of opportunities from corners. Some early luck was on the side of Clarke's men when Merino cracked a shot off the inside of the post, while Morata had the ball in the net but was flagged for offside. You could see that Clarke had done his homework and given his players clear instructions. That was shown when the Spanish wingers Torres and Oyarzabal switched flanks and Andy Robertson and Aaron Hickey also went with them, with Clarke clearly deploying them on man for man duties.

Scotland managed to get to half-time level, but it came at a cost. Robertson had gone up for a ball in the box and had been caught by the Spanish keeper Unai Simón. The Liverpool star had to walk dejectedly off in some pain and discomfort with a shoulder injury. The good thing is that Clarke now has options and cover right across his squad. Nathan Patterson came on at right back while Hickey moved across to fill in for his skipper.

Spanish coach Luis de la Fuente knew his side had been the better team, but had nothing to show for it. He changed two of his wide options although Scotland looked to have snuffed that early threat out and were beginning to offer more of an attacking threat of their own.

A Ryan Porteous effort was easily gathered before the moment of controversy, as Ryan Christie had robbed Dani Carvajal and then been fouled by the Real Madrid full back tight to the right-hand side of the Spanish 18-yard box in the 62nd minute.

Scott McTominay stepped up to take the free kick. He shaped as if he was going to cross it to the back stick – but he surprised everyone in the stadium by thundering the free kick high over a stunned Spanish keeper Simón.

It sparked wild celebrations in the away end and on the pitch, as McTominay ran off to celebrate what could have been a massive, massive goal. Clarke wasn't getting caught up in the moment. His coaching staff, subs and players might have been jumping for joy but he was still on the touchline, trying to keep his players grounded and finishing the job. You could see the message was to keep their focus.

Stephen O'Donnell noted that is one of Clarke's many strengths. He explained: 'His biggest thing is his calmness. You can sense that in the team and on the side of the pitch. When you are playing and things aren't going well he doesn't stress out. Look at the Spain game, even after the buzz of the McTominay free kick he was still calm and focused. That helped him with what happened next. Steve wasn't on the pitch getting carried away. He is always calm and collected and he will celebrate at the right times and get carried away at the right times. Certainly, in the middle of business he doesn't.'

It was VAR and not Clarke and his players that had become the main focus. Referee Serdar Gözübüyük had signalled for the goal but before the restart there was the customary check. It was then the Dutch official was invited to review the footage. Gözübüyük returned after a major delay and much to the delight of the Spanish crowd disallowed the goal. Gözübüyük had returned and clearly signalled for a foul rather than offside. The initial word is that it had been chalked off because Jack Hendry, who had been standing beside Simón, had fouled the Spanish keeper. At that time it had caused fury because it would have been the softest foul ever as Hendry's hand had barely brushed the Spanish No. 1's jersey. Social media and television pundits and commentators, quite rightly, went into meltdown. It had looked to be a complete injustice. Word later emerged that the goal had been ruled out for offside.

It was a blow to the Scotland team but the next one was to be even bigger. Sub Jesús Navas curled in a cross and Morata found time and space to beat Angus Gunn with a diving header. The game had been turned on its head and Clarke had to react. He did. He sent on Che Adams for Dykes and Stuart Armstrong for Christie. It almost worked as a gritty run from Hickey saw him find Adams, but he couldn't get enough power and direction on his shot to beat Simón, while Armstrong had a shot deflected over for a corner. Scotland knew it was all or nothing on the night and going for it left gaps at the back, with Ryan Porteous having to clear off the line. Hope then evaporated when there looked to be little or no danger. Hickey, who had been faultless in the game, slipped and allowed Joselu to cross and Porteous tried gallantly to clear the ball with a sliding challenge in front of Oihan Sancet but ended up putting into his own net with five minutes left on the clock.

Clarke's Scotland team is clearly all in it together. They win and lose as a team and that was to be the case.

Defender Scott McKenna, speaking to Viaplay Sports,

insisted: 'Aaron has been brilliant for us ever since he came into the team and it was just an unfortunate moment. Ryan Porteous nearly bails him out but the clearance hit off their player then goes into the back of the net. So it was one of those moments; it was a mistake but Aaron has been brilliant and unfortunately it went against us.'

With it went Scotland's unbeaten run and the points. It was also a costly goal in terms of the group. It allowed Spain to cancel out their 2-0 defeat at Hampden. If it had been 1-0 then Scotland if they had finished level on points would have had the advantage. Now it would go to goal difference and at that point the free-scoring Spaniards were streets ahead.

A night of frustration was compounded with the news that Norway had thumped Cyprus and so qualification would need to wait for another day.

The aftermath pretty much centred on the furore and con troversy over VAR's decision to disallow the game-changing McTominay goal and with the general performance of the referee Gözübüyük, where it was later claimed he had changed his reason for disallowing it.

John McGinn, speaking passionately to Viaplay Sports after the game, said: 'He changed it in game, which is the frustrating thing. It shows that it was not clear and obvious. I am not sure if clear and obvious is a European VAR thing, but at the moment Jack made a decision to step to the other side and maybe he could have stayed. Is he going to save it? Absolutely no chance. No goal-keeper in the world is going to save that. He is saying at one point it is a foul and then he changes it when he realises it is not a foul to offside. It is a big, big moment. It is a bit of a hammer blow. I feel for big Scott. Sometimes they go for you but it was never going to go for us.'

That was a view shared right across the Scotland team.

'I asked what the referee was checking the VAR for,' Ryan Christie added. 'We were all told it was a push on the goalkeeper. We didn't see it back because we were on the pitch. It wasn't until the full-time whistle went I went back to shake hands with the officials again and I asked the referee why the goal wasn't given again. He told me it was for offside. It has been highlighted by plenty of other people but when the referee comes back and gives the decision he doesn't give offside. You can't just change what you have given 20 minutes later because it fits better. It was a bit of a strange one.'

Cypriot international Alex Gogic was another who was bemused that McTominay's free kick hadn't stood. He insisted: 'The game in Spain, if that free kick, from McTominay, is given then it is a different game for me. I don't know how it was given a foul but that is another argument.'

Aston Villa star McGinn felt aggrieved about the official's performance the entire night. Perhaps it started when he was clearly taken out in a first-half counter and Gözübüyük astoundingly waved play on.

McGinn, speaking to Viaplay Sports, added: 'I need to be very careful what I say. I think everyone from a Scotland point of view, whether you were on the pitch, in the stand or in the dugout, it just felt like we weren't getting a decision; 50/50 balls, going in for fair challenges and not getting them. It made it extremely difficult against a world-class team to try and get anything from the game. The stats will show they had a lot of the ball and a lot better chances. You need everything to be perfect. It is very difficult to win here but in the circumstances it was near enough impossible.'

Clarke was more measured. He didn't want to go too deeply into the VAR argument and preferred to focus on his players and how they deserved to take something from Spain.

The Scotland manager, speaking on Viaplay Sports, claimed:

'You can show the Scott McTominay goal as many times as you want. We're not getting it. It's gone. You have to try and move on. We did that. I thought the second goal was really unfortunate. It puts a little bit of an unfair shine on the game. I didn't think we deserved to lose, to be fair.'

The debate over the McTominay goal continued to rage the next day as the Scotland team made their way back to Glasgow. The SFA confirmed later that day it had written to UEFA asking for clarification.

The UEFA press office had already been in full spin mode earlier in the day. They had claimed Hendry had been standing in an offside position. The response from the UEFA Media Relations was short and to the point: 'Dear Sir, the goal was ruled out for offside.' The statement included a link to UEFA's live text commentary of the game. It claimed: 'Hendry [Scotland] is flagged for offside.'

When I put up that response on X the next day, it was met with an angry response from a number of Scotland fans, accompanied by screenshots from footage of the match that suggested otherwise.

Christie added: 'It would have been nice to do it in Spain to give ourselves a chance to top the group. You look back at the Spain game and we had the Scott McTominay goal that wasn't to be. Doubts maybe started to creep in and maybe people were asking: "Are things going to start turning against us?" Even watching the Spain game and their first goal was ruled out after VAR, I thought: "Here we go again."'

It didn't change anything. Scotland still sat top of Group A, three points ahead of the Spanish who had a game in hand against Norway three days later.

Slightly lost in the McTominay aftermath were the post-match comments of Rodri. He had clearly realised the uproar his initial comments at Hampden had made. He went on to blame his poor English and praised the Scots. It didn't go unnoticed within the Scotland squad.

Christie said: 'I saw he backtracked a bit after the second game. If I am being honest I didn't even see his comments after the first game until somebody else mentioned. Rodri had tried to dig himself out of that one.'

Spain had got themselves out of their own hole with this win that gave them back the advantage to win the group.

Chapter 27

GERMANY, HERE WE COME

SPAIN had caused Steve Clarke and Scotland a whole world of pain with their win in Seville just three days earlier. Now the country's main competitors in the fight to finish top of Group A could go from sinners to saints in the Scots' fight to qualify for the 2024 European Championships. Luis de la Fuente's side could seal Scotland's passage to Germany by getting a result in Norway.

A Spanish win or draw would be enough for the Tartan Army to reach for their passports, if they hadn't already. The ideal scenario was a draw because it would give Scotland the advantage in the fight to finish top of the group. That would have its clear and obvious advantages in terms of the draw for the finals.

A lot of the Scotland support would have been glued to their television sets watching the Norway v Spain game at the Ullevaal Stadium or constantly refreshing their phones for score updates. It was a venue that had given the Scots a big Euro 2024 qualifying result back in June; could it provide another? Maybe the ultimate one? Certainly nobody wanted it to go down to the final Euro 2024 qualifying double-header, with Scotland heading to Georgia and then hosting Norway at Hampden.

Scotland star Ryan Christie said: 'We had made an amazing

start in the group. We went into this camp with the single thought of: "Let's just get this over the line now." We knew the longer we left it the more anxious people would get outside the camp, not so much inside it. A lot of people thought we had already qualified but we knew it could still turn quickly, especially if Norway started to get results, but thankfully Spain put an end to that.'

Clarke and his team's focus was their own job in hand. Their double-header was to be completed with a friendly against France in Lille. It was another tough task for Clarke and his side. Les Bleus had actually got in ahead of Scotland to qualify from their group with a win that weekend over the Netherlands. It was hardly a surprise since they could boast top talents like Kylian Mbappé, Antoine Griezmann and Adrien Rabiot. They had also lost the World Cup final on penalties at the turn of the year and Didier Deschamps' side sat at No. 2 in the world rankings. It was as tough a challenge as you could get. It was another one in the mould of the England friendly at Hampden the previous month for the SFA's centenary.

People questioned why the SFA and Clarke had taken on such challenging friendlies. It was at a time when Scotland were almost at the Euros but not quite. Could these games dent the confidence when the final step was still to be cleared? Clarke, however, wanted to test his side against top teams. The likelihood is that was going to be the level of opposition Scotland would face if they were to make it to Euro 2024.

Clarke put his team through their recovery after the Spain game and turned his attention to the upcoming friendly in Lille's Stade Pierre Mauroy. The team, like the nation, tuned into the Norway v Spain game, awaiting a favourable outcome. Injured skipper Andy Robertson was still nursing his shoulder injury, prior to surgery, but delayed his return to Liverpool so he could be with the squad, just in case. It was another example of the camaraderie of the squad and how important representing their country is to the nation.

It turned out to be the emotional roller coaster of a night that every Scotland fan is now accustomed to. Nothing is straightforward, although Clarke's side in winning their first five qualifying games had done the hard work and made qualification a less nervous proposition than it normally would have been.

Norway were behind the eight ball and they had to win to keep their flickering hopes alive. When you can call on Erling Haaland then you are always going to have a chance. It was a game that Spain dominated but lacked a cutting edge. Alvaro Morata had the ball in the net but VAR intervened and chalked the goal off to ensure that the Norwegians and Spanish went in 0-0 at half-time.

It was the perfect result for Scotland but four minutes into the second period, Spain got their goal through Gavi. There was another VAR sweat before the goal was finally given. Clarke and his team celebrated but a Norwegian equaliser could have been even bigger.

Christie recalled: 'We watched the game in the hotel. It was up on the big screen and we all sat and watched it. We were all buzzing when Spain scored to go 1-0 and then in the last few minutes we were all hoping that Norway would score so we would have a better chance of topping the group. That was just asking too much and we had to accept qualification via Spain's win.'

Spain saw it out and Clarke, his backroom team, players and support staff popped the champagne corks and celebrated another landmark achievement. It was mission accomplished getting Scotland to a second consecutive European Championship finals. Not only doing it but doing it in some style with two qualifying fixtures still to play. It was an absolutely phenomenal achievement.

Clarke, like every great leader, took time to pay tribute to his entire squad, players and staff, to congratulate them and to tell them to make the most of this accomplishment.

'The players and staff all watched it together so we were all buzzing,' Christie said. 'We congratulated each other and had a good celebration. It was a lot different to the Serbia game because that was almost a free hit. Not many people were expecting us to do it out there, but it was different this time around. We had done well and were really close and we got there. The manager congratulated us on qualifying and told us to look forward to it because our performances had earned it. It was a nice touch but it was also great for the manager to see his team get over the line. We all absolutely love playing under him. It was the best way for us to repay him for the work he has put in for the players, the team and the country.'

Absent friends weren't forgotten either. Kieran Tierney was injured and was back in Spain doing his rehabilitation, but Clarke and his Scotland teammates kept in regular contact, so there was nobody feeling left out. That just doesn't happen on Clarke's watch.

The SFA quickly put out statements from Clarke and captain Andy Robertson to mark their Euro 2024 qualification.

Clarke said: 'I would like to congratulate the players for their efforts in qualifying for back-to-back tournaments. I'm not sure they will fully realise the significance of their achievement yet, but to qualify for successive Euros after more than 20 years is phenomenal and testament to their hard work. I would also like to thank my backroom team for their support and, of course, the fans who have packed Hampden Park to capacity and made it a place to be feared once again. They have played a key part in our success, both home and away, and they can now look forward to making their plans for Germany – although I suspect many had done so before tonight. I said after Euro 2020 that we wanted to be serial qualifiers again and reaching successive Euro finals shows the progress we've made. We will raise a glass tonight to celebrate but then it's back to work tomorrow in preparation for our friendly against France. Then we turn our attention to Georgia and Norway next month and finishing with as many points as we can.'

It was a case of job done for Robertson and his fellow players who had been involved in the campaign. The proud skipper said: 'It's a great achievement for this squad to have qualified for Euro 2024 with two games remaining. When we qualified via the play-offs last time, we set ourselves a target of doing it automatically next time – so that's the first mission accomplished. Euro 2020 was a great experience and the objective for us next summer is to build on that previous experience and improve on our last overall tournament performance. Our fans have been immense. We thank them for playing a huge part in our success and we look forward to seeing them in Germany in their tens of thousands.'

Many of the Tartan Army were already on manoeuvres in France. It was a case of no Scotland, no party. The players and staff certainly deserved their night of celebration. Clarke allowed his players out to let their hair down. Their pictures were all over social media as they went out to join their adoring public, from the streets of Glasgow to the city's own Blue Lagoon fish and chip shop.

Those fans who hadn't been celebrating were probably on Skyscanner or looking to beat the rush to get some cheap travel deals to Germany. By the time the hangovers had started to subside the following morning, Clarke had sent out an open letter to members of the Scotland Supporters' Club.

It read: 'I'm writing to you today to simply say: thank you. When I was first appointed as Scotland Head Coach, I said there were two things I wanted to achieve; to return to major tournaments and to put a smile back on the face of our supporters. We've certainly achieved the first of those objectives; through the hard work and commitment of my players and staff we've now qualified for our second European Championships in succession. As for the second goal: it has been immensely gratifying to see you in the stands at Hampden and overseas showing your support for the team. Your backing has driven us on to qualification and I hope that the team's effort during this campaign has given you some memorable moments. To witness the connection between the players and you, the supporters, has been something I take great pride in as Scotland manager. Make no mistake, your support has been instrumental to our successes on the pitch – we have achieved qualification together. So, once again, thank you for your support. We will continue to work hard in the remainder of this campaign as we begin to set our sights on diligently preparing for Euro 2024. I look forward to seeing many of you in France, Georgia, back at Hampden as we round off this memorable campaign – and of course, next summer in Germany.'

Stephen O'Donnell had been there at the start of his Scotland journey with Clarke. Spain may have got the Scots over the line, but O'Donnell is adamant that the national manager and his players had done all the hard work and were always going to get the job done.

O'Donnell claimed: 'I always thought we were going to qualify. We would have got there under our own steam, given how good this squad has been and is. It might have been better for the players if they had clinched it on the pitch, but Spain's win saved us having to wait another month and it didn't lessen the achievement. Scotland did the business in the first five games and the players and coaching team deserve all the credit for that. To win five games in a row and to make it to back-to-back European

Championship finals is amazing. I remember the message the manager gave to us before, during and after Euro 2020 was that we want to be here again. He has been true to his word. Now we go into Euro 2024 with tournament experience. It just puts us in a great position. We've got good players who have been there and done it and it is a really good place to be.'

Cypriot defender Alex Gogic felt that over the course of Group A, Scotland deserved their qualification, alongside much-fancied Spain. Gogic said: 'I think Scotland have been one of the top teams in the group and deserved to qualify. Norway have good players in Erling Haaland and Martin Ødegaard, but I would say they rely more on these individuals and Scotland are more of a team. Norway has other good players but they rely on their world-class players. Spain were very good because they just pass and move and kill you getting into space, but Scotland as a team were as good as there was in our section.'

It was now about preparing for Euro 2024 for Clarke and his team. The next stop was the north of France and Lille. Clarke lost Robertson and fellow full back Aaron Hickey. It saw a surprise call-up for Max Johnston from the Scotland under-21s. The young full back had been the subject of a meteoric rise as he had been on loan at Cove Rangers less than a year previous. He returned to Motherwell where he was named the Scottish Football Writers' Association's young player of the year before he had won a big-money move to Austrian side Sturm Graz. Johnston had just helped the Scotland under-21s to a win over Hungary but was sent off in stoppage time. Instead of serving a suspension he was mixing it with the full Scotland squad.

Johnston admitted: 'I burst out laughing when I was told; I just couldn't believe it. I couldn't wipe the smile off my face. I went back up and the first thing I did was text my mum, Nicola, my dad, Allan, and my sister, Amy, first of all. They were over the moon. They were buzzing and couldn't believe it either! My sister told me my dad was up booking flights at 5 a.m. the next morning.'

Johnston joined up with the Scotland team and trained under Steve Clarke's watchful eye at Lesser Hampden the next morning. The final preparations were completed before the afternoon flight out to France.

Clarke, not surprisingly, made changes to his squad. Players were given the night off while others were handed some long over-due game time. The Scotland boss gave a debut to Motherwell keeper Liam Kelly, while he was to be replaced at the interval by Hearts star Zander Clark, who was to follow him by making his international bow. Clark had been involved in Scotland squads previously but then fell out of the picture after he left St Johnstone and failed to find a club right away. He was determined to wait for the right move. It eventually came when Hearts came calling and his time at Tynecastle not only reopened the Scotland door but saw him win his first caps.

Clark stated: 'It was a tough spell in my career. There was never nothing happening. There was always stuff going on in the background that people didn't see. It looked worse than it was. As time goes on you start to think, right, what am I doing? I signed for Hearts and it was my aim to break into their side and the international set-up. I knew being without a club and not playing a lot of games for six or seven months was always going to be tough for the manager to select me. I got into the Hearts team and I have managed to work my way back into the set-up. To then make my debut in France was hard to put into words.'

Greg Taylor came in at left back, with Scott McTominay named as captain in a total of eight changes from the side that started in Spain.

France had also qualified but still sent out all their big guns.

It was a friendly in name but nothing else for them. They didn't want to see Scotland spoiling their qualification party.

A lot of the Tartan Army had celebrated Spain's win over Norway that sealed Scotland's qualification. Some of them might well have thought they were still drunk when the Scots took a shock 11th-minute lead.

Billy Gilmour put the ball into the box and it fell to Eduardo Camavinga, who uncharacteristically gave it back to the Brighton midfielder and, coming in off the right, he curled it superbly past Mike Maignan.

Could it be a repeat of the famous James McFadden night in Paris back in 2007?

Could there be a better time to be a Scotland fan? Five minutes later they were brought crashing back to reality.

Gilmour savoured the moment, as did the fans, and it was just as well because it lasted just five minutes before the French levelled.

Benjamin Pavard equalised and then netted a second. Mbappé scored from the spot and Kingsley Coman came off the bench to clinch a convincing 4-1 win for the French. There were still positives. Both back-up keepers Kelly and Clark were given a first taste of international football. Lewis Ferguson received a rare start and striker Jacob Brown impressed coming off the bench. Fellow sub John McGinn was also given a run in the final minutes as he came on for his 60th cap.

It wasn't the result that he or Scotland had hoped for, but in terms of the double-header, the ultimate goal – Euro 2024 qualification – had been achieved.

Christie said: 'It was good and amazing qualifying, but it was also a bit weird. Looking back to that double-header we got beat in two games, but everyone was still buzzing. I suppose it was down to our previous results and the great way we had started the group had got the job done. It was a good celebration. All the boys, going into the camp, were just desperate to get over the line. I know we had to rely on another result, but the good thing was that we managed to get over that line to qualify.'

Clarke wasn't about to let his team rest on their laurels. He was unhappy that they were on the back of three defeats, in friendlies to England and France and in the Euro 2024 qualifier to Spain. Clarke demanded that the team get back to winning ways in the upcoming qualifiers in Georgia and at home to Norway. He made it clear that when you play for Scotland there is no such thing as a dead rubber or a meaningless game.

Chapter 28

SUPER SHANKS SAVES CLARKE'S 50TH

IT isn't very often that Scotland have been able to go into the final fixtures with qualification already in the bag. That just sums up the job Steve Clarke and his squad had done in guiding the country to Euro 2024 with two games to spare. So, in reality, the pressure was off for the trip to Georgia and the home game with Norway. Okay, Scotland could still top Group A, but that was not looking very likely with Spain's superior goal difference and their final two matches being away to Cyprus and at home to Georgia.

While there was a way then, you know Clarke wouldn't give up. Even if Scotland couldn't catch them he would still demand his team goes out and wins or at the very least puts on a performance and gives 100 per cent. Anything less just wouldn't be tolerated or accepted.

The game in Georgia was also a landmark one for the Scotland boss. It would be his 50th as national coach. He would join an exclusive band of Scotland managerial greats like Jock Stein, Craig Brown and Andy Roxburgh.

For Clarke, however, it is all about the team and not his own individual milestones. It was about getting his group back to winning ways. He is a winner by nature and you can see anything other than that would gnaw away at him.

Clarke had to name a squad with a few noticeable absentees. Captain Andy Robertson and Aaron Hickey remained injured from the last international meeting and so, for once, it left Scotland short of left back options. Celtic's Greg Taylor was the obvious candidate to step up while Hellas Verona defender Josh Doig was promoted from the Scotland under-21 squad, as Max Johnston had been for the trip to France.

Angus Gunn also remained absent through injury and so Rangers' Robby McCrorie came in as one of the three keepers, alongside Zander Clark and Liam Kelly. McCrorie had found first-team football hard to come by at Rangers, but he has always been there or thereabouts when it comes to Clarke's Scotland squads. Clarke, when naming this Scotland squad, did warn McCrorie that he would need to get more regular first-team football if he wanted to safeguard his place in the international set-up.

There was still time for another squad change before the team met up. Southampton's Che Adams pulled out with a knock and that opened the door for Hearts captain Lawrence Shankland to get back in.

Shankland said: 'I got the shout after the Motherwell game that I was going to be called up, which was great.'

Shankland had been left out of the last squad, so he could concentrate on recapturing his club form, which he had. Hence, the recall.

Hearts manager and former Scotland coach Stevie Naismith confirmed: 'The manager had spoken to Shanks the previous month. That is the time when you want players to be honest. They can quite easily say: "No, I am good," when the gaffer is asking him how he is feeling. When we knew he wasn't going away with Scotland we decided to give him a good break. He hadn't really had one. He also came back early in the summer [to Hearts for pre-season] so he could really be part of things, so he probably was running a bit on empty. That was shown in his early performances. Since the break, he has kicked on and been really good. His performances had been excellent and he was scoring goals. He probably came into this camp disappointed that he hadn't been selected initially, but very quickly we knew he was going to be involved. From then, it was up to Shanks to take his opportunity.'

There was also to be a change to Clarke's backroom team. Naismith pulled out initially as he was waiting for Hearts to decide whether or not he was going to get their top job at Tynecastle on a permanent basis. Clarke turned to his former West Bromwich Albion midfielder James Morrison. The former Scottish international came in to fill that void in the short term and was to be appointed permanently when Naismith's deal at Hearts was eventually rubber-stamped.

The SFA agreed to send their team out to Turkey to acclimatise before the trip to Georgia.

Shankland said: 'I think they [the SFA] anticipated needing points from the last two games and this was a little booster ahead of those games. I don't think anyone expected us to have qualified with two games still to play. The Turkey trip got us together and it was quite chilled and relaxed.'

Georgia is a country that has given the Tartan Army genuine nightmares and has never been a happy hunting ground. Alex McLeish can vouch for that in his first spell as national boss. Scotland were right in the running for the 2008 finals until they came up against an inspired 17-year-old keeper in Giorgi Makaridze. He kept a clean sheet and goals from Levan Mchedlidze and David Siradze saw the Scots shocked. It left their final hopes hanging by a thread and that was cruelly cut as the Italians went on to beat Scotland at Hampden.

Seven years later it was another former Aberdeen player who

was in charge of Scotland, in Gordon Strachan, who suffered at the hands of Georgia. Scotland were already playing catch-up to Germany and Poland and the 1-0 defeat in Tbilisi all but extinguished those qualifying hopes. The Scottish nation had to wait another six years until Clarke finally got them back to the European Championship finals.

Scotland could travel to the Boris Paichadze Dinamo Arena in Tbilisi knowing the heat was off in terms of qualification, although when Clarke is in charge the pressure always remains on.

The game saw Clarke make a few changes. Zander Clark and Liam Kelly had shared the goalkeeping duties in France, but it was the Hearts keeper who got the nod to make his competitive debut.

Clark recalled: 'It was weird. Kels [Liam Kelly] and I spoke about it after the France game. You get nerves. I wasn't overly nervous though because it is what we train to do. You have that thought that it is not just a fan base but a whole nation you are representing so there is that wee bit extra pressure there. I have to say I loved every minute of it though.'

Hearts boss Stevie Naismith knew it was a big thing for his No. 1, who had grabbed his Hearts opportunity with both hands after Craig Gordon's injury.

Naismith acknowledged: 'It was great for Zander getting the start. That was the one decision that everyone was looking at before the game with both Zander and Liam having played a half in the friendly against France. It was great for Zander and us that he got the shout.'

Clark at 31 years and 143 days was the oldest goalkeeper to make his debut for Scotland since Henry Smith back in February 1988.

Boss Clarke also switched away from the back three that the qualification had been built on. He went for a 4-3-3 formation.

There was no doubt he was looking to work on plans B, C, D and probably E, knowing the national coach, with a big summer of football ahead.

Taylor came in at left back, Nathan Patterson on the opposite side, Scott McKenna and Ryan Porteous were the centre halves. Scott McTominay, Callum McGregor and Billy Gilmour made up the midfield with Ryan Christie and John McGinn playing off the sides of Lyndon Dykes.

The pitch was heavily watered before the game, although it was never going to be as wet as Hampden when the two teams met earlier in this campaign. Georgia were determined not to go under again.

It wasn't to be the perfect start for Clark as he had to pick the ball out of the net in the 17th minute and there was very little he could do about it. Otar Kakabadze put in a low cross and Khvicha Kvaratskhelia slid in first to net at the front post.

Spain, at the same time, were taking care of Cyprus and so top spot was slowly slipping from the Scots. The best they could muster in a slow first half was a Lyndon Dykes header that he nodded wide.

Scotland weren't at it but McTominay dismissed that it had anything to do with complacency or a feeling in that camp that the job was done. We all know Clarke and his backroom team wouldn't tolerate that.

McTominay, speaking to Viaplay Sports, said: 'The message since we have been away has been more of a firm talking-to in terms of we need to wake up again. We had lost three games in a row from England, Spain and France. Now we need to get to the pitch and to get back to winning football games. That was part of the message going into the game, if we could play well and hopefully win the game, but most definitely not to lose it.'

Clarke wasn't happy with what he had seen either and decided to make changes. Gilmour and Christie made way for Kenny McLean and Lewis Ferguson at the interval.

It worked because within four minutes Scotland had drawn level and McLean was the creator. He set up McTominay who let fly from the edge of the box and smashed a shot through a defender's legs and past keeper Giorgi Mamardashvili. It saw the Manchester United star take his impressive goal tally to seven for the campaign. It also matched the recent Scotland goal hauls of John McGinn and Steven Fletcher. McTominay's goals had been significant in the campaign and in the Euro 2024 qualifiers only Harry Kane, Kylian Mbappé, Cristiano Ronaldo and Romelu Lukaku would score more. Not bad for a midfielder and one who started the campaign on the bench!

The delighted McTominay, speaking to Viaplay Sports, said: 'I was quite fortunate. I maybe should have had one when John McGinn cut it back. I am just trying to get into areas and to keep trying to score goals and doing my best.'

Scotland would have expected to kick on, but seven minutes later Georgia went ahead again. Kvaratskhelia cut inside from the left and fired in a shot beyond a couple of defenders and the despairing dive of Clark.

Scotland had to pick themselves up again. Dykes got his header on a corner but Mamardashvili made a good stop.

Georgia then did everything in their power to run down the clock, feigning injury to try and hold on to what they had, much to the disgust and frustration of the white-shirted Scots. The antics from the stands weren't much better as Scotland striker Dykes was targeted by a laser pen.

McTominay, speaking to Viaplay Sports, didn't mince his words. He said: 'Every game at this level is big and they have some really, really good footballers. The way they were acting on the pitch in terms of provoking the referee and us, as players – it is not the way you should go. Anyway, that is football and the way it goes. We have to keep our heads but it is difficult. It is hard. They should do something about it, people pretending they are injured when they are not and stuff like that. It is a difficult one to call but rolling around, crying like babies all afternoon is not football. For us, we just wanted to get on with the game and play. We did our best to try and win the game but on the other side they were provoking the referee a lot. You learn a lot. Keeping your head, picking the right passes and showing a bit more patience around their box, trying to move them around.'

Clarke's side continued to push the Georgians back as they went for an equaliser while the manager decided to mix up his team again. Anthony Ralston, on his 25th birthday, came on for Patterson and Stuart Armstrong replaced Taylor, while Shankland replaced Dykes in the 85th minute.

Shankland said: 'I had been on the bench and we had pinned Georgia in. We had a lot of pressure in and around their box and I was itching to get on with some of the areas we were getting into. You could see how things were developing and it would maybe suit me. I got the shout. The gaffer never really said anything apart from good luck. I knew what I needed to do. I was close to a couple of balls and I had the feeling I might get on to something.'

Scotland kept hammering away. Seven minutes of added time went up on the board but the visitors only needed three of them. Armstrong curled in a cross from the left and fellow replacement Shankland managed to get his head on it and to beat Mamardashvili.

'Stuart put in a great ball at the end and I managed to put my head on it,' the Scotland hero recalled: 'It was an important goal in the end because we didn't want to go losing four games on the bounce. My goal put an end to that. Personally, it was a good moment for me because I had been a bit of a bit-part player through the years and you want to prove your worth to the manager and the boys that you can do something significant in this group stage and that was my moment. The manager laughed and gave me a smile – knowing the gaffer, that might have been a bit of approval from him.'

Shankland had tried to play down his intervention after the game but his club manager was having none of it.

'It was great for Shanks to get his goal,' Naismith proudly claimed. 'I watched Shanks's interview after it and he did himself something of a disservice by saying he was fortunate to be there and get on the end of it. I mean his movement is brilliant and he puts himself in a position where he is in full control, the defender doesn't know where he is. He is in a position where Shanks can get in front or in behind his marker. When the ball comes in like that then you are not going to get any better in that position.'

Many people feel Shankland is the most natural goalscorer that Scotland has and that is something Naismith agrees with.

The Hearts manager said: 'I would say he is the best finisher we have. The way the squad is, there is not one striker that is similar to the other. Che is not like Shanks, Che is not like Dykes and Jacob is a different type of striker again. That is why when Shanks goes away there is a chance he could be involved, depending on how each game unfolds. If Scotland are winning and looking to see the game out then Shanks might not go on, but when you need a goal then there is a chance he will be involved because there is not a better goalscorer in that squad than him. I know Shanks is confident if he gets a chance he will take it and that is what he did in Georgia.'

McTominay knew Scotland hadn't been at their best and praised the subs for lifting the levels and giving the team a well-earned jab. 'We have had some really good nights and there will be other nights where we don't play so well,' McTominay, on

Viaplay Sports, acknowledged. 'It is important on these nights that we stick together, don't lose the game and we definitely try to win. The subs made a big difference. That is what the manager demands whenever you come on the pitch. You show something and bring something additional to the team. All the guys who came on made a big impact and a brilliant goal from Shanks.'

It was enough for the Scots to stop any potential rot and to salvage their first point in Georgia. It also meant that Clarke had hit the big 50 with an impressive record of 24 wins, 11 draws and just 15 defeats.

Naismith said: 'It is a brilliant achievement. Look at his record and his win ratio. I am delighted for Steve. There will be loads of pundits and ex-pros out there with egg on their face now. I remember, way back at the start, they weren't giving Steve enough time. They quickly had the opinions set, it wasn't going to work. One of my first camps we got beat quite heavily and there was a bit of backlash from it. Now some of these same pundits are applauding him for how good he has been. It is something I am sure the gaffer would have a nice wee smile on his face over now.'

Chapter 29

THE QUALIFICATION PARTY

WHEN the fixtures for Group A were announced, it looked like Scotland v Norway at Hampden on the final day was going to be a big one. Both countries were expected to slug it out for second spot behind favourites Spain. That was in theory, but in practice things turned out very differently. The game was effectively a dead rubber, albeit Scotland could still have topped the section but that was unlikely. It would have required a home win and Spain to lose at home to Georgia, with the latter always looking like something of a long shot.

The bottom line was that Scotland had done their job and wrapped up second spot and Euro 2024 qualification after Spain had beaten Norway. It meant the Georgia and Norway games were pretty meaningless, especially with the Spaniards back on form and on a relentless charge towards Germany.

Ryan Christie said: 'It was good. It was a bit strange going into it because probably at the start of the group we'd looked at this game as the one it would come down to for qualifying. But then, to be over the line with two games to go made it a bit strange going into it. It was good being able to take everything all in having known we had already qualified, although we still wanted to finish off with a win against Norway. It's 100 per cent one of the happiest times of my life. When I was growing up I hoped to play for my country. I never thought I'd get the chance to represent my country at a Euros. I did that at Euro 2020. Hopefully I'll get to do it again in 2024. To do that is one of the biggest achievements in football and I certainly won't be taking anything for granted.'

Norway had pretty much failed to recover from Scotland's dramatic late win in Oslo six months earlier. Clarke's side had stolen victory from the jaws of defeat.

Norway and Brentford defender Kris Ajer conceded: 'Yes, that was the killer. We played well up to the crazy two goals [at the end]. That was obviously disappointing.'

Steve Clarke still wanted to win the final game. His team had stopped the rot of three losses with a draw in Georgia and was looking to sign off the campaign in style with another win.

Hampden was already sold out and it was billed as Scotland's Euro 2024 qualifying party. It was the first time Clarke and his squad had been back at Hampden since they had sealed their qualification. It was a chance for their adoring Scottish public to go and show their appreciation to the class of 2023. They certainly did that on a dark and wet November night.

Clarke mixed his squad up again from the Georgia game. Zander Clark kept the No. 1 spot and fulfilled a lifelong ambition. He was no stranger to Hampden as he had lifted both domestic cups there with St Johnstone, but that was during Covid. This was for his country and in front of a capacity crowd. It helped that he had a few friendly faces there with his wife and a lot of his friends in the stands.

The Hearts keeper said: 'To be involved in it is a huge honour, but to get minutes in games makes it even more special. When we met up we knew Angus [Gunn] wasn't going to be here and it was a case of Liam Kelly, Robby McCrorie and myself training as hard as we could to put ourselves in the manager's thoughts. I would have been delighted with just the 45 minutes in Lille, but then to go on and play two 90 minutes after that was special. As a kid, you want to go and represent your country. I did that in France and Georgia and doing it in front of the home support makes it that bit more special. These are the ones you dream of in front of a sold-out Hampden. It was a proud moment.'

Scotland boss Clarke sprung a surprise at the top end of the park as he gave Luton Town striker Jacob Brown his first start. He had made the move from Stoke City to the English Premier League new boys that summer.

Brown said: 'It was a great feeling. I got goosebumps when I was walking out; the atmosphere was really good. It was something I've obviously been waiting a long time for, so I'm just happy for it to finally come. It meant a lot for me and I think for all the players and staff as well, having already qualified, we all wanted to end on a high.'

It has been a long, patient wait for Brown. He added: 'My first camp was around this time two years ago, and obviously, everyone wants to come and start. I think you've just got to be patient, bide your time and keep working hard, and luckily I got the chance against Norway. That was my eighth appearance, but my first start, so it was good.'

The teams walked out to fireworks and a big tifo that ran from behind both goals along the North Stand, with German flags on both sides and a large sky blue banner which read: We'll be coming. The Tartan Army's very own trademark anthem.

'Flower of Scotland' was then played by a piper before he stopped for the second verse and let the Hampden crowd take over for their own spine-tingling rendition. It was powerful stuff.

Norway had travelled without their star turns Erling Haaland and Martin Ødegaard, but the visitors were determined to sign off a disappointing Euro 2024 campaign on a high. It took them just three minutes to go in front. They got lucky as Julian Ryerson's cross came back off the back of Jørgen Strand Larsen and fell to Aron Dønnum, who had been afforded too much time and space to get his shot away as it deflected off Nathan Patterson and flew into the net.

Dønnum's joy was relatively short-lived. He went from villain to hero for Scotland. Callum McGregor cracked in a shot and the Norwegian striker blocked it with his hand inside the area. Referee Horațiu Feșnic immediately pointed to the spot. The VAR check backed up Feșnic's initial call and the penalty was awarded. Stand-in captain John McGinn sent Egil Selvik the wrong way from the spot in the 13th minute. He ran off to celebrate with his trademark glasses celebration with 'We've Got McGinn, Super John McGinn' bellowing out from the jubilant home stands. It was McGinn's 18th goal and took him joint sixth in Scotland's all-time scorers chart, level with Kenny Miller.

This game ebbed and flowed from end to end and Norway went ahead again. Ryerson's cross came off McGregor and wrong-footed Clark, allowing Larsen to squeeze the ball over him in the 20th minute. Both teams went at it toe to toe although Norway gave Scotland another big helping hand. Scott McTominay's corner was flicked on by Kenny McLean and it came off Leo Østigård and dropped into the Norwegian net.

It meant the sides went in level and maintained the feel-good factor. The Scotland support were treated to some of the many highlights of the Euro 2024 qualifying campaign over the big screens at the interval. It just added to the occasion and fired up the crowd ahead of the second period.

It looked like another big moment had been produced when Scotland went ahead just before the hour. Stuart Armstrong got away from a defender and played it into John McGinn, who drove into the box and then intelligently pulled the ball back for

Armstrong to fire in a low shot that went through a defender's legs before it nestled in low at the near post. That sparked the Scotland support with chants of: 'Germany, we are the famous Tartan Army and we are off to Germany.'

Clarke made a number of changes as Lewis Ferguson, Lyndon Dykes and Ryan Christie came on for McLean, Brown and Armstrong, while the injured McGinn made way for Ryan Jack.

It looked like Scotland would see out the win, but Norway had other ideas and it was down to Mohamed Elyounoussi, who was no stranger to Glasgow. He had two loan spells at Celtic and he spoiled the party with a late header four minutes from time. Lawrence Shankland came on for McGregor in the final minutes but didn't have enough time to grab another late goal.

Shankland revealed: 'Liam Cooper was ready to go on and the gaffer changed it within seconds because we needed a goal. It was great to get on, get another cap and to have played a little part of the night before we got involved in the celebrations.'

Clark had let in five goals in his two competitive games but still managed to boast an unbeaten run in competitive games.

He stated: '[It was] Still a qualifier and we were disappointed that we couldn't see it out for the win. The job was done and thankfully there wasn't too much riding on it. It is a positive and good not to lose either game.'

By the time the final whistle had gone, the Scotland subs and bench already had T-shirts on which read: 'We're off to Germany'. The Hampden PA was keen to get the party started and played all the Hampden classics from 'Yes Sir, I Can Boogie' to 'Freed From Desire'.

Steve Clarke and his Scotland players took a well-deserved lap of honour around the Hampden pitch, soaking up the acclaim, taking their bows and having celebratory snaps taken by the waiting press photographers. It was a moment the entire nation wanted to milk and rightly so. There was no Covid to curtail the celebrations.

Christie had been part of both Euro qualifying celebrations. The first one in Serbia he had been emotionally reduced to tears on national television, in a Covid bubble with no fans. This time around the supporters were there to savour Scotland's big moment.

Christie said: 'This was definitely better [than Serbia]. That was a strange night. I'm not as emotional tonight but you'll get me going! I've grown up a little bit. I'm used to it now! It's important to enjoy these moments when they come along. Over the last couple of generations it's not happened much. So when it does happen you need to enjoy it, especially with how close this squad is. Everyone enjoys it together, the whole staff and everybody. Credit to the manager for instilling that feeling. It's definitely played a massive part in getting us where we are [Euro 2024].'

It had been six years since Christie had made his Scotland debut and it was very much changed days. The Hampden Roar was back with a vengeance and the Tartan Army was almost going hoarse with the amount of big nights they were getting to savour under Clarke and his team of heroes.

'The feeling between now and then is a bit chalk and cheese,' the former Inverness and Celtic star acknowledged. 'You go into these games full of confidence. You feel like you've got the whole of Hampden at your back. It's a special time to be part of this squad and fingers crossed I get to go to these Euros and see all the Scotland fans cheer us on in Germany. Everybody is buzzing for it already. We have to try and put it on the back burner and not think about it. There's a break before we meet up in March and then the preparations start for Germany. I'm pretty sure Scotland fans will travel in their numbers and take over certain parts of Germany so I can't wait.'

Lyndon Dykes had firmly established himself as a Hampden favourite and this was another big night.

'To play at Hampden in front of a sold-out Scotland support is just amazing,' Dykes said. 'We had some big nights in the Euro 2024 qualifying campaign both home and away. We didn't get the win we wanted but the celebrations at the end were great. The manager, staff, players and fans had all been on some journey in this qualifying campaign. It was just great for everybody to share that moment together. Nights like that will live with you forever.'

It ended up as very much a family affair as Clarke got his players, staff and their nearest and dearest together for a celebration back at the team hotel in Glasgow city centre.

Shankland said: 'We had a wee get-together. All the players and backroom team and our families, which was good. We had a meal and a few drinks and we enjoyed the night and the achievement of what the team had done. It was good to have our families there because we don't see them a lot during the camps and so it is important to enjoy these moments with those closest to you.'

Chapter 30

CLARKE'S INNER CIRCLE

STEVE Clarke is a man who has worked with some of the biggest names in the game in his long and distinguished coaching and managerial career in England. He has built up dozens of relationships and trust through his many spells at different clubs and he was able to use that when he stepped up to become Scotland manager in 2019.

It was no real surprise to see him make Alex Dyer his first appointment. The Englishman came in as one of his assistant head coaches. He has worked previously with Clarke at West Ham United and he turned to him to be his assistant when he landed the Kilmarnock manager's job.

Dyer, a former Charlton Athletic and Huddersfield Town defender, had trained as a PE teacher before he went into coaching at West Ham United. He went on to have assistant manager spells at Charlton and Huddersfield before he had a stint in management with Welling United. He had been working as first-team coach with National League South side Whitehawk when Clarke offered him a route back to full-time football with Killie.

Dyer came north and Clarke and the Rugby Park players would be first to admit that the pair together were a big part of their success that led to their manager becoming the Scotland national coach. They worked well together and so it made sense to take that partnership and see if it worked at the top level. Dyer came in on a part-time basis while continuing his role as assistant manager with Kilmarnock.

Dyer said: 'Steve has a lot of strengths as a man, a coach and a manager. Trust and loyalty are definitely big things for him in all walks of life. Everyone talks about him being a top coach or manager, but he is also a top human being and that is why people want to do so well for him.'

Clarke had also turned to another coach he had worked with in his time at Reading, Steven Reid. He was slightly younger than both Clarke and Dyer and would be more of a link to the Scotland players. Reid also had international experience thanks to his 23 caps and a World Cup visit with the Republic of Ireland. He was a highly rated coach. He had spells at Crystal Palace and AFC Wimbledon but was out of work after leaving his role as assistant after caretaker Jimmy Shan had failed to land the West Bromwich Albion job on a permanent basis. So the timing was right for Clarke to make his move.

The final piece of that initial jigsaw was goalkeeping coach Stevie Woods. He was the goalkeeping coach at Celtic and had also held the position under Clarke's predecessor, Alex McLeish. Clarke spoke with Woods and convinced him to remain as part of the Scotland set-up.

Quite simply, the Scotland boss knew it was his job and that of his staff to make the Scotland players and team better. He also wanted to improve himself and his coaches to continue their education and development. Both Dyer and Reid were well regarded in their respective fields, but they were also highly ambitious and that was another thing that attracted them to Clarke.

Subsequently, Clarke's own success at Kilmarnock inadvertently cost him assistant coach Dyer. The Rugby Park board had turned to Italian Angelo Alessio to try and maintain their lofty fortunes after Clarke's departure. It turned out to be an absolute disaster and he lasted just seven months before he was replaced. The Kilmarnock board felt they needed a safe pair of hands, somebody who knew the club and could get them back on the same lines that had brought success under Clarke.

The man they turned to was their assistant Dyer. He had the backing of the Kilmarnock squad and it meant that at the end of the Euro 2020 qualifying campaign that Dyer stepped down as Scotland assistant coach to fully focus on Killie. The Englishman left knowing he owed a debt of gratitude to the Scotland manager.

Dyer said: 'The gaffer knew I wanted to be a manager in my own right. I had never hidden that fact and so when I got the chance at Kilmarnock it was one I couldn't turn down. It was a good club, one where I was working and had done so well under Steve. The gaffer understood my situation and in fairness he told me I should take the job because he felt it was a good fit for me and I could do well there. That was good to hear. It was a great, great time for me working under Steve. I learned so much. From tactics and organisation to the way he handled himself with the players. The respect he gave and got. We had three great years or so working with him and that will always keep me in good stead.'

It left a major void in the Scotland backroom team. The manager once again delved into the Clarke archive. He turned to Englishman John Carver. Another man who had worked with him in his time at Newcastle United under Ruud Gullit. Carver had been taken up from the Newcastle academy to the first team during their time together. It was there that Clarke and Carver's professional and personal relationship blossomed, living in neighbouring villages.

Clarke even left Newcastle to return to Chelsea to help ensure Carver remained part of the St James' Park coaching set-up. They maintained their friendship as both their careers moved in different directions.

Carver was already doing some scouting for Clarke and the SFA before his appointment, watching games in the Championship and English Premier League.

The Englishman had a wealth of coaching experience. He had spells at Leeds United and Luton Town before he went into management in his own right with Major League Soccer side Toronto. Carver returned to become assistant at Plymouth Argyle and first-team coach at Sheffield United before he returned to coach at Newcastle again. He went out again on his own as head coach of Cypriot club Omonia Nicosia before Clarke offered him the Scotland gig.

Carver came in for the 2020–21 Nations League campaign, kicking off against Israel and the Czech Republic in the September 2020 international window.

Dyer said: 'When I left, Steven Reid stepped up and John Carver came in. John is a good coach and a good person. The gaffer knew him for a long time and it was a perfect match. They worked together previously but they are a good match and you can see that with the way they have taken the team on to another level again.'

The team of Clarke, Carver and Reid took Scotland through a Nations League campaign, to Euro 2020 and kicked off the start of the 2022 World Cup qualifiers. It was after the delayed Euro 2020 finals that there was another changing of the guard. Reid had taken up a first-team coaching role at Nottingham Forest and Woods was also stretched, juggling the non-stop commitments of Celtic's domestic and European campaigns along with Scotland. Both stepped down after the finals and Clarke was again charged with revamping his backroom team.

Clarke, in an SFA statement, said: 'I would like to thank Steven Reid and Stevie Woods for their contributions to the national team, not only during the summer but especially in my early months in the job, when we had some tough times and results, but they were always there to support me. I appreciate how demanding it is to have a club job and still find time and enthusiasm to travel with the national team in the international breaks. They both have big seasons ahead for their respective clubs and I wish them well for the future.'

Clarke signed his new contract after Euro 2020 which would take him into the World Cup qualifiers and the Euro 2024 qualifying campaign. He brought in two replacements who had international experience.

Austin MacPhee had been a coach with the Northern Irish national team. He came into Clarke's team as a coach, analyst and set-piece specialist. The Kirkcaldy-born coach also held a club position at Aston Villa. MacPhee had previously been assistant coach at Cowdenbeath, St Mirren, Hearts and Midtjylland.

Former England and Rangers No. 1 Chris Woods came in to replace his namesake. He had been goalkeeping coach at Everton, Manchester United and West Ham United, while he had also held the same position for the United States international team.

Clarke added: 'Austin has major tournament experience with Northern Ireland and is now a respected set-piece coach in England's Premier League. He is a specialist coach and his approach to coaching on the field and use of data off it will be an asset to the existing backroom staff. Chris brings a wealth of experience both as a top-class international goalkeeper and as a respected goalkeeping coach in the English Premier League and the United States. I am sure our goalkeepers will enjoy working with Chris and benefit from the knowledge he has accumulated throughout his career.'

MacPhee's Scotland career had to be delayed as a positive Covid test meant he had to sit out of his first gathering. It opened the door for Clarke to bring in one of his former Scotland players, in Steven Naismith. He had been coaching at Hearts since he retired that summer and was brought in for the World Cup qualifying triple-header against Denmark, Moldova and Austria.

Naismith, who was still cutting his coaching teeth, recalled: 'I turned up for my first camp because Austin MacPhee had Covid. I had a relationship with the manager. I had played under him for Scotland and he had also tried to sign me a couple of times when he was in club management. I was going in there as a coach for the first time but I wasn't sure how I was going to play it. We had a good relationship, but when you are part of the manager's inner circle, I was like: do I just sit there quietly, pick up the bibs and balls and do whatever he wants me to do? Very quickly because of my personality I thought I needed to say what I think in the meetings. We started to look over the games and preparations for what we were going to do and come up against. I decided that I was going to be honest and come out and say what I thought. I think he liked that. The credit, though, must go to the gaffer for creating an environment for us to feel comfortable enough to do that.'

Clarke might be the boss, but he gives everyone their place and doesn't want yes men to agree with his every move.

Naismith added: 'It is the biggest learning experience I have had as a coach and now as a manager. I learned so many things. A lot of things I saw the manager do or I asked him about them. The biggest thing for me is the dynamic within his coaching team. Everybody, and I mean everybody, gets their opinion. The manager wants to listen to people's points of view. He takes it all on board and then he will use them, put them into the mix and then decide what he feels is best.'

The former Rangers and Everton striker was only meant to be with Scotland for the one camp but he made a real impression under Clarke, who made the move a more permanent one, alongside MacPhee and Carver.

Naismith said: 'Originally, I was only in for the first camp, but after it he said he would like me to continue for the duration. It ended up working well. When I was there as a player we had a lot of good conversations. It showed football-wise we were maybe on the same wavelength. What was fortunate for me was that I wasn't long out of the squad as a player. I had good relationships with the players and the manager saw the value in that. I had good honest chats with players, to see how they were. I would pass on some of my experiences, especially to the guys who come away thinking they are going to play and they don't. It is about resetting. Like Lawrence Shankland against Georgia! Be ready because you don't know when you are going to get that opportunity. It is about building relationships and as things grow, the gaffer gives you a bit of leeway to do a bit of coaching and it goes from there. I can't speak highly enough of him and I learned so much.'

It was just as well because Clarke puts demands on his coaching staff and is always challenging them and looking at ways to make his team stronger – on and off the park.

Naismith explained: 'I remember one of the early squads, he put up a team on the board and left two players out. He then asked me to fill in the gaps and put in the other two players. Looking back now, it was probably a bit of a test to see if my mindset was similar to where Steve was. The two players I picked were thankfully the two who made up his starting XI the next day. That maybe gave me a bit of credit going forward, knowing we were on a similar wavelength. These are the types of things that make him so good. As a member of his staff, you feel valued and appreciated, knowing he also wants your input and opinions at the right moments. The manager made it clear he wants and needs that as part of his process. When we were reviewing anything, a camp or a position, he is happy for you to speak your mind and to tell him what you think, good or bad. He wants to know, good or bad, because he wants to get better. Over the period, he has shown that.'

In March 2023, Carver criticised Scotland's training base at the Oriam in Edinburgh. It grabbed more than a few headlines and a lot of time on the airwaves. Clarke tried to defuse the comments but it was clear that the training camp was an issue and had been a major topic of discussion for the Scotland boss and his team. The Scotland manager had publicly made it clear that he would eventually like the SFA to have its own top-level facility or training base, like England have with St George's Park. It was no surprise to see Scotland quit Oriam and set up base in Glasgow, using Queen's Park's rebuilt Lesser Hampden as their training base for a lot of the Euro 2024 qualifiers. Carver had publicly lit the fuse for Clarke on that front.

Naismith believes Carver and the Scotland manager are good foils for each other. 'You need to give a real acknowledgement to JC as well,' Naismith claimed. 'He is his right-hand man. Their relationship and understanding of each other is incredible. It is a great team that works really well.'

Carver has remained the one constant in Clarke's most recent backroom team. Naismith stepped down at the start of the Euro 2024 qualifying campaign. He was the next of Clarke's assistant coaches to land a manager's job in his own right. Naismith had been the interim boss at Hearts but was handed it on a permanent basis in June 2023.

He insisted it was a tough call to walk away from Scotland, knowing they were on the verge of something special.

Naismith said: 'It is one of the hardest decisions I have had to make, playing or as a coach. I knew how well we had started the qualifying campaign and I really believed we would go to the Euros. I am giving up this chance of going to the Euros and being part of an unbelievable campaign but I was taking up a massive, massive job at Hearts. One of the top jobs in Scottish football. I leaned on the manager a lot when I was put in interim charge at Hearts. I didn't know whether I was going to get the job or not. Things overlapped because I was meant to go away with Scotland for their training camp but I was still waiting to see what was going to happen at Hearts. I was a bit in limbo and Steve likes to have his plans in place and ready to go, but he was really understanding, spoke to me about it a lot and gave me good pointers. It was difficult but it is credit to the man, he made it as easy as it could be for me to make my decision. We still speak quite regularly.'

Naismith was replaced by another former Scotland cap, James Morrison. Clarke knew him from their time together at West Bromwich Albion, where he was coaching. It was all part of Clarke's master plan to keep bringing through top, young Scottish coaches.

Naismith said: 'The manager is big on that to give boys opportunities. His path, where he has been and the hard work he has done to start with as a coach – he knows how hard it could be. He feels it is important to give people an opportunity, which I was lucky enough to be rewarded with – at such a great level with the international squad and I have now gone into frontline management myself. It is great because Steve has done that to give young Scottish coaches the best opportunities they can possibly get to be the best they can be. If we can have a fraction of the success that the gaffer has had then we will have a lot of top, top future Scottish managers and coaches. He has a real passion for that, but he is more interested in the long term than short-term gains. He wants to do something that lasts.'

Charlie Adam, who is now a manager in his own right at Fleetwood Town after coaching at Burnley, is one who hopes to benefit from Clarke's experience and know-how.

Adam said: 'In the future, I would love to go and see how his Scotland camps operate. Just to see how he has evolved and moulded into a top international manager. Listening and watching people like that can only help you on your own journey, learning from the best. Yes, he has some very good players – but you still need to get them playing in the right way and winning games. Steve Clarke has done that and in some style.'

Chapter 31

SOLVING THE TACTICAL PUZZLE

WHEN Steve Clarke took over the Scotland job he had a core of experienced players. However, it is fair to say he didn't exactly have strength in depth across his squad. There were glaring deficiencies and shortcomings. Like every Scotland manager before him, it was a case of getting everything out of what you have. Sometimes it is about coming up with tactics or game plans that bring the best out of your team or players individually. It is exactly what the job had entailed for Clarke at Kilmarnock, Reading and West Bromwich Albion.

Clarke had also worked at the top with the likes of Chelsea, Liverpool, West Ham United and Newcastle United. As a coach and manager, he had worked at all levels. He has a standing in the game that commands respect.

'You can see that in abundance,' former Scotland defender Declan Gallagher said. 'The way he talks and the presence he has about the place. You see in football a lot these days that the players think they have got more power, but when you look at Steve Clarke and his aura and the way he is, you can see he gets total respect from every player and person in the camp. Everyone gives him massive respect because everybody can see he is a top manager and why he did great things at Kilmarnock and going back in all his coaching roles and managerial roles from Newcastle United and Chelsea. The gaffer has brought it all together and shown he can do it at the top level.'

That respect buys you time but you have to be able to back it up on the training pitch and with results on the park. Clarke inherited a team that had arguably two world-class left backs in Liverpool's Andy Robertson and Celtic's Kieran Tierney. It was a case of how do you get them both into a Scotland team? Clarke had a bit of time to come up with a solution as Tierney, who had left Celtic to seal a big money move to Arsenal, missed his opening European 2020 Championship qualifiers because of injury.

The first team Clarke went with was in a 4-3-3 formation for the Euro qualifier with Cyprus back in June 2019. David Marshall had a defence of Stephen O'Donnell, Charlie Mulgrew, Scott McKenna and Andy Robertson in front of him. The midfield was John McGinn, Kenny McLean and Callum McGregor while the front three was Ryan Fraser and James Forrest flanking Eamonn Brophy. Yet it took a tactical switch, with sub Oliver Burke coming on to score the only goal.

Clarke knew his side had to come out and take the game to Cyprus, especially at Hampden. The next run of games were a different proposition altogether, with Belgium and Russia both home and away. It was a case of tinkering and working out tactics on the job. There were some heavy defeats. He went with a back four with various formations in front of that. A 4-4-1-1 formation was tried in the away defeat in Belgium and then a 4-3-3 in the narrow Hampden loss to the Russians. It was back to a more conservative starting 4-4-2 in the home mauling from Belgium and then it was switched to a 4-2-3-1 for the trip to Russia, but that also ended up being a sore one against two quality sides. Clarke was at a real low point as national boss around that time.

He was still finding his feet internationally but would have been infuriated that he hadn't laid a glove on Belgium or Russia. Clarke had made a name for himself by regularly upsetting the odds at Kilmarnock, getting big results against Celtic and Rangers.

Clarke stuck with the same 4-2-3-1 shape for the six-goal win over San Marino to show that it can work, albeit against much weaker opposition. It allowed hat-trick netting John McGinn to shine. Clarke finished off with the win in Cyprus with a 4-4-1-1 shape and went with a 4-2-3-1 to see off Kazakhstan.

The 2020 Nations League finally gave Clarke the headache he wanted, fitting Robertson and Arsenal's Tierney into the one team. Clarke went for a three-man defence for the first time as he threw a couple of curveballs in for the opening home game against Israel. Midfielder Scott McTominay was pushed back into the right of the central defence, Scott McKenna in the centre and Tierney on the left. James Forrest was the right wing back, with Andy Robertson on the left.

Ex-Scotland frontman Charlie Nicholas said: 'Everyone knew Scotland's problems before Steve came in, but it was a case of how was he going to solve them? He has solved the majority of them and shown why he has been at the top level in England because he is a bright, inventive coach. The job Steve has done has been remarkable. His team and players have continually improved because more and more of them are playing at a better and higher level in England. We've always had the top guys at Celtic and Rangers but that English Premier League exposure is massive in the modern game. Steve has fitted in Robertson and Tierney. He has put them both together and got the best out of them. He looked at the shape and made us hard to beat. I can go back to the late Craig Brown and 1998 when we were a good compact team. Steve has shown he also knows how to get the best out of the players he had at his disposal.'

That first selection also saw Ryan Jack and Callum McGregor as the midfield heartbeat with John McGinn and Ryan Christie looking to get forward to support Lyndon Dykes. The three-man defence remained in place for the Nations League and was the basis to get Scotland through the play-offs and at the Euro 2020 finals, showing that Robertson and Tierney can both be big players in the one Scotland team.

'People who say we can't play together have been proven wrong,' captain Robertson, speaking to the SFA's media team, stated: 'A lot is said about KT and me but we don't compete against each other. We don't make a big deal about it and we are just happy to play anywhere for the Scotland shirt. Now he is fully fit and flying at Arsenal. He has shown that in these three games and in the Serbia game I thought we linked up pretty well, down that left-hand side. When he goes, I sit, and he always gives us an option down that left-hand side. I always try to help him in defence and going forward.'

McTominay looked uneasy at times, especially in his early games, in defence, but Clarke continued to persist until he found a right-sided defender he could bring in and move McTominay forward into midfield, where he has gone on to shine as top scorer in the Euro 2024 qualifying campaign. He was also named Scotland's men's Player of the Year for 2023.

Former Scotland cap Billy Dodds acknowledged: 'It hasn't always been perfect. You look at Scott McTominay when he was right of a back three and now he is an attacking midfielder. Clarke has had to chip away to get a shape and structure. Now he is in a position where he has options all over the park. McTominay is now a first-pick midfielder and scoring goals for fun. He has become a massive player for Scotland.'

Stephen O'Donnell played a lot of the time at right back or right wing back at the start of Clarke's time. Winger Ryan Fraser was then employed there as a more attacking option until the emergence of Nathan Patterson and Aaron Hickey, who can play full back on either side.

Players are willing to play out of position for Clarke because it is for the benefit of the team. He also does his homework, sets it out in black and white and his players know what they are going into. Clarke has them prepared as best he can.

Fleetwood Town boss and former Scotland cap Charlie Adam said: 'You have to understand the whole game and Steve Clarke is an example of that. I don't think you can be a defensive or an attacking coach. You need to understand both sides, especially at the top level. Steve has an excellent knowledge of how the game should be played and how to problem solve and adapt to different scenarios his team finds itself in. Steve has played the game at the highest level. That helps as well. I always feel his personality and aura around the top players is really, really impressive. It is important how you handle the big players. When Steve was at Liverpool he wasn't one to tiptoe around them. If something was to be said then he would say it. That is a real strength because that is the only way you maintain top standards. Steve is strong in his beliefs and I was impressed with the way he treated everyone from the young players up to the top, top players.'

There have been tactical changes where Clarke has gone with one striker and two attacking midfielders and other times two centre forwards. The three-man defence has been the basis although Clarke moved away from that at the end of the Euro 2024 qualifying campaign to go back to a back four. He has previously said a four-man defence was his preference although Scotland haven't been as strong in terms of keeping clean sheets, but the emergence of Jack Hendry and Ryan Porteous, along with Scott McKenna, gives his defence more pace to play a higher line and a more forward press.

The middle of the park is where Clarke has real strength in depth. John McGinn is often the first name on the team sheet in terms of an attacking midfielder, while Callum McGregor and Scott McTominay's recent goalscoring surge makes them pretty much nailed on and then you have the likes of Billy Gilmour, Kenny McLean, Ryan Jack, Lewis Ferguson and Stuart Armstrong to come into the equation, whether he wants to play with two sitting midfielders, a flat four, diamond or a variation.

Clarke revealed he spoke to McTominay at the start of the Euro 2024 qualifying campaign and changed his position slightly. It is fair to say it worked and saw him hit the goal trail. He had been struggling at Manchester United and had looked to be on the way out, but Clarke believes Scotland was a trigger for him to spark his season into life at Old Trafford.

The Scotland striking options are pretty much Lyndon Dykes, Che Adams or Ryan Christie and beyond that you have the likes of Kevin Nisbet, Lawrence Shankland and Jacob Brown all vying for the sole or dual striking roles or if he decides to go for a three, which is more than likely to see Christie and McGinn down the sides of a central striker.

Clarke may not be blessed with some of the great striking options that Scotland teams of the past have had, but he does have forwards who leave everything on the pitch. Their work rate and commitment can never be questioned. They also play unselfish roles and get players from other areas to chip in, with McTominay in the last campaign and John McGinn before that. The Scotland boss openly concedes that his teams are structured for the strikers to take the brunt and to make space and goalscoring opportunities for the midfielders and defenders who are bursting forward.

Charlie Nicholas knows Clarke's Scotland sides have evolved and are becoming more dangerous going forward. He explained:

'Steve was gradually looking to be more creative and to bring better players in and to become a decent attacking side. In all honesty, he has done it without any top-class strikers, with what he has currently achieved. We have strikers who work hard and do a good job for the team, but you wouldn't class them as top-class strikers. That makes his achievements an even more remarkable story.'

Clarke is also not afraid to mix it up and to try something different. It keeps his own players and the opposition on their toes. His squad also has an adaptability where they can go out and take the game to the opposition or they can sit in and defend as they showed in the Nations League fixture away to Ukraine that saw them win their group. Clarke might know how to make his teams hard to beat, but is also mindful of the importance of maximising the transitions and being a threat on the counter-attack, as his team showed to devastating effect in the Euro 2024 qualifying win in Norway.

Naismith said: 'Tactically, he is very good and he is not scared to do things if he feels it is right or in the best interests of the team. Look at the Georgia game away. I don't think anyone would have expected Scotland to line up with a back four. Steve understands what is coming, where we are going and what the country might face this summer at Euro 2024. His understanding and knowledge of that is brilliant. That is what has got him his success. Most of the time he makes the right decision and that isn't easy.'

Adam knows that Clarke's eye for the finest detail sees him stand out. He also isn't scared to make changes when things aren't going their way, as was seen by the attacking switches that led to Scotland's dramatic Euro 2024 win in Norway.

The former Liverpool star claimed: 'The biggest surprise for me is that Steve has never been involved in bigger jobs, on his own, in his own right. He did well at West Bromwich Albion and did really well at Kilmarnock and got the Scotland job. Steve has had a lot of years coaching and as a No. 2, but when you sit down and look at what he has done in his own right he has done really, really well. You always knew the way he planned, he was so meticulous. His knowledge of the game is brilliant.'

Naismith is now in management himself. He is cutting his teeth and knows that you can't avoid mistakes. Clarke has made his own but Naismith believes he has learned from them and made himself a better manager and the Scotland team even more formidable.

Naismith said: 'We had such a good Euro 2024 campaign because he has learned from previous campaigns. He has looked at where we could do better and implemented it. Getting to two consecutive Euros hasn't been done for so long and will give him a lot of credit. There will be spells when it is difficult but I don't think he will get the same flak and heat that he got before. He has gained and earned that respect in his time as Scotland manager.'

Chapter 32

EURO 2024: WRITING NEW CHAPTERS

THE eyes of a nation looked and dreamed towards the Euro 2024 draw as soon as Steve Clarke's Scotland had sealed their qualification. It was made in Hamburg – one of Germany's host cities – on Saturday, 2 December 2023 in the Elbphilharmonie concert hall. It was a typical all glitz and glamour UEFA affair with some of the biggest international managers and powerbrokers in attendance. National boss Clarke, the SFA's chief executive Ian Maxwell and chairman Mike Mulraney were amongst the distinguished guests there to discover their fate.

As is always the case, legends of the game were drafted in to give the occasion the X factor. Italian goalkeeping phenomenon Gianluigi Buffon drew the Pot A teams, apart from Germany who automatically went into Group A as the tournament hosts.

Former Dutch midfielder Wesley Sneijder drew the teams from Pot B and Scotland's fate was left in the hands of ex-French cap Blaise Matuidi, who picked out the balls from Pot C. It didn't take him long to get his hands on Scotland. He pulled Clarke's side out first and they went into Group A alongside the already drawn top two seeds, Germany and Hungary.

They were then drawn as A2 in terms of what sequence the group games would be played. It was confirmed that Scotland would kick off the competition against Germany in Munich's Allianz Arena in the opening game. It brought an approving nod from Clarke watching in the auditorium. It mirrored France 98 where Craig Brown's side had famously been part of the World Cup curtain-raiser against Brazil.

It was then a case of waiting for the Pot D draw to see who would make up Group A. Rangers and Denmark legend Brian Laudrup was the man in control of that and drew out Switzerland to finalise Group A.

Clarke, speaking to the SFA's website team, gave his early reaction. He said: 'My first thought is that it is nice to have clarity. We know who we're going to face, we know the opposition and now we can start preparing. It will be nice to open the tournament, nice to get the first game and hopefully it will be a good match. We've got to make sure it's not about the occasion, that it's about the match. We look forward to it, it's an exciting draw, but I don't think it really mattered who we were going to get, it was always going to be exciting for us. We've also been drawn against two good teams. We will be competitive in the matches, I'm sure they will be competitive too. It's a good group – I think an evenly balanced group – and we look forward to it. The aim is to be competitive in every match, that's always the aim. Respect your opponent and be competitive.'

The dates of Scotland's games were also confirmed. The opener would be on 14 June in Bayern Munich's impressive Allianz Arena. Scotland would then travel to Cologne to play Switzerland on 19 June and head to Stuttgart to take on Hungary on 23 June.

There was a real excitement within the Scotland squad that they were not only going to the finals but they were also going to be part of the opening ceremony. The message was clear, though: they weren't going to Germany as a support act but to try and make history.

Striker Lyndon Dykes claimed: 'I think it is an interesting group. There are some good teams and a few wildcards in there. We have the opening game against Germany in Munich which will be very hostile and tough. Germany has been a solid team for a number of years and we know how hard that will be. We also have Hungary and Switzerland who we know have good creative players. They will both be dangerous and challenging opponents.

'It is not going to be easy but we have to be confident in what we have and we will go to Germany trying to qualify for the knockout stages. The players and staff all want to make history by getting out of the group for the first time. It is going to be tough and we will all need to chip in. The squad is our big strength and we have to make sure we turn up at Euro 2024. Going into tournament football you can't slip up at any point. We need to be solid throughout. We have learned that from our experience at Euro 2020.'

Callum McGregor got Scotland's only goal at the last Euros and Dykes is desperate to emulate him. The striker has been keeping his head down, hoping to ensure he is on that plane to Germany. It is a burning ambition to score for Scotland in a major finals, although he would put the team's success ahead of any personal glory.

Dykes said: 'It is a major tournament and I want to be playing in that. I am focused on my club football at Queens Park Rangers and we will see what happens come the finals. If I was to get selected and play it would be good to get a goal or two. The most important thing though is the team. As long as we progress that is the most important thing for me. I know what it would mean to everyone connected with the Scotland national team.'

The draw forced Scotland back to the drawing board when it came to friendlies for the March and pre-tournament inter-national windows. The SFA chief Maxwell confirmed a friendly with Switzerland had bitten the dust because they had been paired together in their Euro 2024 group. It meant a swift change of direction and the SFA confirmed March 2024 friendlies against the Netherlands and Northern Ireland. Scotland would travel to the Netherlands on 22 March and then host the Irish at Hampden four days later. Scotland went on to confirm the two final pieces of the jigsaw, with friendlies against Gibraltar at the Estadio Algarve in Portugal on 3 June before a Hampden Park send-off against Finland four days later.

The SFA already had rough plans and locations in place for the Euro 2024 final bases before the draw. It was just a case of nailing them down. Clarke settled on his team being in Garmisch-Partenkirchen, just south of Munich, ahead of the opening game.

A lot of the Tartan Army had already gambled on booking flights and accommodation when Scotland had been on the verge of qualifying. Hundreds had taken their chances before the draw and others would flood the travel websites when the Euro 2024 plans were down in black and white. Maxwell knows that tens of thousands are expected to travel to Germany, so supply was never going to meet demand in simple economic terms when it came to match-day tickets!

Dykes wants to make it a trip to remember for them all. He said: 'We know there are a lot of fans travelling and we want to try and make them happy. It was amazing to see the whole of Scotland buzzing for Euro 2020. We saw it on the bus on the way to Hampden and the flags from all the houses and just the general backing we got from the entire country. That is what football is all about and we want to do that all again. You look at all the team's experience. We made the last finals and although we didn't get the results we want to learn from it. We need to take that experience and use it to our advantage.'

Fellow Scotland star Ryan Christie knows the Tartan Army

will be, as it so often is, the team's 12th man. He said: 'Everyone loved getting to the Euros last time and we were just desperate to do it again. We know this time the Scotland support will be travelling in their numbers and we will have a big, big following in Germany. They are important and can play a big part for the team at the finals.'

Former assistant national coach Alex Dyer knows Germany, Switzerland and Hungary won't be relishing facing Clarke's Scotland. They have already shown that reputations count for nothing as Spain can justify from the Euro 2024 qualifiers.

Dyer claimed: 'Steve has been brilliant and I think this team has exceeded expectations especially in qualifying for Germany. They made it look easy at times. They worked hard home and away, especially in the first five games. You have to take your hat off to them all; as a group, they were outstanding. The players and Steve and his coaching staff's hard work has paid off and I am delighted for them. All the lads have bought into what Steve has put in place. There is a core of players that Steve knows he can rely on, but there have been a few new players who have come into the squad and added a bit more. They all know their roles and have carried out their jobs to perfection.'

Former international frontman Charlie Nicholas was part of the Scotland squad that qualified for the 1986 World Cup in Mexico. Sir Alex Ferguson's side never got out of their group after some cynical final game tactics from Uruguay. That campaign Scotland also faced Denmark and pushed West Germany all the way. Nicholas believes this time Clarke's side can go where no other Scotland side has dared to venture, predicting Scotland can finish in the top two.

'I don't think it is a bad draw,' Nicholas excitedly claimed. 'I look back to France 98 when we played Brazil in the opening game. Germany aren't the force they once were but they will still be a good team. I don't think Steve will sit in against Germany. He wants to have a go and that it is encouraging. I firmly believe we have a chance of finishing in the top two. If we can take something from Germany in the first game then I think we will be well positioned. I think we are maybe outside of the top two, as it stands just now, but we are good enough to muscle in there and there is also the added possibility that we could also qualify as one of the best third-placed teams. We have done the hard work in qualifying. Sometimes as a nation we can feel a bit nervous but I believe Steve can get us going at Euro 2024. I don't think this team ever feels inferior but they have shown that on their day they can compete with the top teams in Europe.'

Legend Michael Ballack may have dismissed Scotland with a stereotypical German confidence in the aftermath of the draw, but former Scotland star Billy Dodds doesn't see anything in Group A to fear.

Dodds said: 'It is a really good opportunity, especially when you get Germany as the top team. They haven't really done themselves justice at recent finals and it gives us a chance and a bit of hope. Pot 2 with Hungary wasn't that bad although Pot 4 was probably the biggest disappointment in getting Switzerland. I would have preferred one of the play-off winners. What I would say is that I don't think too many teams would have fancied getting Scotland in Pot 3 either. Switzerland was a naughty one but I would say there are four teams who are pretty evenly balanced.'

Now the dreaming can start and that will vary from the sublime to the ridiculous. Stephen O'Donnell was part of the Euro 2020 squad and knows a finals win would be a step forward.

The Motherwell full back said: 'The first target will be a win. We only got one point last time at Euro 2020 and if the team could do that it would be a good starting point for Euro 2024.'

Scotland are still searching for the holy grail of making history and getting into the knockout stages of one of the big tournaments for the first time.

'Clarke has done an incredible job,' Dodds said. 'We have genuine quality and a togetherness. I would say we have some quality of player and that is even stronger when you put it all together in a team and squad. You wouldn't bet against Scotland getting to the knockout stages. If you beat Spain 2-0 at home and then give them a scare in Spain then you are capable of doing that to any of the teams in our group. We had the friendlies against France and England and they were a good challenge because it will stand the team in good stead for the Euros. We will face teams at the Euros we know we can be competitive against. Steve and his players will fancy their chances.'

Norwegian defender Kristoffer Ajer came up against Scotland in Euro 2024 qualifying and reckons, as they have shown, they can cause anyone problems.

Ajer said: 'They are a very strong team. They play for each other and are a nice squad. I think they have a great chance. They make it tough for every single team. They beat Spain 2-0 here and so they can beat anyone when they have their day. It will be exciting to see them play.'

Before then Clarke's biggest headache will be picking his 23-man squad. It will be narrowed down from the additional Covid cover that was allowed for Euro 2020. It means that Clarke will have to leave players disappointed.

Newcastle United winger Harvey Barnes is one player who could be a late gate-crasher to the squad. He has one England cap in a friendly and so can still switch to Scotland via the grandparent rule. Barnes has missed most of the season through injury but certainly hasn't closed the door on a switch north of the border. Clarke has already made it clear there won't be too many changes away from his own tried and trusted.

Clarke spent the first-half of 2024 keeping a watchful eye on his potential picks and doing his analysis, with a fine-tooth comb, on Scotland's Euro 2024 opponents. It has been about Scotland's players and hopefuls doing their best for their clubs and hoping it is enough to get them on that plane to Germany.

Hearts and Scotland striker Shankland said: 'Everyone will want to be involved. These things take care of themselves. The reason you are in contention for Scotland is because you have done well or are doing well for your club. For me, the task in hand is simple. I need to keep playing well and scoring goals for Hearts. Hopefully when the time comes I am in form. I just need to keep my head down, work hard and make sure I remain in the thoughts of the gaffer. Every Scottish player will have the same mindset.'

Scotland's qualification, it is estimated, will land the SFA around £10 million in prize money before lucrative sponsorship deals. That is major money for the Association and will help them invest heavily in Hampden for their part as Euro 2028 hosts.

Steve Clarke and his squad have already helped to create their own and future legacies. You get the feeling that they are not finished yet and they are ready to write a few more chapters. Starting at Euro 2024.

Deutschland – wir werden kommen!